barry humphries'

flashacks

barry humphries'
flashbacks

text written by Roger McDonald

adapted from the television series written by Barry Humphries
and David Mitchell and produced by John McLean

HarperCollins*Entertainment*
An Imprint of HarperCollins*Publishers*

HarperCollins*Entertainment*
An Imprint of HarperCollins*Publishers*
77–85 Fulham Palace Road,
Hammersmith, London W6 8JB

www.fireandwater.com

This paperback edition 1999
1 3 5 7 9 8 6 4 2

First published in Australia in 1999 by
HarperCollins*Publishers* Pty Limited
A member of the HarperCollins*Publishers* (Australia) Pty Limited Group
Copyright © 1999 Flashbacks Limited Pty

The Authors assert the moral right to
be identified as the authors of this work

ISBN 0 00 255896 3

Design: Melanie Feddersen

Printed and bound in Great Britain by
Scotprint Ltd, Musselburgh

contents

Barry Humphries

Dame Edna Everage

Sandy Stone

Sir Les Patterson

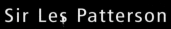

foreword by Barry Humphries

The decades Roger McDonald so entertainingly chronicles in this book correspond 'spookily', as Dame Edna might say, with my own career as an author and entertainer. The text is interlarded with the pronouncements of Edna herself, Les Patterson, the feisty and libidinous diplomat, and ghostly old Sandy Stone, the phantom of Glen Iris, the returned man. Elsewhere, lesser-known characters, who have long since passed their sell-by date, are quoted alongside the commentaries of real people, like Clive James and the incomparable Kathy Lette.

I confess that until reading this book I had no idea that my theatrical inventions had so many opinions about so many subjects. At the time of their creation they were certainly never intended to be in any way typical, or exemplars of their epochs. They were just Australian types who amused me and fell within my somewhat limited range as a comic actor. They also made people laugh.

I believe that in the 1960s when I was beginning to perform my one-man shows in larger Australian theatres – compared with the 'alternative' playhouses in which I had appeared in the fifties – some critics saw me as a kind of amateur sociologist with an edifying agenda. It was briefly fashionable to call me 'cruel' because I depicted – albeit in caricature – ordinary people who had previously been ignored by humorists and indeed, by serious writers. The housewife with her narrow preoccupations of food, family and flower arrangement was certainly the Cinderella of Australian art, and lower middle-class suburbia, with its lemon trees and pin oaks, and its streets of dull and comfortable prewar bungalows, was terra incognito to the satirist. Mrs Edna Everage's immediate popularity from the day of her creation on 13 December 1955 can only be attributed to the joy of recognition; the excitement of an audience long fed on British and American theatrical stereotypes, beholding at last a familiar image. For some, this image was painfully familiar, and I was rebuked for attacking the defenceless, as I was later to be excoriated for tarnishing Australia's 'international image'.

For a nation that has always prided itself – and Australia has never ceased to pride itself somewhat stridently on most things – on its toughness and resilience, we have always been very touchy about jokes at our expense. Beneath out rugged exterior there lurks a deep insecurity, sometimes amounting to paranoia. This seemed to reach a peak of hysteria in the seventies when the greatest accolade an Australian could receive was the epithet 'internationally acclaimed'. We weren't any good unless someone abroad or 'overseas', or both, gave us the nod of approbation.

I grew up during these decades of self-doubt on the one hand and excessive chauvinism on the other, but I never cease to look back on my formative years without an intense nostalgia. It is true to say that when I started to set down on paper my observations on the society in which I lived, they were sometimes inspired by rage and boredom. Everything seemed so cosy, so certain, and above all, so 'nice'. How priggish and infuriating my Young Self now seems, as from the armchair and slippers of the present I look back on that long-haired youth who preferred to frequent 'continental' restaurants, watch foreign-language films and read books translated from the French and German. Anything that brought a savoury or even rancid whiff of Europe into the too-clean environment of suburban Melbourne, acted upon me with the potency of a drug.

The parents of a Jewish school friend who had escaped from Poland by the skin of their teeth via Lithuania and Shanghai amazed me when they said, 'Hitler did one great thing in his life.' 'What was that?' I asked, incredulous. 'He gave Australia chamber music and decent coffee' was the refugees' reply.

Sometime in the fifties, we Australians were confronted with a 'traumatic' glimpse of ourselves, to use a seventies epithet. It happened at the time of the first parliamentary broadcasts, when the national network relayed to wireless sets all over the Commonwealth the voices of our Government and its Opposition. Shrill, coarsely abusive, rancorous and unequivocally from 'the wrong side of the tracks', these loutish exchanges did little for our self-confidence. Could our rulers really be such hayseeds and guttersnipes? It was only the voice of Robert Gordon Menzies, our longest serving prime minister, that reassured the genteel, though listening to him now one hears little but the sound of sanctimony.

To follow the great Australian adventure from the folksy fifties right through to the eighties, when we had begun to live dangerously beyond our means, is an exciting and sometimes alarming journey. In this volume and in the television series to which it is a corollary, we have dwelled rather selectively on but a few aspects of the story. There is not, for example, much about sport, even though this is the major preoccupation of many Australians. The reason for this is that I have no knowledge of, or interest in, this topic and would prove woefully unconvincing were I to address it.

On the other hand, there is much in Roger McDonald's survey about the world of entertainment and of television especially, since the introduction of this medium was one of the great educative influences in our lifetime. It is true that Australian television never really tried to educate, sometimes quite the opposite, but it did entertain, and it gave a geographically isolated society a glimpse of the outside world, which the radio never really provided. It also assisted in the rise of the ad man as universal guru and it nourished that new and terrifying animal, the Consumer Society. In the eighties and nineties, however, the influence of these genial hucksters seems positively benign beside that of the men who now rule Australia: the venal politician, the mendacious accountant and the power-crazed lawyer.

This is not a definitive history. It is, we hope, an entertainment; personal, quirky, opinionated, often to be consumed with a grain of salt. One of the things which does emerge from these pages is our devotion to fashion in words as much as things, and the shift in our allegiance from our British heritage to the seductive influence of the United States. It would be interesting to know exactly when the Australian Labour Party became the Labor Party, since loyalists might see this obeisance to the now accepted American mis-spelling as the thin edge of the wedge. I well remember when we decimalised in the sixties, and there was huge excitement that we could at last refer to our money as 'bucks' and even, a little self-consciously at first, tell our deeply impressed friends how many 'grand' our new American car cost. To a nation educated by Hollywood movies it was thrilling to use, however clumsily, the vernacular of the flicks, and a decade later even educated people were referring to men as 'guys', and saying 'hi' to each other, and even 'not a problem' apropos of anything. Deeply concerned by the ubiquity of the rough-and-ready Australian phrase 'no worries', the guest-relations personnel of our new 'internationally acclaimed' hotels were begging their young employees to abandon this parochial knee-jerk courtesy in favour of the trans-Pacific 'not a problem'. Only recently in Brisbane I said 'Good morning' to the concierge of my hotel and received the surrealistic reply, 'not a problem'.

When Australians get hold of a word or phrase we really work it to death. For example, although 'hopefully' was an American invention in the early seventies, we cornered the world rights, as we later did with 'uptight', 'heavy' and 'hassle', not seldom in the same sentence. We now can't get by without 'basically' in every utterance, as in the bad old days we couldn't eat a meal without tomato sauce. These are not so much words for communication of thought as useful footholds on the treacherous precipice of grown-up discourse.

We did, and despite economic depredations still do, live in a nouveau-riche society, which is what makes Australia so much fun. For as long as I can remember, people have desperately tried to be 'with it', up-to-date, in-tune, au fait, hip and, with any luck, miles ahead of the rest of the world. Like Switzerland, our inventions are few but ingenious: the boomerang, Redi-mix concrete, the combine harvester, the lamington cake, the rotary clothes hoist, and the Bakelite teledex. But our winemakers are beginning to teach the French a thing or two, and as the Koreans buy less and less of our minerals, we are still exporting huge numbers of artists and opera singers. We are beginning to explore our own infinitely varied continent with the zeal with which we formerly explored Earls Court and that beach in Bali we subsequently managed to destroy. Yet, if you look up at night in most parts of Australia, you can still see the best and brightest stars in the world.

Barry Humphries

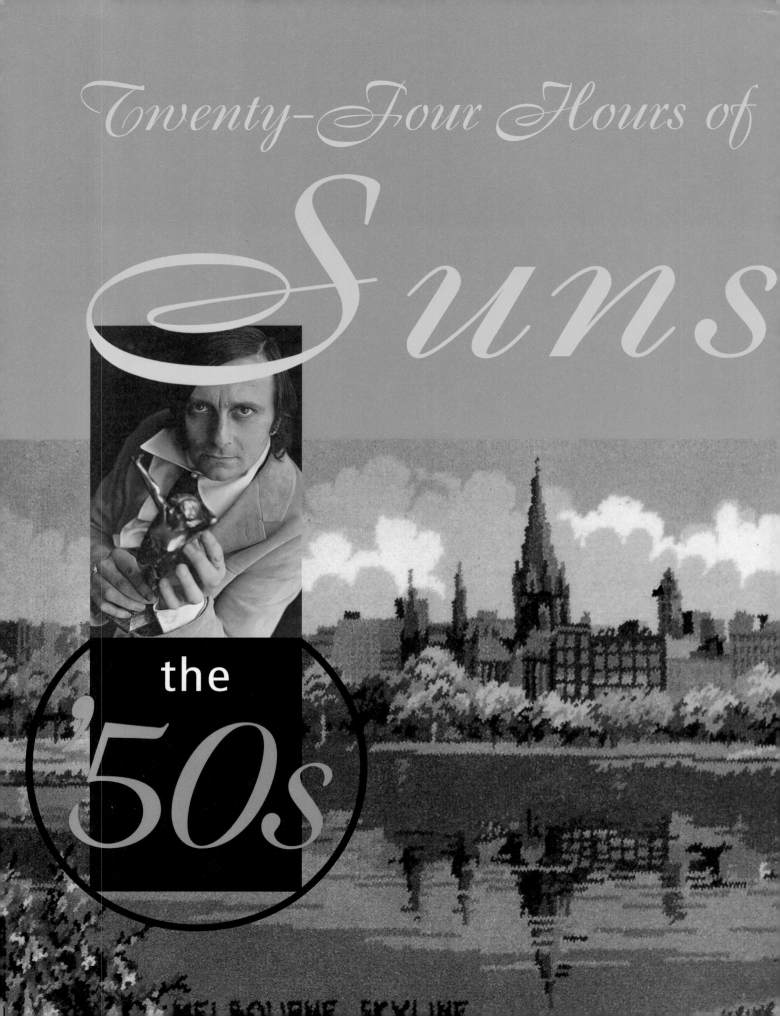

nine

Souvenir Programme
PRICE 2/-

ROYAL
VISIT - 1954
SURF
CARNIVAL

BONDI BEACH — SATURDAY 6th FEBRUARY 1954
Conducted by
THE SURF LIFE SAVING ASSOCIATION OF AUSTRALIA

Eileen Mayo

AUSTRALIA

PARTICULARS AT GOVERNMENT, SHIPPING, AIRLINE & TRAVEL OFFICES

The fifties

would be a time when Australians could snooze away the hardships of war, confident in having a benevolent young monarch looking down on them from afar, a nicely spoken prime minister, Mr R. G. Menzies, to govern them into the foreseeable future, and the assurance that, when the paperboy woke them in the morning with the slap of the tightly rolled-up *Sydney Morning Herald* or Melbourne *Age*, there would be news of health, wealth and perpetual happiness. It was to be twenty-four hours of sunshine beneath Australian skies.

The slide into the unreal future started at the end of 1949 with a good old-fashioned warning about socialist Labor being a threat to family values and about the dangers of 'Reds under the beds'. Such was the burden of the conservative campaign against the ruling proletarians and the genial engine-driver turned prime minister, Ben Chifley.

Above: AUSTRALIANS EMBARKED ON POSTWAR LIFE WITH WARLIKE ENTHUSIASM. IN OCTOBER 1949, ENTERTAINMENT-STARVED CITIZENS GATHERED AROUND THE RADIO TO LISTEN AS THE GOVERNOR-GENERAL, WILLIAM MCKELL, SET OFF AN EXPLOSIVE CHARGE THAT MARKED THE BEGINNING OF THE SNOWY MOUNTAINS SCHEME. **Previous pages:** 'MELBOURNE ON THE YARRA' (main picture) WAS CELEBRATED IN THIS 1950S RUG WHICH TAKES PRIDE OF PLACE AT CHEZ HUMPHRIES. IMAGES OF SURF (inset top) AND KANGAROOS (inset right) WERE KEY SELLING POINTS TO POTENTIAL MIGRANTS NOT IMPRESSED BY AUSTRALIA'S URBAN SOPHISTICATION.

The warning worked and the Liberals stepped into power under Robert Gordon Menzies in December 1949. The mystical date of 1950 loomed. Then it was roll on the Indian summer of Australian innocence, when spirits would soar like Royal Doulton pottery geese across a living-room wall. There was to be no rude awakening, if Mr Menzies had his way, from Australia's white-people's dreaming of pounds, shillings and pence, 'God Save the King', Barossa Pearl wine, Laminex household surfaces and the delusion that Australia was an exotic lump of the Home Counties that had somehow slipped its moorings and drifted into South-East Asia.

To children of the 1940s the new half century loomed ahead as a gateway to a changed reality, with a feeling of almost exquisite modernity about it.

At schools across the country young Australians were mustered and instructed as a group to understand the kind of power that was being unleashed in the coming decade. Gathered in close to the standard-issue Department of Education loudspeaker boxes, they were asked to listen for an explosion. They needed no encouragement to be quiet. It was October 1949. The governor-general, Mr William McKell, made an on-the-spot broadcast from the site of the future Adaminaby dam in the Snowy Mountains. He spoke about mountains being moved, rivers changing their course, towns being established in the arid inland to take pressure off burgeoning coastal cities. As he spoke, McKell stood over an explosives detonation plunger. It was a kind of positive war being declared. The Snowy Mountains Authority, which was to run the whole thing, had been set up by the Commonwealth

Government under its defence provisions Acts. A country so long inspired by the war of 1939–45 was to carry the feeling over into peacetime. That was the thought. A brief acknowledgement was made of the several hundred people whose homes would be flooded in the national interest. Then Mr McKell set off the charge, and Australia's future leaders strained forward to see the silk loudspeaker covers tremble as the earth rumbled.

It was a time when visions of flying cars and space travel from *Popular Mechanics* magazines would become a reality. A common fantasy was the flying car. The promise was to live where you liked, fly to where you had to be, land, unclip the wings and drive away. Children did their sums and worked out how old they would be when the year 2000 came around. It was such an impossibly distant date that to think they would live that long was almost a guarantee of immortality.

Rockets, jet planes and the atomic bomb were already a reality. What was coming next? Soon it would no longer be necessary to stare at the dusty speakers of radio receivers and imagine pictures, but to have them happen by the magic of television.

BETWEEN 1948 AND 1959 ALMOST 2.5 MILLION MIGRANTS ARRIVED IN AUSTRALIA. THE 'BRIDE SHIP' (left) WAS PERHAPS THE MOST EAGERLY RECEIVED CARGO EVER UNLOADED ON AN AUSTRALIAN WHARF. WHILE SOME VIEWED THE NEW ARRIVALS AS 'A DISAGREEABLE NECESSITY', THEIR INDUSTRIAL AND CULTURAL INPUT WERE INVALUABLE TO AN UNDERPOPULATED COUNTRY. IMMIGRATION CONTRACTS MEANT THAT NO MATTER WHAT THEIR QUALIFICATIONS, ALL NEW AUSTRALIANS HAD TO COMMIT TO TWO YEARS OF CIVIC LABOUR. THE BLOKE WITH THE SLEDGEHAMMER (right) MAY WELL HAVE BEEN A DOCTOR.

There was a mood of the cargo cult waiting to happen. Petrol rationing had only just ended, but there were still shortages of raw materials after wartime restructuring. Australia was open for the taking and willing hands were needed to dig its dirt, tunnel its hills, build its houses and roads, till its vegetable patches on outer-suburban farms, and lay pipes for its sewerage systems.

Stranger than any imagined future was the coming of the first of millions of new arrivals who would get their hands dirty doing this work.

Foreigners, according to Lord Casey [formerly a minister in the Menzies Government], were a disagreeable necessity – populate or perish – and real Australians were forced to welcome large numbers of Greeks and Italians who did not necessarily wish to sell fish and chips or fruit and vegetables. In an official attempt to curb our natural resentment of these swarthy intruders, Australians were encouraged to drop the generic term 'Balt' (for Baltic states) and adopt the nicer epithet 'New Australian'. There was, however, a growing disquiet that this might be the thin end of the wedge, a fear confirmed by isolated public outrages as, for example, when Hector Crawford conducted the national anthem at the Myer Music Bowl and a few Latin music-lovers failed to rise to the occasion. 🖝

BRITISH MIGRANTS WERE ESPECIALLY FAVOURED IN THE POSTWAR IMMIGRATION BOOM. BUT EVEN AT 10 QUID, NOT ENOUGH BRITS WERE WILLING TO COME IN ORDER TO MEET THE TARGET OF 70 000 A YEAR, SO EUROPEAN MIGRANTS WERE ADDED TO THE MIX.

It did not take long for the new migrants' way of life to start a series of changes in the standard Australian lifestyle. All it took was an Australian chef in a migrant hostel to serve an Italian his spaghetti cooked in dripping. Then the New Australians knew that they had better make changes around the Old Australians or they would never get a drink on Sundays or find a café worthy of a passionate conversation. What it took after that was the ripple effect. Let's say it started when a university student seeking instant sophistication asked for his first cappuccino or 'cup of chino'.

Australia's postwar boost to migration was one of the biggest and boldest government-organised migration schemes the twentieth century has seen. Between 1948 and 1959 almost 2.5 million migrants arrived. Latvians, Estonians, Lithuanians, Hungarians, Germans and Maltese came by the boatload. The greatest numbers among the non-English-speakers were Greek and Italian. British migrants found themselves especially favoured. A satellite city to Adelaide was created, named Elizabeth after the new young Queen, and it was filled with families from the Midlands as surely as if an ant trail led from Manchester to the City of Light. This implied huge respect for British heritage, as well as an unquestioned racial theory that held British stock to be of the best. It also showed complacency that living conditions in Australia would make British newcomers fall over themselves to migrate. How could they fail to? And so they did. A few treated the passage – for which they were required to pay £10 – as just an extended tourist jaunt, and complained self-righteously if conditions weren't as they expected. Dull news days on Australia's afternoon papers could always be enlivened by the editor's instruction: 'Go out and find a whingeing Pom.' Even more newsworthy was the returnee who declared, back in England, that Australia was the promised land after all, and so applied to re-migrate.

Robin Gibb and his brothers (of Bee Gees fame) were 'ten-pounders' in the late fifties. The family came from the cold northern English city of Manchester and settled in tropical Brisbane. Robin, eight at the time, recalls travelling the 600 miles from Sydney to Brisbane by train and 'feeling the hot air in my face and seeing this rugged bush that I'd never seen before'. Once there, suburban Brisbane was in many respects the promised land of milk and honey. 'It was a very free kind of environment for children of our age. All the kids walked around barefoot. Fruit grew wild – there were pawpaw, mango and banana trees in the back garden. Coming straight from Manchester to that was a culture shock. It was great.'

Children came face to face with the migrant era in the schoolyard or over the back fence. From the kid's-eye-view, all Europeans coming to Australia – if they weren't Greek – were wartime enemies. In games in the dirt, the words 'Nazi' and 'Jap' were interchangeable. It was a requirement of migrants' contracts to take two years' public work to earn their passage, and it didn't matter whether they were doctors, engineers or lawyers, they took mattock and spade in hand and built roads or went down six feet in the back lanes of remote towns laying water pipes or installing the sewerage system. In reality the indentured labourers were a quizzical, interested and somewhat superior bunch. One of the Estonians in the team that gave a family their first flush lavatory might have been a doctor. Eventually his qualifications would be recognised in Australia, but he would first have to improve his English and then have to resit his medical exams. Admission to the full privileges of Australian society was hard unless you were born into them. But if his daughter attended the local school, then within a very short time she could be dux – top of her year.

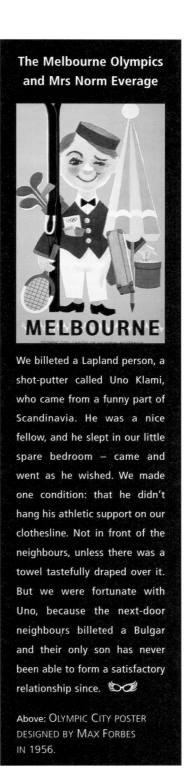

The Melbourne Olympics and Mrs Norm Everage

We billeted a Lapland person, a shot-putter called Uno Klami, who came from a funny part of Scandinavia. He was a nice fellow, and he slept in our little spare bedroom – came and went as he wished. We made one condition: that he didn't hang his athletic support on our clothesline. Not in front of the neighbours, unless there was a towel tastefully draped over it. But we were fortunate with Uno, because the next-door neighbours billeted a Bulgar and their only son has never been able to form a satisfactory relationship since.

Above: OLYMPIC CITY POSTER DESIGNED BY MAX FORBES IN 1956.

TANIA VERSTAK CAME TO AUSTRALIA IN THE EARLY FIFTIES WITH HER WHITE RUSSIAN PARENTS, WHO WERE REFUGEES FROM COMMUNIST CHINA. SHE WENT ON TO BECOME THE FIRST MIGRANT MISS AUSTRALIA IN 1961.

Or, a few years later, Miss Australia. Tania Verstak, Russian migrant and Miss Australia 1961, arrived in Sydney in the early 1950s when she was 12. With her family she moved to suburban Bexley North. 'I didn't speak much English to start with, but not once did I feel as though I was unwelcome or that there was a problem about being a New Australian.' Be that as it may, Tania did feel it necessary to take elocution lessons through which she successfully lost all trace of her migrant past. She now says, 'I'm actually quite sad I did it, because I'd love to have a bit of a Russian accent … I think it's so charming.'

Once the migrants arrived, the urge to prove that Australia was better than the rest of the world continued. The way of proving it was to imitate the rest of the world as much as possible. For too long Australians had been hearing about things long before they saw them: news, fashions, and inventions ranging from fountain pens to refrigerated cabinets. It was time to begin ending the isolation in a rush.

CAPPUCCINO, OR 'CUP OF CHINO' AS IT WAS SOMETIMES PRONOUNCED, WAS A NEW BREW IN THE AUSTRALIAN DIET, THANKS TO THE POSTWAR INFLUX OF ITALIAN MIGRANTS. IT WAS MOST FASHIONABLY DRUNK AT COFFEE LOUNGES SUCH AS THIS, WHICH OFTEN FEATURED ABORIGINAL MOTIFS IN THE DECOR.

And so Australia spent the 1950s bulldozing its bushland and expanding its suburbia – marching across the hills, valleys and plains fringing the south- and east-coast cities of Adelaide, Melbourne, Sydney and Brisbane.

The suburbs of Melbourne really went ahead in leaps and bounds in the fifties. I can remember that where we were there was nothing more than a grocer's shop and a little newsagent's. And then slowly the houses came, filling up all the paddocks. It was an amazing thing, but by the time we got to the fifties the young couples were wanting to move into newer and bigger homes. Sometimes two-storey homes! 🎙️

The fifties were a time when the possession of an electric washing machine, a gas or electric oven and possibly a motor car could almost be considered a spiritual aspiration. It was the decade when Australia bid for and won an Olympic Games, held in Melbourne in 1956 – although a year before the Games happened Avery Brundage, President of the International Olympic Committee, felt that Melbourne was appallingly unprepared and could possibly have its privilege taken away.

It was also the time when Australia kept its Anglicised accents on radio but invited in an Americanised kind of television. It was when Australians manufactured their own car, the Holden, under the auspices of an American company, General Motors.

It was when Australians showed their political up-to-dateness by generating a Red Scare of international proportions. It was when Australia's part-Aboriginal children continued to be taken from their families, because the benefits of living white were unquestioned. It was the decade when atomic bombs were exploded in South Australia and Western Australia as a gesture of solidarity with Britain – and as a thumbs-up to America – and when any concerns about radiation fallout were smoothed away in the assurances of politicians whose job it was to know everything.

All these changes were delivered from above. Newspapers and magazines, radio and newsreels, all gave the impression that the future was in good hands. Australians had never taken to using the phrase 'the authorities' as the British had, but they had a deep reliance on authoritative voices all the same. It made little difference whether this was thanks to the convict heritage of first settlement, when the higher-ups dangled the noose and threatened the whipping triangle against every

And well she might smile! This lucky housewife has lifted the lid on a Pope washing machine, the first in the country to feature dual automatic functions – no more washboards or manual manglers. White goods were almost a spiritual aspiration for the housewife at a time when cars, electric ovens and, later, televisions, were the trophies of postwar prosperity.

IN THE 1950S THE LAWN MOWER BECAME A NATIONAL OBSESSION, AN ESSENTIAL INSTRUMENT FOR TAMING THE WILD GRASSES OF SUBURBIA AND A MACHINE WHICH FORMED A CRUCIAL PART OF A BOY'S RITE OF PASSAGE TO MANHOOD.

misdemeanour, or because democratically Australia was an over-governed entity and proud of it (the various colonies ceding important powers to the Commonwealth in 1901 and thus creating a nation with seven houses of parliament). The famous Australian assertiveness hid a deep belief that someone else always knew best. In the 1950s, the pinnacle of that belief was centred abroad.

The epithet which carried with it the very highest promise of artistic excellence was 'continental'. No more improving an evening could be spent than in a continental restaurant eating a continental meal before a continental film, followed by a continental supper in a continental coffee lounge preferably inhaling a continental cigarette. Black Balkan Sobranies were very popular with affected youth, and black coffee was still a slightly exotic novelty in a society that either sipped tea or swilled beer. At symphony concerts in the Melbourne Town Hall, it was the visiting continental artists who attracted the biggest crowds, although Australia's Bernard Heinz (later Sir Bernard) was a popular conductor, probably because his name sounded foreign and yet reassuringly the same as the tomato sauce (Australia's alternative beverage).

This was a time when Australians were leaving for Europe by the boatload. Nice young physiotherapists, primary-school teachers and mothercraft nurses, all off on the Big Trip in order to make up their minds about some local beau to whom, after brief and catastrophic experiments with Italian ship's stewards and Austrian ski instructors, they would inevitably return and marry. The older couples, like my parents, usually had some Royal objective: a glimpse of the Queen perhaps, or several hundred Kodachromes of an English phenomenon known as 'pageantry'. They never returned to Australia without first purchasing several copies of the My Fair Lady *album for culture-starved friends and relations. They also preferred to visit only what they commonly described as 'the clean countries', i.e. Holland, Switzerland, the Lake District and Scandinavia. And in handbags and hip pockets they carried, neatly folded, yards of toilet paper with which to upholster the infested lavatory seats of Europe.*

The 1950s were a time when most Australians lived in cities but the national image was one of woolgrowers, shearers, wheat farmers, miners, steelworkers and stevedores – along with soldiers and cricketers. The office worker, clerk, salesman, shop assistant and ordinary labourer may have been the statistical majority, but were not elevated as national icons. The small struggles of forgotten people, which is how most Australians lived their lives, had no place in the annals of Australian experience. If you were an authentic Australian you looked towards the horizon with eyes narrowed against the glare and approached every task with laconic self-deprecation and an understated physical and mental strength.

It was a sun-sizzled hybrid culture: defiantly English in inheritance, defensively self-sufficient in pride. The archetypal mainstream Australian was white, middle class – or else fiercely and pridefully working class – and almost certainly a male. He was nominally Christian, preferably non-Catholic, English-speaking, albeit in an accent that left many English-speakers dumbfounded. He was a vigorous, outdoor, rugby-football-playing, Victorian-football-playing, swimming, surfing, horseracing, running, cycling, tennis-playing and cricketing sportsman. He was uncomplicated psychologically and politically (and for that matter sexually) as a matter of state policy. Where the archetype was a woman – and she sometimes was – she was someone's wife, and backed her husband in his chosen career, which was certainly his lifetime career. She maintained the family house, invariably called 'the home', and produced healthy, practical, outdoors-orientated children. There was a literary life and an artistic life in Australia, but it made people uncomfortable if it drew too much on the socially unacceptable parts of Australian experience – that is, if the characters created by novelists and playwrights reflected too accurately the way Australians actually spoke, thought, and lived in all their rough variety.

THIS TYPICALLY AUSTRALIAN BIRTHDAY CELEBRATION TOOK PLACE AT LAMINATED TABLES AROUND THE COUNTRY. HOWEVER, THE MIGRANT ASSAULT ON OUR MEAT-AND-THREE-VEG CULTURE SOON LED TO THE USE OF GARLIC AND THE CONSUMPTION OF SPAGHETTI THAT MR HEINZ HAD NOT CANNED.

From Panto Dame to Superstar – The Birth of Edna

In the mid 1950s on bus trips touring Shakespeare around Victoria with the Union Rep (under the direction of Ray Lawler), we'd all entertain each other, usually at the expense of the town we'd just been to or were just about to visit. My party turn from the back of the bus was a very successful Australian falsetto I had developed.

The voice from the back of the bus between Mirboo North and wherever, was that unmistakable voice of the genteel Melbourne housewife. She was loosely based on all the people who surrounded me in my youth, and she spoke at the supper party which the mayor or the lady mayoress would offer us after a perfomance of *Twelfth Night*. A speech of gratitude for bringing Shakespeare to the town.

Ray said, when the time for the annual revue approached, 'Why don't you write a sketch for that character you did in the bus? What's she called?' I plucked a name out of the air: 'Edna,' I suggested, since I'd once had a kind of nanny called Edna, of whom I was very fond. I said, 'Her name is Edna, and she comes from Moonee Ponds.' I thought, I daren't say Camberwell, or my mother will think it's based on her.

Indeed, Edna is more of a Camberwell character than a Moonee Ponds character. Moonee Ponds was a suburb of Melbourne I'd never been to, at the time. The name was chosen partly for its associations with a famous poem by Kendall called 'Moonee'. It was also a good euphonious name, and it still is a wonderful name – it's evocative, and has a hint of something elusively humorous about it.

'Well, if I write a sketch about this character, who will play Edna? Will I do the voice from offstage?' Ray said, 'You do it yourself.' 'Can't Zoe [Caldwell] be Edna?' I asked. He replied, 'No, you be Edna. Do it like a pantomime dame ...'

The response to the early Edna sketches was rapturous and surprised us all. Edna was a person obsessed with the beauty of her own home, and no one had really talked about Australian houses before. Since my father was a builder, a creator of a number of substantial Melbourne houses, in jazz moderne with manganese bricks, or Spanish mission with the barley-sugar columns and little grilled windows, I was interested in houses. I still am interested in the places in which people live, the shells they inhabit. No one thought of them as even funny, or thought that life in the suburbs could be funny. In fact it was felt to be intractable dramatic material ... So I found that I'd discovered something I could write about, not by putting the telescope to my eye and trying to write something in the manner of Coward or Alan Melville, but by just looking through my venetian blinds onto my own front lawn.

So Edna was born – Edna Everage as in 'average', husband Norm as in 'normal'.

Mrs Norm Everage (left) on the set of a 1959 Melbourne television show. The set depicts a typical fifties Australian lounge room, complete with a 'feature wall' of crazy stonework and a comfy 'poof' for resting weary feet.
Above: Edna on a Melbourne city street in the late fifties, looking somewhat distraught having read that the 'female convenience' is closed for renovation.

A DISTURBING TREND TOWARDS INDIVIDUALITY IN YOUTH
CULTURE GAVE RISE TO THE BODGIES AND WIDGIES OF THE FIFTIES.
SIR LES PATTERSON REMEMBERS ENCOUNTERS WITH THE LESSER-
KNOWN 'ABOWIDGINES'.

In the fifties I was knee-high to a grasshopper. But I was a scallywag; I gave a little bit of aggro. I was a naughty boy; I was a bodgie. I was proud to be a bodgie. And my girlfriend – can't remember her other name – she was a widgie. Bodgies and widgies. We were in the milk bars, we had fun. Our regular milk bar was frequented solely by an all-white, Caucasian group of kids – though there were areas in Sydney which had black bodgies and widgies, or 'Abowidgines', as they were known.

It was better to stick to the safe and tested models from overseas, with high culture winning every time over the home-grown product. To be an artistic and interested male in matters of taste and style was to be branded effeminate.

The emphasis was on sunshine. There seemed to be 24 hours of it a day in Australia and never a dark side to the experience at all. To look outward, not to be moody and introspective, to join in, to co-operate, to band together – this was the ruling spirit of the times.

And it found expression in dance. The young were interested in square-dancing, which was an absolute craze in the first half of the fifties – the clothes, the music and the callers, who received press coverage and considerable publicity. People went to square-dancing parties. Girls wore bobby socks, ponytails and gingham – it was a uniform. Callers learnt American dialects, since it was an American dance form. The most notable caller was Jim Vickers Willis. He was a remarkable phenomenon.

Barry Crocker, the Australian singer and entertainer, recalls that it could be pretty horrific being a teenager in the fifties. 'I remember, because the clothes were so revolting. We look back at them with a great deal of affection now, but I mean, we were so poor, you'd get one jacket a year. Your mum would buy you one jacket and you'd sweat on it all year … And we looked pretty terrible, I think – you know, the slicked-back sides, all trying to look like Tony Curtis, with a duck's tail. Mine looked more like a chook's bum really, very tacky.'

Bodgies had barely made their first appearance in the land with their cheekily free-and-easy widgie consorts. It was scarcely rumoured – even faintly – that such males would emerge into the broad sunlight of Brisbane, Sydney, Melbourne or Perth with sallow complexions, leering expressions, disdainfully curled lips and hair even longer than Cornel Wilde's in the Chopin movie. Most couldn't afford motorbikes or heavy leather like Marlon Brando in *The Wild One*, but they could bouffant their hair with Brylcreem and wear a 'zoot suit' – with wide, draped shoulders and padded collars. Their girlfriends wore strapless polka-dotted sun frocks, went bare-shinned and flat-heeled, and mocked their conventional sisters in milk bars and dance halls.

The music of this epoch was predominantly sentimental, and Mantovani's syrupy strings provided an authentic background to the simple pastimes of the period. Before rock 'n roll exploded from the radio and early television it was Doris Day, Bing Crosby, Betty Hutton. Jazz was generally played late at night on the radio – a sophisticated taste and an upper middle-class pursuit. The two musical elements that most vividly evoked the early 1950s were Khachaturian's 'Sabre Dance' and Frankie Laine's 'Cry of the Wild Goose'.

Indeed, geese were potent symbols of the period. One of the great bestsellers of those years was Paul Gallico's mawkish epic The Snow Goose and, early in the decade, the porcelain variety began their optimistic, diagonal ascent across the walls of thousands of suburban lounges.

EVERYTHING WORTH REMEMBERING COULD BE PRESERVED ON COLOUR SLIDES. FOR THE NEXT 25 YEARS, THE 'SLIDE EVENING' WAS A POPULAR FORM OF HOME ENTERTAINMENT.

The time had come to give an unconscious heave and to be ready for change, whatever the consequences. It happened in the national election of December 1949. Could the world already have come so far as to have used up half its twentieth century? So many marvels already and the future still in hand. So many terrors, too, but then war was an adventure game in young eyes.

Stories of London in the Blitz and the adventures of secret agents on the Continent were closer to heart for many Australians than events on Australia's doorstep. The reality was that Australia had been bombed along its northern settlements (with more than 200 killed in Darwin in February 1942, and repeated raids on Townsville, Wyndham and Broome to follow). Australians had fought and died in the New Guinea and Islands campaigns, leaving few families untouched by tragedy and concern. The stories of Kokoda Trail, Changi (where 16 000 Australians were incarcerated by the Japanese) and the Burma Railway were often told, and hatred of the Japanese was deeply ingrained as a result of savage executions and enforced starvation of ordinary soldiers. The truly adventurous reality for a generation growing up in the 1950s lay in the flood of literature dealing with war on the European front: Guy Gibson's *Enemy Coast Ahead*, Paul Brickhill's *The Dam Busters* and *Reach For the Sky* (about Douglas 'Tin Legs' Bader), and other authors' stories of escape – *Escape to Danger*, *The Great Escape*, *The Wooden Horse*, *Boldness Be My Friend* and *The Colditz Story*.

The Menzies era was ushered in with the Liberal–Country Party Coalition victory over Labor. The decade of the 1950s was (by common resolve) to be as different as possible from the 1940s, with that decade's six years of world war, social upheaval, grief, hardship, shortages and, to top it off for rural people, the worst drought on record. Under Ben Chifley, Labor had relied on a steady record of achievement, but it was not enough to remain in power. A former train-driver from Bathurst, and one of the working-class gentlemen of Australian politics, Chifley served as opposition leader for another year and a half, dying alone in 1951 in his room at Canberra's Kurrajong Hotel on the night of the Jubilee Ball at Parliament House.

Robert Gordon Menzies' soothing tones were heard throughout the land. His eyebrows were like a shady verandah. The hair on his slightly elongated head was as smooth as a barnyard egg. His manners were polished

but not necessarily overbearing – he was like an extremely distinguished private-school headmaster. The mood of a stern but benevolent government filtered its way down to the suburbs. In popular memory, Menzies was the man who had approved the sale of Australian pig-iron to Japan on the brink of World War II. When the electorate kicked Labor out at the end of 1949 and elected Mr Menzies he was never *Mr* to most Australians: merely Bob – or Pig-Iron Bob to Labor and communist opponents. Those less caustic, perhaps even affectionate, towards him called him Ming after 'Mingies', the Scottish pronunciation of his name. Through a widespread psychological quirk, children thought of Menzies' eyebrows as fatherly. He was of Presbyterian background, was mercantile

WITH EYEBROWS LIKE A SHADY VERANDAH AND THE MANNERS OF A PRIVATE-SCHOOL HEADMASTER, THE BENEVOLENT AND 'NICELY SPOKEN' PRIME MINISTER ROBERT MENZIES STEERED AUSTRALIA COMFORTABLY THROUGH THE FIFTIES.

Melbourne in sympathy, and his social class was the ruling elite of Australia. Melbourne was the financial capital of Australia. The boardrooms of all the great companies were there – BHP, CSR, Colonial Mutual.

When Menzies' new government brought down its first budget for the decade, in October 1950, the headlines ran: 'Australia set to prosper'. Matters were in good hands, the country was assured. The treasurer, Mr Fadden, said as much: 'Governments and all their connected authorities are pushing on with large programmes of works to provide power, fuel, water, transport, housing, hospitals and schools for a larger population and a more highly developed economy.' The mood was that of a national cleanup after some sort of unspecified disaster – the past.

It was a private-enterprise government – but the long hand of public spending reached out. A loan of $US100 million was obtained from Washington for the country to buy agricultural equipment. Those who tilled the soil needed help but those who grazed it bare were, by contrast, doing extraordinarily well. This was when Australia 'rode on the sheep's back' and woolgrowers were harvesting pound notes. In 1951 they voted against any form of government-backed reserve price scheme for their industry, and no wonder: the price of wool had jumped from 76 pence a pound in 1949 to 375 pence. It would soon rise even more, bringing a bonanza to woolgrowers and allowing them to spend like lords. In the 1950s stories were told of them carting rolls of barbed wire around the paddocks in the boots of Rolls Royces. Workers in the wool industry meanwhile struggled until 1956 to get increased wages out of the boom, only to have their wages almost immediately cut again when wool prices fell. This led to a bitter six-month-long shearers' strike nationwide in an attempt to have wages kept at the newly raised level. Strikes were invariably depicted by Menzies as fomented by communist agitators, allowing the Cold War and the Red Menace to be taken to every corner of Australian life, even to remote and dusty corners of the bush, where hardworking, courageous people were exposed to scare tactics in their very hearts.

Australia was a democracy, a free society in its political definitions of itself. But it was far from free in matters of social control and the pressure of standardised thinking.

The most widely sought-after books of the time were banned – James Joyce's *Ulysses* (since 1929) and D. H. Lawrence's *Lady Chatterly's Lover* being top of the list. Norman Lindsay's raucous romp, *Redheap*, had been banned since the 1930s. It seemed mystifyingly tame to those who got hold of a copy and pored over its pages with hot breath. Locally, communist Frank Hardy's *Power Without Glory* was banned for libel reasons, so ensuring it bestseller status when the ban was lifted – along with a clutch of other novels deemed unsuitable for Australian eyes, including *Love Me Sailor*, *The Postman Always Rings Twice* and *Peyton Place*. Mostly it was because they contained the very same language heard every day on the streets, and suggested that love was a physical act.

If you came across one of these banned volumes, the trick was to drop it onto the floor and, by magic, it would open at the offending passage. Australia had to be purged of all political and sexual innuendo.

One of the great scandals of the decade erupted in 1956 when Sir Eugene Goossens, conductor of the Sydney Symphony Orchestra, was arrested at Sydney airport for bringing in a substantial quantity of compromising items of a sadomasochistic and satanic nature. He was fined £100 and would later leave the country in disgrace.

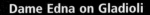

The gladdie is a very complex flower. It's not as simple and adorable as it seems. I had a moment in my life when I was very disappointed in gladdies, having loved them since I was a child. Since I was, in fact, knee-high to a gladiolus. I found out just by accident from a botanist friend of mine that the gladiolus is a bisexual hermaphrodite. Well, that didn't worry me at the time, because I didn't know what those things meant. But I looked them up in a spooky old book, and I was not pleased with what I read. In fact, I was embarrassed. And to this day I can't have them in the bedroom, unless the light is on. You never know what they're going to get up to in a vase.

Another of my new interests, which disappointed my parents, was my enthusiasm for second-hand bookshops; indeed, for anything that had the patina of age. 'Do you have to buy those old bits and pieces?' my mother would say if I came home with some dusty old volume after a visit to Mrs Bird. 'You never know where things like that have been.' Some of my books, like the Tales of D. H. Lawrence, *disappeared mysteriously from my shelves and when I mentioned this my mother said, passing the buck, 'Your father thought it was quite unsuitable, unnecessary and completely uncalled-for!' I never saw the books again, though I suspect they were consigned to some secret bibliocaust in the incinerator at the back of the garden.*

The present nostalgia for the 1950s is shorthand for wanting the whip-hand to be held by conservative, British-heritage Australians. The White Australia Policy was still in force (and not removed from the platform of the Australian Labor Party even until 1965). Australian governments from colonial times believed in the domination of whites over all other people, and therefore when Australia federated in 1901 the policy became national. In the words of the historian Manning Clark, Australians 'were terrified that a day might come when the coloured people of the world humiliated the whites. They were terrified that the higher races of mankind would be thrust aside by the people of the world characterised by the servility the white races loathed and condemned. They, therefore, wanted to prohibit the migration of all coloured people to Australia and possibly discriminate against those already resident in the country.'

And if you were an *indigenous* Australian, you were by no means free: absurdly, yet intractably, you were condemned for not acting white and were denied the rights of whites. Indeed, it was best for you if you kept entirely out of the way of whites, and tried to cultivate a certain reticence and distance.

Country children always knew other children who worked in shearing sheds when they should have been at school. They would disappear from the classroom for weeks on end, and return boasting of the money they'd earned 'picking up'. Even the dead wool from carcasses rotting in the sun, or strands of wool caught on barbed-wire fences, had a value and were sought after. This wasn't riding on the sheep's back, it was looking up from underneath. A life was led completely outside the structures of anything others knew or would ever know, and the reason was plain: they were Aboriginal kids, or, as the word was then, half-castes. Mostly they lived in tin shanties on the edge of towns. Nice children never went to visit the area known as 'the common'. It wasn't something

40 000 YEARS OF MYTH AND LEGEND PROVIDED QUAINT MOTIFS FOR COFFEE-SHOP INTERIORS, FABRIC DESIGN AND TRAVEL POSTERS LIKE THIS ONE WHICH FEATURES THE BOOMERANG, THE PRE-EMINENT ICON OF AUSTRALIANA UNTIL THE SYDNEY OPERA HOUSE WAS BUILT.

UNTIL 1956 AUSTRALIAN HOTELS CLOSED AT 6 PM IN AN ATTEMPT TO ENCOURAGE THE MALE TO RETURN HOME IN TIME FOR THE EVENING MEAL. THE FRANTIC 'SIX O'CLOCK SWILL' WAS A SIGHT TO BEHOLD AS ANXIOUS DRINKERS PUSHED TOWARDS THE BAR AND BRACED THEMSELVES FOR THE LONG, DRY HOURS AHEAD.

that fitted inside anyone's thinking. The common was regarded as a place where dirt, disease and drunkenness flourished. Aborigines were banned from buying alcohol and from drinking in pubs, and so they drank it as sly grog sold by whites at exorbitant markups, a potion called 'white lady' in Western Australia and 'goom' in Queensland, a mixture of boot polish, methylated spirits and wine.

In that generation of white Australians, it was an unquestioned fact that living on what amounted to a rubbish tip was somehow the fault of the people themselves and that they were to blame for it. This was a given in Australian society, as much as the paternal twitch of Mr Menzies' eyebrows was a given. But as the anthropologist C. H. Stanner was to say, in his 1962 ABC Boyer Lecture, the old man down there on the rubbish tip at the edge of town carries inside his head a heritage of myth and story richer than all of Homer's. Meanwhile, welfare workers were taking children away, destroying loving families in the name of good hygiene, tidiness and a sense of order – and a dozen other reasons all masking non-acceptance. Children came and went from school and there was no way of telling where they had gone. They never came back, and were considered by classmates to be the lucky ones.

It was the 1950s. Someone else always knew best.

The house was where a man found refuge when he came in from work. It was where the woman as wife and mother ruled in the daytime and instituted a degree of feminine values against the exterior all-male domains of pub and sports field. It was where the shades were pulled against the glare of too much reality in the outside world. The house was where the ordinary Australian turned for confirmation of identity as husband, father, property-owner and individualist. Then 'house' truly became 'home'.

THE GREAT AUSTRALIAN SUBURBAN DREAM IS DEPICTED IN THIS VIEW OF NEWLY BUILT BRICK-VENEER HOMES IN SYDNEY'S WEST. IT PORTRAYS MUCH OF WHAT THE FIFTIES WERE ABOUT: THE HOME AS A WOMAN'S DOMAIN, THE COMPOUND FOR CHILD-REARING AND THE CANVAS FOR EXPRESSION OF LONG-STUDIED DOMESTIC SCIENCES. THIS WAS A PLACE WHERE INDIVIDUALISM IN ANY FORM WAS AKIN TO COMMUNISM AND WHERE THE ANONYMITY OF THE REPETITIOUS STREETSCAPES WAS A COMFORT TO ALL AND CONFIRMATION OF A TRULY EGALITARIAN SPIRIT.

Pubs closed at six o'clock in a near-riot of last-minute guzzling, followed by a parade of males staggering through the hot streets. It was called the 'six o'clock swill' and was soon over.

Until the repeal of six o'clock closing in 1956, and the extension of hotel hours to ten o'clock, the evening streets of Australian cities and towns were a mass of drunks lurching, yelling, bailing people up and being sick in the gutter or directly onto the footpath. Men urinating against walls, or crying over a smashed half-dozen long-necked bottles slipped clumsily from their arms, were a common sight in the murky twilight around seven in the evening. Broken glass posed a danger to any barefooted kid passing by.

And the sun hadn't yet set. Men straightening their ties and squaring their shoulders were hungry when they arrived through the front door at home, their appetites sharpened by schooners, middies, ponies, pots, sevens and pints – all varieties of beer-glass sizes and inevitably topped by a small collar of legally insisted-upon foam. And so a hot meal would be ready and whipped onto the table. Grey and bleached-out overcooked colours predominated – mutton chops, mashed potatoes, boiled pumpkin, peas with Worcestershire sauce on the side, a stack of white bread and butter, and a pot of tea. A popular snack was mince on toast. Spaghetti, until the mid 1950s, came from tins – and then, when it was shown to have other origins, was embraced as a 'special treat'. Any food out of the ordinary was called that, and was given gourmet status on the family table.

Left: Domestic appliances presented as erotic or spiritual icons reflected a society not just obsessed with material possessions, but genuinely moved by advances in home comfort. Above: Furniture too was beginning to break new ground with designs like this Douglas Snelling ensemble. These pieces were modern, clean and light, in contrast to the heavy 'Genoa style' so loved by Sandy Stone and his generation.

The 1950s credo for women related to serving the needs of her man. She must never seem dour or depressed when he rolled in. Making complaints about her day was an absolute no-no. *His* day was, by definition, more stressful than hers. She therefore listened, nodded her head, spoke in a low soothing voice, and let him unwind.

Home was where individual taste could be indulged to the limit. By 1950, furniture could be bought on time payment; indeed, the more interesting, colourful furnishings were only available in stores that offered such terms. Cash dealers specialised in the drab, whereas, by signing a hire-purchase agreement and apportioning a part of one's weekly income, an instant transformation of the home interiors was possible. The armchair was usually a wide, low, broad-armed object, swathed in coarse, patterned, carpet-like material called Genoa velvet, and boasting varnished hand-rests made from plywood. Positioned off-centre in the room, this armchair resembled a stylised, low-slung, flying brick. To one side stood an electric lamp, around 5 feet high, incorporating a circular drinks tray and a beehive-shaped metal

Sandy Stone on Breakdowns

People never had nervous breakdowns in my day and age. It was completely unheard of. I remember reading in a Digest once about nervous breakdowns, but we didn't know anyone who'd had one. You knew people who were a little bit nervy. But no one who was dippy. I mean, there might have been people who were dippy, but they didn't live in Glen Iris. I think it was more of an overseas thing altogether. Though Beryl did know a woman at the bowling club. Or said she knew her. Or knew of her. Or knew a woman who knew her or knew of her, who knew of Beryl, who knew her, whose niece — I think it was her niece — had gone a little bit odd. And she put her head in the gas oven. Apparently the medical people said that it was a cry for help. In which case it was even more serious, because, I mean, if you're going to cry for help, you'd put your head out the window, wouldn't you?

EDNA EVERAGE: 'WE ALWAYS USED TO LEAVE A LITTLE BIT ON OUR PLATES FOR MR MANNERS. AND MR MANNERS WAS A VERY IMPORTANT PERSON IN OUR LIVES, ALONG WITH JESUS AND FATHER CHRISTMAS. AND MY MOTHER USED TO SAY TO US, CLOSING THE BIBLE: 'BE NICE AND PEOPLE WILL BE NICE TO YOU.' I DON'T KNOW WHERE THAT IS IN THE BIBLE, BUT IT'S THERE, I CAN ASSURE YOU OF THAT.'

ashtray rising from the chrome edge with cobra-like insistence. Nearby were a walnut cocktail cabinet and a plastic radio. Glazed china cats and shepherdesses preened themselves in a special glass-shelved display cabinet, and scenes of English rural life on the wall portrayed haymaking, ploughing and fox-hunting.

It was the culmination of more than a century of suburbanisation of southern Australia. The aim was to have a custom-built home, in a private garden, for every householder. This airless, small-windowed cube was the outback reduced to a postage stamp, and was how most Australians in the cities lived, or aspired to live.

As white Anglo-Saxon Australians moved in their thousands to their new cream-brick Shangri-la's in the outer suburbs, the old inner-city working-class areas were filling up with European migrants being briefed and caringly brainwashed. It was all very well for migrants to appear in their varieties of national dress at their own gatherings, or to parade for colourful effect on Australia Day, but the real business of being a New Australian from the Australian point of view was to place emphasis on the word Australian. This meant classes where people who could barely manage the basic courtesies in English were taught the surreal words of the national song, 'Waltzing Matilda'. Even when their English was good they had to start afresh hearing the clanging consonants and screeching vowels of Australian English. They began this induction under the national roofing material, corrugated iron, which was in the process of being rejected by suburban builders everywhere except Adelaide, where its properties were still valued.

It was assumed the migrants had been used to living in slums back home. So they ended up in the inner-city suburbs. But, as quick as they could move into these quaint working-class terraces, the Housing Commission would pull them down.

From the outside the 1950s house was as squat and clumsy-looking as the armchair within. More interesting styles of house were things of the past. The picturesque turn-of-the-century villa with its dark red tiles was gone. False 1920s gables and frilled ridges were gone. By 1950 there was no wooden or tiled verandah floor out the front. There wasn't even a verandah any more. The house was like a wooden crate or a stack of blocks. The connection from the verandah to the stream of life was largely gone from Australian towns and cities. Gone or going.

The roughcast touches to the 1930s bungalow style were gone as well. Also gone was the rugged, simple homespun look of earlier decades, the characteristic low flat roof over the porch and thick pylon supports made from brick, cement, timber or tin. Even such basic decorative touches as rounded corners were no longer around. It was a time of shortages.

The 1950s-style suburban house was an L-shaped box-like structure, as tidy and as tight as a long-held breath. Postwar unavailability of materials and cost-savings dictated the shape. Imagination was never allowed to get around them into a more 'vernacular' response. Not even the individualism of the World War II brick bungalow got past the building restrictions and rising costs of the postwar period. The thought of adding a verandah – the most vernacular touch available to Australian builders since early in the 1800s, when adaptation to climate was the theme – was out of the question.

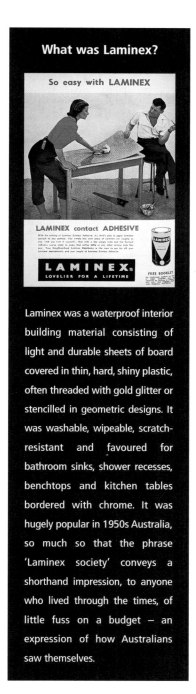

What was Laminex?

Laminex was a waterproof interior building material consisting of light and durable sheets of board covered in thin, hard, shiny plastic, often threaded with gold glitter or stencilled in geometric designs. It was washable, wipeable, scratch-resistant and favoured for bathroom sinks, shower recesses, benchtops and kitchen tables bordered with chrome. It was hugely popular in 1950s Australia, so much so that the phrase 'Laminex society' conveys a shorthand impression, to anyone who lived through the times, of little fuss on a budget – an expression of how Australians saw themselves.

The two men, my father and uncle, planned to build a weekend shack together at Healesville, a beauty spot about 40 miles from town. Accordingly, they bought 30 acres of virgin bush about a mile from the township, up a dusty track. There, in a small clearing with a blue view of Mount Riddell and the lavender-coloured foothills of the Great Divide, my father, assisted by Pat and Alec, built a house, known thereafter as 'the shack'. It was a rudimentary structure of weatherboard, asbestos sheeting and corrugated iron, and there were none of the cosy amenities of Camberwell. No water, electricity or sewerage, so we had a galvanised-iron tank at the side of the house, spirit lamps and an outdoor dunny, built of split logs over a very deep hole. This was furnished with little more than a huge desiccated tarantula on the ceiling and, for the convenience of visitors, a mutilated Melbourne telephone book suspended by a string from a bent nail …

EXPRESSIONIST VISIONARIES SUCH AS ARTHUR BOYD (above) AND SIDNEY NOLAN FLED AUSTRALIA IN THE FIFTIES AND FOUND ACCLAIM OVERSEAS. ONLY THEN, WITH REVIEWS OF THEIR WORK REPRINTED FROM OVERSEAS NEWSPAPERS, DID MANY AUSTRALIANS SWAP SCORN FOR ADMIRATION.

Soon our shack in the bush became a regular weekend haven for all the relations. There were beds everywhere, and at night on my lumpy mattress in my little 'sleep-out', I could hear the adults in the living room playing whist and mah-jong late into the night …

The economic realities of 1950 suited the Australian imagination. It was a time for the expression of security and conformity. It was not a time when indulgence of imagination received public approval. The artistic mavericks of the time were Sidney Nolan, Arthur Boyd and Patrick White. They were not yet mainstream status symbols.

A lot of the staidness came from an appreciation of how far Australians had come from Depression-era privations and in many cases from rural simplicities – they were tired of constant water shortages, incessant dust, lack of electricity, backbreaking chores, of 'making do' in a time of widespread unemployment. They came in from the brown land to the cities seeking relief. The journey was a long one from the bush shack to the neat suburban block, to the brick or fibro house with inside plumbing and light and power at the flick of a switch. The generation of children who grew up in the 1920s and 1930s, with their deprived Depression-era realities, had entered World War II as young adults. Fathers had seen horrors and experienced losses that could hardly be imagined by their children and wives. They were content with their self-owned brick-and-tile share

THE HILLS HOIST WAS INVENTED IN 1946 AND SOON BECAME AN ESSENTIAL PIECE OF AUSTRALIAN BACKYARD FURNITURE. WHILE MUM MADE THE MOST OF THE ROTARY CLOTHESLINE'S PRACTICAL APPLICATIONS, THE KIDS SOON LEARNT IT MADE A MAGNIFICENT SWING, A DISCOVERY WHICH WOULD EVENTUALLY DESTROY THE WHOLE DEVICE.

of a much-reduced dream. They settled for a bathroom with a small handbasin and awkward stubby taps, and a toilet bowl wedged up against their knees whenever they wanted to perform the simplest task of hygiene. It would do them very well. 'Be thankful for small mercies' was uttered with a sigh of relief by such battlers as they got older: but the words were a dreadful stifling to young ears.

If they were better off, they could build in a more flamboyant style. But imagination wasn't a necessity in that direction either. A Tudor villa, a Spanish mission or a Gothic castle were all possibilities. It was a certainty, though, that the home would be a barrier of some sort between the inside and the outside. The ideal seemed to be to live as differently as possible from the way life was conducted in one's youth. It was progress to have it this way. And healthier, too, if it meant sewage pipes were being laid in the vicinity. 'Progress' was the constant promise on the radio, in the newspapers, in the coloured magazines. It was the energised word dangled by politicians and representing the future. Bigger, cheaper, *more*, better. The consumerism marking the second half of the twentieth century was beginning its push.

Women were identified as the major users of new appliances coming onto the market – the washing machine with motorised wringers, the electric vacuum cleaner, the spacious and efficient refrigerator. The entire backyard was planned around a centrepiece – a concrete slab in which was embedded a Hills hoist. It was Australia's gift to the world, but needed plenty of backyard space and open-air breezes. There were as many ways to haul a load of washing out to the Hills hoist as there were ideas for attaching small solid wheels to laundry carts and having a woman propel them along. Advertising was directed at women as the ultimate consumers for home and family. Devices were often billed as labour-saving – and so, in theory, should have freed women to get out of the house. But nobody believed that, really. As time went on, pride in the woman as a skilled household worker gave way to the idea that she had an obligation to stay at home, freed or not, and be hostess, wife, helpmate and mother. In other words, to be the cornerstone of Family Values. But in any case, *would* she be freed? The imperative associated with a 'washable surface' was that someone be there to give it a wash.

The kitchen was the hub of our home. It was Beryl's domain. I think she spent most of our married life in there. She had everything absolutely as she wanted it. Her surfaces – my wife's surfaces were probably the most beautiful in Australia. She cared about her surfaces; she looked after them. And she knew where everything was. She could walk into that kitchen in the dark and put her hand on anything she wanted. She cooked and had the tins there, and the condiments in different-sized tins. She was a great one for condiments. There was plain flour, self-raising flour, and the rice and sugar. And then there was the coffee and tea. We didn't go in for the coffee, it wasn't our cup of tea. We tended to have, if we so required, the coffee essence. And she used another tin for the desiccated coconut. 📖

There was conformity, too, in dress. Australians loved uniforms. The working man's uniform consisted of an old-style Akubra hat, a 'half Norfolk' jacket, single-breasted, with a half belt across the back, generally in fawn, sometimes with a large over-check – usually from Fletcher Jones, but cheaper varieties were available. It was worn with grey trousers, boots, an open-neck shirt with its collar over the lapel, a maroon and fawn two-tone cardigan in the colder months, and a collapsed Gladstone bag which carried the man's lunch but could bring back from work at least four bottles of Tooheys beer. This was the real man's uniform through the 1950s.

Middle-class male students, on the other hand, wore a sports coat with a crew-neck sweater. And suede shoes, depending on their sexual orientation. Suede shoes were called 'poofters' shoes' – crepe soles were a dead giveaway for being gay.

While parents raised the drawbridge, poured a cuppa, relaxed on the lounge, drew close to the radio serial and blessed the roof over their heads, their children remained an outdoor tribe right across Australia. As Robin Boyd wrote in his 1952 classic, *Australia's Home*, childhood 'remained so, even when the cities developed and the playing paddocks were overgrown with buildings and fences. From earliest infancy, the weather and the private garden drew the child outside the house. The infant left the pram earlier than his European contemporary, playing with his woolly toys and saucepan lids on the grass...'

So echoes of an earlier Australia could still be heard in newly built streets with their smells of newly laid tar and freshly sawn timber. Look, too,

Sandy Stone and the Great Desiccated Coconut Shortage

There was a tragedy in the fifties when a boat bringing desiccated coconut to Australia discovered they had a leper on board, and this old leper had got into the desiccated coconut somehow or other. I don't know what he did to it or with it, but they had to dump the lot in the middle of the sea. And again, who knows what happened with the desiccated coconut or the effect it had down there? Who knows, maybe one day it will rise to the surface and there'll be a coconut slick in the Pacific.

We used it for the lamingtons. My wife won several lamington competitions. She got the sponge just right and iced it beautifully with the chocolate and then rolled them in the coconut. But for a whole generation coconut was off the market due to the leprosy. And that generation missed out on lamingtons. And they're the ones who are giving us the trouble now. Because I think – I'm not a scientist, but I think there's an enzyme in lamingtons.

at school photographs taken in the late 1940s and early 1950s and you might be looking down a long barrel of time to the 1920s and 1930s. Bad dentistry in the smiles. Girls in pleated frocks and with plaits so tight they are almost screaming. Evidence of fatty diets, excessive protein, shortage of fibre and fresh greens. Boys in collarless shirts, flannel shorts held up by Police and Fireman braces, and bare feet with callused, splayed toes. A sleepy look from energetic use of time.

There were plenty of part-time jobs around, as well as full-time ones. Home delivery was a theme. The baker had a horsedrawn cart and so did the milkman. They began their rounds well before dawn, often with a schoolchild doing the fetching. Milk was decanted from solid-metal, sour-smelling tubs and poured into billycans on the front steps of the house. In the grocery trade, bulk handling was done close to the customer – sugar and salt were scooped into paper bags over the counter, everything measured and weighed in person. Or the grocer went out in a spluttering truck, getting his deliveries in before nightfall. This vehicle, a Dodge, Ford or Chrysler, was known as a 'ute' in the eastern states, or a 'buckboard' in parts of Victoria and South Australia. Sometimes an old dray would come grinding along the newly tarred streets of the suburbs with a cadaverous figure at the reins calling, 'Clothes props!' These were long, green eucalyptus saplings cut from an outlying farm. They had a fork at the end to hold the clothesline wire up, but when a strong wind blew they

THE CORNER GROCERY STORE BELONGED TO AN ERA WHEN GROCERS KNEW BETTER THAN MOST THE INTIMATE FINANCIAL DETAILS OF FAMILY LIFE. PUTTING ITEMS 'ON TICK' UNTIL PAYDAY WAS THE ONLY WAY MANY FAMILIES GOT THROUGH THE WEEK.

flipped over to the other side, like a yacht's boom going about, and the washing fell in the dirt.

A powerful figure in children's imaginations was the abysmal Dunny Man. He came down the back lane in a noisy old truck and dragged the full pan out and pushed an empty one into the back of the narrow little shed known as the dunny. Luckily his truck was noisy, because the thought of being caught sitting on the seat when he came was frightening. Children remembered him as a giant, red-headed man with a face the colour of his business. They would ask him how he could stand the stink. He would put his hands to his hips, arch his throat to the sun and look thoughtful. 'I get the first fresh pan of the morning, I stick my finger in, I wipe it across my upper lip, and I don't smell a thing for the rest of the day.'

A decade is never exactly the years it covers. While the cities of Australia in the 1950s moved into an era of urban growth that was in part an international phenomenon, other parts of the country stayed in the mood of the 1940s or even the 1930s. In many ways it is this blast from the even more distant past that summarises the style-mood of the fifties. They were like the thirties, re-run with atomic bombs in the offing, and so had a kind of science-fiction feel. The fifties were the first full decade when the appalling destructive power of humanity's genius for knowledge stared mankind in the face. For Australia, the admixture of horror and rural-type innocence was perfectly reflected in Neville Shute's *On the Beach* – both the book and the movie made from it.

Legend has it that, when she arrived to make the film of Neville Shute's story of nuclear holocaust, Ava Gardner was asked how she liked Melbourne. The actress is said to have replied: 'Where better than Melbourne to make a film about the end of the world?' This is probably quite apocryphal, but it has been repeated by masochistic Melburnians ever since.

For young people in the cities there were the Saturday 'arvo' flicks, a scene of yelling, jostling hysteria brought to silent anxiety only by the climax of the weekly serial. Entertainment in a country town meant Friday-night pictures (most of the films being in black and white), the reading of comics and books, playing with mates, and the telling of stories. Sometimes the circus came. In western New South Wales and Queensland, rodeos were a drawcard. At other times a tent-show housed a visiting evangelist, whose attraction for kids was the chance to compete for free gifts. The fact that they were

Sandy Stone on Home Deliveries

We had a lot of deliveries by horse and cart in the early fifties. You'd hear 'clip-clop' down Gallipoli Crescent and there'd be the milkman at six o'clock in the morning. They'd get up early then, you know. Bread would be delivered – beautiful bread. Horsedrawn again. Manure on the street. You'd go out when they'd gone and shovel it up and put it on the strawbs or on the shrubs.

We'd also have grocery deliveries most mornings. You ask kiddies these days to go down to the shop and get a few groceries and they wouldn't know what you meant by groceries – the word groceries. It's like blotting paper. You tell a kiddie to get some blotting paper at the newsagency and they'd say 'blotting paper, what's it for?' They don't know because they don't have fountain pens.

AN EARLY FACILITATOR OF THE SEXUAL REVOLUTION, THE DRIVE-IN THEATRE WAS A PHENOMENON OF THE LATE FIFTIES. DRIVING OFF THROUGH THE CLOSING CREDITS WITH THE LOUDSPEAKER STILL ATTACHED TO THE DOOR AND WITH THE WINDOWS STEAMED UP WAS A HAZARD FOR MANY AUSTRALIAN TEENAGERS.

tawdry scripture stickers and flimsy cardboard boomerangs studded with biblical quotes made no difference. It was something to do.

Some of the country picture theatres were of indoor–outdoor construction, with a rail where the projector was trundled under the stars in the hot, dry months of the year. The outdoor seats were stretches of canvas between two poles. Bugs flocked to the projector beam. Going to the 'flicks' on a Friday night was an event for the entire school, and there was no question of its being unsafe to go without parents. Kids trailed through the streets and made their way home as late as they liked – after cartoons, newsreels, shorts of forthcoming features (they were never called movies then) and then the double feature: first up a comedy – Danny Kaye, Red Skelton in *The Yellow Cab Man*, or *The Three Stooges* – and finally the main feature. Westerns were wildly popular, 'Cowboys and Indians' being a nonstop game among children, with cowboy tents, cowboy suits and cap-guns being the preferred Christmas presents. Ushers walked the aisles with long silver torches like New York cops keeping order. There was a kind of picket fence separating the first few rows of the stalls from the rest of the theatre. The front side of that fence was for Aborigines. Of these, the adults knew the rules, but kids who were cheeky enough to flaunt them or wanted to be with their friends in the back stalls or (much more rarely) in the dress circle, would be hunted down to the front again.

It was the same old reaction from the time of the earliest settlers, who were greeted by fellow humans smeared with grease and dirt. A metaphor for it all was germs. You might 'catch something'. Hookworm and ringworm were believed to fester in Aboriginal camps, with special hookworm clinics being set up in some places. The worst proof of the viciousness of communicable disease in the wider community was the polio epidemic, which scared nice kids off eating ice-cream cones because of the hand contact involved. Thus middle-class Australia exercised its control and achieved its supremacy in many small ways. Imagine how black mothers felt with white

LONG BEFORE THE WONDERBRA AND PLASTIC SURGERY, THE BIGGEST-SELLING BRA OF THE FIFTIES WAS THE HOLLYWOOD-MAXWELL. THIS MARVEL OF ENGINEERING MEANT THAT AUSTRALIAN WOMEN COULD EMULATE THE POINTED 'SWEATER GIRL' LOOK POPULARISED BY MOVIE STARS LIKE JANE RUSSELL.

mothers putting all this around. Addressing a white readership, Kath Walker wrote in later years: 'In those days, Aboriginal people didn't draw attention to themselves at all. It was the most you could do to appear inconspicuous and make your day as smooth as possible.'

The only schoolmaster I really liked was Mr Albert Greed, the chapel organist [at Melbourne Grammar], who took us for musical-appreciation classes one afternoon a week. Albert was usually in a convivial mood after lunch, having had a few beers up the road at the Botanical Hotel, and could sometimes be persuaded to break off a lesson on Schubert and, whilst still seated at the piano, launch into a sprightly rendition of 'Nola' or 'Kitten on the Keys', during which he would blush and giggle immoderately. Albert also organised lunchtime concerts in the War Memorial Hall and to one of these he invited the Aboriginal tenor, Harold Blair. He was the first Aborigine I ever set eyes on, for if there were any of Australia's original inhabitants living in Melbourne, they were kept well out of the way of nice people; unless, of course, they could sing…

Certainly we dwelt in a kind of postwar time-lag, still trying to catch up with the American thirties. Air travel was becoming fashionable and we invented somewhere called 'Interstate': a place to go when we couldn't go 'Overseas'. Moreover, momentous things started happening at airports. Mrs Petrov's not entirely voluntary trip back to Russia was dramatically intercepted at Darwin airport by a Chips Rafferty lookalike; and another Goose – Sir Eugene – was escorted, ashen-faced, from Kingsford Smith customs for importing a suitcase bulging with the equivocal accoutrements of old-fashioned Satanism. The autocratic, puritan, anti-intellectual Administration chalked up a pyrrhic victory. To the strains of Mantovani, the politics of Niceness had avenged itself.

Communism was another kind of virus, a scarlet fever changing the colour of those who brushed up against any idea that connected to it. During an earlier prime ministership, Menzies had taken a stab at banning the Communist Party and succeeded. That was in 1940, at the time of the Nazi–Soviet nonaggression pact. When Labor came to power in 1941 the ban was maintained. It was lifted a year later, however, at the end of 1942, twelve months after the Soviet Union entered the war against Germany – and when it was clear that Australian communists had done a turnaround and now unreservedly supported the Australian and Allied war effort.

PRIME MINISTER MENZIES LEGISLATED TO OUTLAW THE 'COMMUNIST MENACE' IN 1950, BUT WAS LATER REBUFFED IN A REFERENDUM ON THE ISSUE.

An opinion poll conducted at the start of the 1950s found that Australians were ahead of the rest of the world in believing that another world war was inevitable – and that it would be against the Reds. It would be a more confusing war than any other because of the enemy within. Not just the front line would need to be on guard in this war, but the home front as well. Communists were marked as infiltrating trade unions, undermining national security, destroying religion and being contemptuous of law and order. Indeed, it was an avowed communist aim to do some or all of these things at any one time or when the opportunity presented. Yet with pitifully few card-carrying communists living in Australia the party was no looming monolith. There were people who had joined the Communist Party because the party offered the only ear that would listen to them. One was the poet Kath Walker, who joined in 1943: 'You see, in those days, Aboriginal people just didn't vote, and even if they did, they had to choose between Liberal, Labor and Country parties in Queensland, who all had racist politics. At least the

Communist Party said that they believed in racial equality.'

Immediately after being elected to office in 1950, Menzies introduced legislation calling for the outlawing of the Communist Party.

I decided to become a communist. Furtively I bought a copy of The Communist Manifesto *in a backstreet bookshop in the industrial suburb of Brunswick, but I found it practically unreadable. The next best thing, so I thought, was to appear to be a communist, and this was a path down which I was sure Mr Sutcliffe [the headmaster of Melbourne Grammar] would not follow me. My political period — the only one in my life — was*

Les Patterson and Mrs Petrov's Shoe

It's a strange fact of life, but in any big event, world event, Les seems to have been there. I'm drawn like a moth to the flame of events — a blowfly to the bull's bum of history. And I was at that airport when that poor old commo sheila, Mrs Petrov, was dragged off by the K.B.GEES. And like Prince Charming, I grabbed hold of her shoe. I did! And I've still got it, readers. It's a commo sheila's shoe. It's red, and it's been under the bed. Are you with me? I thought I'd hang on to it all these years in case I fell in love with a sheila with one leg. It'd be a nice tasteful present for her, wouldn't it? But you sniff this shoe — mmm — and to this day, what do you smell? The smell of fear.

A SHOELESS MRS PETROV IS MANHANDLED AT DARWIN AIRPORT IN 1954.

short-lived, since the manifesto left ostentatiously on my desk so that it could be seen by the most fanatically right-wing schoolmaster in Australia was swiftly confiscated and I never saw it again. However I had discovered that there was a very special pleasure and excitement to be derived from shocking people. I suppose it gave a schoolboy, who was in fact completely powerless, the illusion of power.

Back-and-forth smearing was an inhibiting factor in the public exchange of ideas. It mattered little that communists were individuals, and that some of them acted according to principles unthreatening to Australia. Nor that many anti-communists were appalled by Menzies' proposal to ban the Communist Party. A member of the Liberal Party at the time was Gordon Barton, a student at Sydney University, and later to be a well-known businessman. He said: 'My mind boggled in contemplation of a new Australian era of thought police, purge trials and political concentration camps. I thought the Bill was opportunistic, pernicious and contrary to democratic principles.' Communism was branded an 'alien fifth column', and soon enough so were non-communist socialist sympathisers, and so the Labor Party was tarred with the same brush in the interests of political expediency.

It happens in every decade — as one threat recedes another is perceived, and there will always be an accorded enemy given a new name. In the 1950s the enemy was often the ordinary Australian with a social conscience, labelled a 'pinko' or 'fellow traveller'.

They keep Australia strong

IN THE EARLY FIFTIES AN OPINION POLL REVEALED THAT NERVOUS AUSTRALIANS LED THE WORLD IN THEIR BELIEF THAT ANOTHER WORLD WAR WAS INEVITABLE. DISAPPOINTED BY THE WAR'S NON-APPEARANCE, PRIME MINISTER MENZIES LAUNCHED A CAMPAIGN AGAINST COMMUNISTS AT HOME AND RALLIED THE TROOPS FOR A FIGHT IN KOREA WITH THE RE-ISSUE OF THIS WORLD WAR II RECRUITMENT POSTER.

Apart from declaring the Communist Party invalid, the legislation gave the government the power to name communists, required the onus of proof of innocence to be on the accused, barred communists from official positions in the unions and banned them from the public service. The Bill passed into law six months after being introduced in Parliament, but was overturned by the High Court by a majority of 6–1. A referendum followed, with a narrow win to the 'no' vote. Thus by a margin of around 50 000, Australians avoided a bitter McCarthyite era and a declared war against ideas at the government level. Not that any encouragement of political rivalries was needed: it was all bitter enough. Australian soldiers had fought North Korean and Chinese Communists in Korea, and then in Malaya. Communists were continually being identified publicly as the enemies of industrial peace. But would the public feel enough fear to get the right result in the next election? A good result for the government in 1954 was a matter of touch and go. Menzies needed a gift from heaven.

Menzies had introduced to Australia a more genial version of McCarthyism so that in some circles communism became ideologically titillating. The fact that there really were Reds under the beds may well have eluded the prime minister, who was trying to run Australia like Wesley College [his old school]: short back and sides and hands above the bedclothes. ✍

Six weeks before the 1954 election Menzies announced the defection to Australia of a Soviet diplomat, Vladimir Petrov. Suddenly Australia was at the centre of the international news. It gave the national inferiority complex a boost. A drama unfolded: Petrov wasn't just an ordinary diplomat, announced Menzies, he was a member of the Russian secret police (KGB). He knew things about traitorous Australians. And, giving the affair a nasty twist, Menzies implied that when the full truth came out, 'people in close association with politicians would be named'. Obviously the politicians would be Labor – so how were they to be trusted?

The drama intensified. Mrs Petrov asked for asylum but almost at the same moment, tearful and distressed, departed Sydney for Moscow on a BOAC Constellation. During a stopover in Darwin she was manhandled back to the steps of her plane by burly Russian security guards. After argument, crowd pressure and almost unbearable tension, during which her shoe was lost in the struggle and held aloft (to be shown on newsreels flashed around the world), Northern Territory police disarmed the Soviet guards and took her into protection, where she too (after three more hours) asked for asylum. It was ten days before the election and the drama did not just unfold: it was a controlled release as the government fed the press pieces of information, spiced with innuendo. In the election the Liberals' slogan was 'Don't give the Reds a second chance'. It was a not-so-subtle brainwash to identify Labor with a world enemy. In the event, members of Labor leader Dr H. V. Evatt's staff would be among those named in Petrov's documents. Menzies slipped home with a narrow win. Six months later it was announced by the Petrov Royal Commission that 'prosecution of none of the persons whose acts we have considered in our Report would be warranted'.

Many Australians were less than impressed with Menzies' actions. One of them was Jack Mundey, who was to come to prominence as the New South Wales secretary of the left-wing Builders' Labourers Federation and later as an environmental activist. Mundey recalls: 'I believed that each country should find its own way to socialism based on the history, culture and tradition of that country, and not blindly genuflect at Russia or China. Of course, amongst the ordinary Australians who had been brainwashed by the Cold War there was hostility to the word "communist" – to anything socialistic, in fact.' And he adds: 'Menzies maintained his rule by using the defectors from the Labor Party – the clerical side, the Democratic Labor Party, so-called – to keep himself in power … he used the communist bogey very much during those long years he was in power.'

People in the 1950s lived closer to where they worked, and in industrial or semi-industrial areas there was no doubt about the nature of the work done – a new sample of it was wafted to the nose at every change of wind. In Sydney, at Homebush Primary School (close to where the 2000 Olympics would be held 50 years later), there was a gramophone record factory. An Arnott's biscuit factory was over the way. The vast Homebush and Flemington saleyards were not far distant, and the main western railway line ran past the end of the playground. The mixture of smells was poisonous. Melted vinyl, for its part, made a chemical brew that sent children home with headaches. There was increased production as 78 rpm records gave way to 45 rpm's and

the fashion became a craze for long-playing 33⅓ rpm's (making a concert in the home possible without having to jump up and change sides of a record every couple of minutes). The smell of roasting biscuits tantalised and eventually sickened. The pall of cattle and sheep saleyards was a sour, wet experience when the wind changed. The only consolation lay with the trains: coal smoke appealed to pre-adolescent dreamers, and boys lined the school fence noting down train numbers on narrow, thick notepads. The futuristic 'Garratt', with its curved front-mounted water tank, was the most esteemed prize. The trains rocketed and thundered past, carrying dreams in a westward direction.

There was another odour surrounding the asphalt playground – one that Homebush shared with all primary schools of the 1950s – the smell of sour milk. At morning break (called 'playtime') it was the job of the milk monitor to hand out bottles which were to be drunk for the benefit of growing children's bones. It was delivered to schools under a Commonwealth Government scheme begun in 1950. This was a huge bonanza for the nation's dairy farmers, while the art of emptying a milk bottle down a drain without being spotted by a teacher was widely practised. The other pervading smell was dust. It gathered in school floorboards and drifted from chalk, and rose in small, ever-present mites spread by the feather dusters wielded by room monitors.

Many of my schoolmasters had been hauled out of retirement during World War II to replace teachers who had been 'called up', and most of these remained on the staff for the duration of my schooldays. Looked upon as wonderful 'characters' by sentimental Old Boys and younger staff members, and like my mother's housekeepers kept on for their eccentricities rather than their abilities, these ignorant dotards made no effort to communicate knowledge since they had no store of this article on which to draw. Basking in the titillating propinquity of small boys, they filled whole periods, terms and years with boring reminiscence, bluff and sadism. Thus I was 'taught' mathematics and divinity by a senile football coach, art and algebra by a desiccated athletics instructor, and English literature by a major of cadets.

Mrs Norm Everage on Australia's Own Car

My Norm's done quite well for himself. He's got himself one of those wonderful new Holdens. I think General Motors are absolutely marvellous, don't you? I mean, letting us call it 'Australia's Own Car'. They didn't have to do that. Such a wonderful gesture. If there were more people like them in the world it would be a happier place.

Above: The Holden 48/215 or 'FX' is pictured at a construction site with the architect and builder in concentrated discussion. The association of development with 'Australia's Own Car' – even if it was American – was no doubt intentional; this was the decade of 'progress'.

In cities there was little casual entertainment for families, most outings having to be planned ahead and restricted to weekends. Going for a 'Sunday drive' was popular, and the most popular car was the Holden, 'Australia's own car'. The thinking behind this vehicle was that if Japan and Germany could produce their own cars – and they were defeated in World War II – then why not Australia, which was one of the victors? The Holden was a considerable luxury in most families. When the first Holdens came out they cost £760 including registration and insurance. This was almost twice the average annual male wage, and three times the average female wage. By 1956 the Holden was established as the most desirable Australian motoring icon. It was given a nuggety, no-nonsense personality all of its own, and seemed to the loving eye to have grown out of the Australian landscape in familiar boulder-like ute or family-sedan form. (Non-Australians found the Australian ute ugly and absurd – a sedan with its back chopped off and an undersized tray or cargo well slapped on.) In the larger cities most of the driving time entailed getting to a drab outer-suburban picnic spot and then turning around to drive home again. In Sydney the legendary beach culture and the miles of sandstone-framed surf stretching from Cronulla to Palm Beach were not accessible to the whole population. The geography made sure of it.

Sydney was vast and overextended, without a reachable edge when it came to ambling around. Boys bought excursion train tickets and rode the full length of Sydney's rail system in a few hours – up to Hornsby, back down over the Bridge, down to Cronulla and back to Strathfield. They played golf on public courses with clubs bought from op shops. They rode bikes to the Olympic pools. They snatched golf balls from the private courses, dashing out onto the fairway as the balls came driving down, scooping them up and disappearing into the scrub, and then selling them to players on the public course and using the proceeds to buy cigarettes and milkshakes. They put coins on the railway line and watched the wheels squash them flat. If they lived near the harbour or adjacent to bushland and the wild, rocky gullies of Sydney's north-shore sandstone country, they had a better time of it – finding they could launch a canoe or a small sailboat, or go bushwalking and camping in places that gave the impression of never having experienced the footprint of an adventurer in all of time.

To Clive James, the writer and television presenter, those were days to treasure in the mind's eye. 'We had a big adventure when I dressed up as the Black Commando and went out with my gang in the evening. I remember the sounds. I remember the sound of the sprinklers towards evening, and the sound of the southerly buster coming. And the sound of the cowboy beetles hitting the enamel rim of the street lights – ping, ping, ping… There was a peppercorn tree full of cicadas – the row they kicked up! And you got one of these in your hands –

Wowsers

'Wowser' (noun) was one of the most expressive words in the lexicon of Australian English. It was widely used shorthand in the 1950s to denote a person 'who, being entirely destitute of the greater virtues, makes up for his lack by a continuous denunciation of little vices'. The muckraking turn-of-the-century journalist John Norton claimed to have coined the word. Wowserism peaked in the 1950s in such incidents as the banning of bikinis on Bondi Beach and the banning of books that were in any way sexually explicit.

Opposite: THE VOLUNTEER SURF LIFESAVER WAS THE PRIDE OF THE NATION IN THE FIFTIES. AN INHERITOR OF THE BRONZED ANZAC TRADITION, AN EXAMPLE OF PHYSICAL PERFECTION AND DEVOTED PUBLIC SERVICE, HE WAS ALSO GUARANTEED A GOOD TIME AFTER HOURS BY THE INNUMERABLE YOUNG WOMEN WHO REGARDED HIM AS AN OBJECT OF DESIRE. WITH A BELT AROUND HIS WAIST AND A LONG ROPE UNWINDING BEHIND HIM HE NEEDED TO BE A POWERFUL SWIMMER. IN THE FIFTIES, SMOKING WASN'T CONSIDERED TO BE INCONSISTENT WITH THIS REQUIREMENT.

when you were, say, eight years old – and it was terror! You know, *your* terror, not its. Because you felt it pulse in your hand.'

He goes on, reflectively: 'It was a very rich experience, sensually, to grow up in what was a city that had the attributes of the country. That's what the suburb does for people. And I think it was essential to Australian culture and to Australian life that we never had the really densely populated city. There were never any Hong Kongs, even in Chinatown. Each little house in its little piece of ground was a little country. And each street was a nation. And the way you had just enough space in order to explore, I think, was crucial.'

To run around healthy and free was the definition of Australian childhood and of life in Australia in general. But when prominent Australians spoke on the radio, or, as elected national represent-atives, addressed a national

A DAY AT THE BEACH HAS LONG BEEN AN AUSTRALIAN INSTITUTION. IN THE FIFTIES IT WAS AN OUTING WHICH COULD BE ENJOYED BY THE WHOLE FAMILY AND AUSTRALIANS PURSUED IT IN BLISSFUL IGNORANCE OF THE PERILS OF THE SCORCHING SUN. THIS *AUSTRALIAN WOMEN'S WEEKLY* COVER ILLUSTRATION IS BY WILLIAM E. PIDGEON (WEP), A THREE-TIMES WINNER OF THE ARCHIBALD PRIZE FOR PORTRAITURE IN THE FIFTIES AND SIXTIES.

audience, they did not sound particularly free at all. They sounded culturally trapped. The accent they chose wasn't noticeably Australian – it was more like a public approximation of a non-Australian accent in which the Australianness was hidden by rounded, sun-warmed vowels. It pretended to be southern Standard English and had a vigorous, upper-crust, no-nonsense lilt to it. It was the accent of social control, but at the same time it implied a rejection of what it lorded over, and so lacked an easy identity. It wasn't grown-up yet, wasn't grown-out. Australia was a country where it didn't do to stand out from the crowd, unless it was on the sports field or in other manly pursuits. Usually, those who stood out from the crowd were called 'ratbags'.

A ratbag, in the general use of the term, was a fool and a loudmouth. But on the political or cultural scene the word was used to counter the impact of anyone with opinions standing out from the crowd. Artists were ratbags. Writers were ratbags. Composers were ratbags. Youth was a ratbag grouping. If you were from Melbourne, Sydneysiders were ratbags. Supporters of Aboriginal rights were ratbags one and all. Socialists were ratbags. Where else could ratbags go except into the streets, squeezed sideways by the pressures of conformity? The eccentric Bea Miles was a ratbag – an overweight woman wearing an army greatcoat and scuttling around Sydney with a placard hung from her neck advertising recitations from Shakespeare for a few shillings. Schoolboys of the 1950s remember her very well. She was frightening, pinning them with a bloodshot eye almost hidden in rolls of fat, smelling unwashed, urinous, dusty. She favoured the hub of the city around Central Station, where taxis crawled and buses and trams wedged every inch of the roadway. She declaimed in a polished, upper-crust manner and crossed against red lights, against the policeman's hand, against the current of society moving in the opposite direction.

I still felt like an exile in Sydney. I was stranded amongst people who could not even muster the glottal energy to pronounce the 'd' in the name of their own city. They looked so different from their Melbourne counterparts. They wore beach clothes in town, they were shorter and taller and flasher and poorer, and their faces told a story in which beer, cigarettes and strong sunlight played a dominant role. At the time, they seemed to me like parodies of people; like the Toby jugs on the curio ledge at the

THE RADIOGRAM WAS AN ICON BEFORE WE'D EVEN HEARD OF ICONS. UNTIL THE ARRIVAL OF TELEVISION IN 1956 IT WAS THE ENTERTAINMENT CENTREPIECE OF THE LOUNGE ROOM. CHILDREN LISTENED TO 'THE ARGONAUTS', WHILE THEIR PARENTS WOULD TUNE IN TO 'THE VILLAGE GLEE CLUB' OR THE NEW PARLIAMENTARY BROADCASTS. DESPITE THE EFFORTS OF ACTORS, NEWSREADERS AND POLITICIANS TO SPEAK IN THEIR BEST QUEEN'S ENGLISH, THE SOUNDS OF THE AUSTRALIAN ACCENT SLIPPED THROUGH THE RADIO WAVES AND SPARKED WIDE DEBATE ABOUT THE PROPER WAY TO ENUNCIATE.

Dame Edna Speaks

Someone once said to me I had an Oxford accent. I don't know why – I didn't go to the University of Oxford. But it was a lovely compliment, because although I like the Australian accent I would hate to have a broad, ugly, common Australian accent. So I'm very pleased. I think it may be that in another life I went to Oxford. When I was Anne Hathaway or Florence Nightingale, I don't know which – whichever one of them went to Oxford – and it doesn't matter. But niceness is something that comes through, I think. People have said to me: 'Edna, you sound such a nice person.' They say that on the phone. And people write to me and they say: 'We saw you on TV and you seem so nice.' And I am. But it's an instinctive thing. We people from Melbourne are nice, whereas a lot of people from Sydney may be nice but they seem to be a little bit C-O-M-M-O-N, or as my mother used to say, O-R-D-I-N-A-R-Y. Oh!

Wattle Tea Rooms. William Dobell, perhaps the greatest Australian artist, has painted the Sydney face a thousand times, and at the time he was vilified for being a mere caricaturist. At the Granville Returned Servicemen's Club, at 11.30 on Sunday morning, the faces looking up at me as I stood on the small stage were all Dobell creations.

If you tweaked the wrong buttons on the new ripple-fronted, blond-wood veneer radiogram, a very nasty thing could happen: you could get Parliament. When Australians heard, for the first time, the accents and syntax of their elected governors, a deep shudder of revulsion and paranoia shook the nation. 'Surely these marsupial and cockatoo voices were those of the Labor Party!', expostulated the affronted middle classes. Or did they come from Sydney?

Was Robert Menzies the only Australian with a nice speaking voice? It should be noted that in the fifties, Australians had speaking voices as distinct, presumably, from thinking voices, eating voices or farting voices. Radio announcers, those last adenoidal custodians of the Queen's English, tried even harder to redress the cultural balance, but to no avail. We began to feel that we might all be irredeemably common.

In 1952 there was public debate, quite inconceivable now, over the extent to which the Australian accent should be admitted to the airwaves. Most radio actors were so immured to British accents (so-called Standard English and the various dialects of the United Kingdom and Ireland) that they were unable to speak in a natural Australian accent at all – just sometimes one would catch a vowel. In 1952 the *Current Affairs Bulletin* surveyed the question of whether an Australian manner of speech was a good and desirable thing as a sign or symbol of our national independence. Dame Enid Lyons, widow of the United Australia Party/Country Party prime minister Joe Lyons (a conservative politician who died in office in 1939), weighed in with the refined (though somewhat ungrammatical) comment: 'That there is such an "animile" as an Australian accent and that, at his worst, he is singularly unbeautiful, no one, I think, will deny. The question is should he be killed on the spot, or merely groomed into respectability. Personally, I'm all for letting it live.'

Radio was 95 per cent commercial in the cities, but in the country radio meant the ABC – the Children's Session and 'The Argonauts'. There were no other stations on the dial. The radio itself was a heavy, warm-smelling object around the size of two Besser brick blocks. Inside it had domed glass valves that glowed like dying light bulbs, and nests of wires and blobs of solder. Some family radios were homemade by men who had served as wartime radio operators. The leadlike weight came from condenser plates stacked and compressed in layers. The nearest transmitter was usually hundreds of miles away, and reception improved at night, when little that was interesting reached kids' ears, while adults never missed the News, sat glued to Parliament, or listened to orchestral concerts.

'The Village Glee Club' was a whimsical music and chat show, a hangover from pre-radio days. It was entirely scripted, arch and artificial. The word 'camp' had limited currency then, and so wasn't available as a description for what it was. Publicity stills of the time reveal its actors in situations so staged that they mock the situations themselves – an air of sexual naughtiness. This glutinous mix appealed to older listeners because it reflected their childhood era, somehow, when there was little entertainment except what people made for themselves. The format of 'The Village Glee Club' was choral singing as if presented by a small village choir. The concept also reflected a certain hankering over 'English' niceties, a kind of gold standard of the 1950s when it came to pointing out the shortcomings of anything too 'Orstralian' in Australian speech. This gold standard was gradually being eroded, however.

The Assembly Hotel was Sydney's 'bohemian' pub. It was conveniently located one block from the theatre, and I took to calling in there every evening before the show. Very different from the Swanston Family Hotel in Melbourne, where amongst the boozers and hangers-on real artists could sometimes be found, the Assembly was patronised by actors from the radio studios next door. Here, propped up at the bar, and already the worse for too many gin-and-tonics, were the heroines of all the soap operas I had listened to as a child. Many of the old serials were still on air, and these permed and sozzled harridans who practically lived at the Assembly would, from time to time, fall off their stools and totter to the adjacent Macquarie Studios to impersonate yet another sexy ingenue, pert minx or warm-hearted wife and mother. Their male counterparts were equally unappetising, with faces the colour of condemned veal. They possessed, none the less, voices that were famous throughout Australia, and on the wireless these burnt-out old hacks became handsome doctors, benevolent family solicitors and likeable cads – whatever the

AUSTRALIA WAS AN EAGER AND ACCOMMODATING NATION IN THE FIFTIES. WHEN THE BRITISH HAD NO PLACE TO TEST THEIR ATOMIC WEAPONS, AUSTRALIA OFFERED ITS DESERTS. THE MENZIES GOVERNMENT ASSURED AUSTRALIANS THAT THEY 'SHOULD NOT ATTACH ANY IMPORTANCE TO GEIGER COUNTER READINGS OF RADIOACTIVITY'.

script required. They took great pains to suppress their natural accents, since in the limbo of soap opera they were never asked to impersonate Australians. Hence they all adopted a fruity and adenoidal singsong which they supposed to be 'international', and which can still sometimes be heard from older radio announcers. Today, Australian actors have gone to the opposite extreme. Convinced that they don't sound faintly Australian when they speak naturally, they assume a grotesque parodic accent unknown outside the Australian film industry. Consequently, the dialogue in most Australian movies is incomprehensible. ✎

When the Woomera Rocket Range was established in 1946 (under Ben Chifley's Labor Government) it raised protests from many concerned for the welfare of Aboriginal people living in the test area. The minister responsible for the negotiations, Mr J. Dedman, explained to Parliament that the risk was negligible: 'The probability of a missile falling on them would be extremely remote,' he said. 'The area is vast, and the average density of population is probably about one native in every 50 or 100 square miles.' Later, during the atomic testing period, people were trucked out of the desert, but in at least one group the women were in a different place from the men when the vehicles came to their camp, and the women were taken to the Port Hedland area, far from their home country, while the men are believed to have remained in the desert throughout the entire test period.

A-bombs were exploded on the Western Australian coast and in South Australia. There was little or no public outcry over this during the 1952 and 1953 tests. Government policy and the prime minister's public statements were unequivocally pro-atom and free of anxiety altogether. The reasons advanced for sending Australian troops to Korea (stop them there or they will be here next) hovered around the reasons for developing uranium for export. 'The United States and the United Kingdom carry the main burden of the defence of the free world; it is surely our first duty to make our uranium available to their combined agency.' Early public objections were based not on fallout considerations but on concern as to whether Australia was letting go its uranium fuel too willingly – by keeping it to ourselves we could develop a nuclear-power industry within five or ten years. When Britain's first nuclear bomb was exploded in Western Australia, at the Monte Bello Islands, it was frighteningly close. People on sheep and cattle stations felt the shock, and within minutes the mushroom-shaped cloud rose 10 000 feet above the horizon. Publicly, though, there was pride that the device detonated was 'of a much smaller and more efficient design than anything the Americans currently possess'. It is curious how convoluted this Australian pride at the time was: trusting nuclear bombs to define or at least nudge at the idea of a national spirit, but not an intellectual culture so much.

QUEEN ELIZABETH IS GREETED ON HER ARRIVAL AT SYDNEY'S FARM COVE IN 1954 – THE FIRST-EVER VISIT TO AUSTRALIA BY A REIGNING MONARCH. OVER ONE MILLION OF HER DEVOTED SUBJECTS PACKED THE STREETS OF THE CITY. LATER, IN MELBOURNE, A YOUNG NATIONAL SERVICEMAN, BARRY HUMPHRIES, SPARKED THE 'SAUSAGE CONTROVERSY' WHEN HE DROPPED HIS RIFLE IN FRONT OF THE ROYAL COUPLE.

But by 1956, with a series of tests at Maralinga in South Australia, the public was increasingly concerned about the Australian mainland being offered to Britain as a nuclear testing site. The answer from the Menzies Government was soothing: 'The public should not attach any importance to Geiger counter readings of radioactivity from rainfall after the tests. These instruments are extremely sensitive, but their readings are not significant unless read by scientists in association with many other matters.' If anything was an object lesson in the need to question the certainties of ruling governments, this was it.

Early in 1954 the Queen and the Duke of Edinburgh arrived on the Royal Visit. A kind of swooning, anxious, grasping, breathless psychology got to work. The idea of a reigning monarch coming to Australia for the first time was one thing. That it was *her* was another. Queen Elizabeth's youth, her position and her rarity made her a beautiful phenomenon, even if she wasn't (and nobody said or even saw that she wasn't).

In Sydney she landed at Farm Cove near the Botanic Gardens and it was estimated that more than one million people lined the city streets and the gardens area. The Queen's every gesture, movement and reaction were noted – there was a magic in the way the breeze lifted her hat and she grabbed it and held on to it with a gloved hand! She was on Australian soil, actually touched by Australian wind! The visit created the worst traffic jams in Sydney's history. Cars stretched back to Watsons Bay in the east and from the Harbour Bridge to Lane Cove and the Spit Bridge in the north. Families set out from the suburbs intending to drive to the city but were blocked at every turn. Children squeezed forward to the front of the barricades, and there she was – such a good, close view of the woman and her husband, both looking like their photographs but in three dimensions. Children noticed how pink their faces were in the February heat, and were proud – and also a little dismayed – that they had got so near to the couple so easily. Royalty was meant to be magic and unreachable.

MARGARET TOUGHER (NÉE BUTTEL) READS THE SCHOOLCHILDREN'S ADDRESS OF WELCOME. MARGARET LEARNED THE HARD WAY THE USEFULNESS OF HEAVY-DUTY HAT ELASTIC AS STRONG WINDS GREETED THE QUEEN AND PRINCE PHILIP ON THEIR VISIT TO WOLLONGONG.

Schoolgirl Margaret Tougher read the address of welcome to the Royal couple on their visit to her home town of Wollongong in New South Wales. Margaret recalls the excitement of the occasion. 'The Queen had a beautiful tulle frock on. She just smiled. The Duke was lovely. He said, 'You're going to have trouble with that hat.' It was blowing a gale and the hat, despite the big pin in it, was flapping around. I still meet people who say, 'Oh, you're the girl who met the Queen and

PRIME MINISTER MENZIES TURNED ON A SPECTACLE TO RIVAL NUREMBURG AND THE BERLIN OLYMPICS AS MILLIONS OF AUSTRALIAN KIDDIES LINED THE STREETS TO PAY HOMAGE TO THE ROYAL COUPLE.

nearly lost your hat.' Even today, without prompting, Margaret is still able to recite her speech: '... We pledge to you our loyalty and service, and pray that God may grant you a long life and a prosperous, peaceful reign.' Says Margaret, 'It was quite funny, because I have a rather Australian accent, and the teachers insisted that I say "grant" with a long "a" sound, rather than the local drawled "grant" with a flat "a". They said it sounded a bit raspy.'

The excitement began with children hanging royal portraits in schools, with staging re-creations of the Coronation, and with young women being crowned festival queens. All over the country, Queen Elizabeth lookalikes were being installed by Archbishop of Canterbury wannabes. Sceptres made of local materials were employed, including marsupial skin.

I was amongst the children of Melbourne lining the route from the airport. I was a national serviceman at the time. Prophetically, it was probably in the vicinity of Moonee Ponds. We were holding rifles and had to present arms as the Royal couple passed. As they came into view I accidentally dropped my rifle. There was a terrible clatter and, for one second, my eyes and the Duke of Edinburgh's met. He muttered something to the Queen,

THE ORIGINAL CAST OF RAY LAWLER'S *SUMMER OF THE SEVENTEENTH DOLL*. LEFT TO RIGHT: RAY LAWLER, JUNE JAGO, CARMEL DUNN (AT PIANO), ROMA JOHNSTON, NOEL FERRIER AND FENELLA MAGUIRE. FROM ITS PREMIERE IN 1955, 'THE DOLL' PACKED THEATRES ACROSS THE COUNTRY. AUDIENCES THAT HAD BEEN FED A STRICT DIET OF BRITISH THEATRE FELT A SHOCK OF RECOGNITION AS THEY HEARD ACTORS SPEAKING WITH AUSTRALIAN ACCENTS IN A STORY ABOUT ORDINARY PEOPLE.

which was caught on film, and a deaf person read his lips, later claiming that the Duke had said to the Queen: 'Chin up, Sausage.' The newspaper report of this was rebutted by the Palace, which drew screaming headlines in the Melbourne press: 'I Did Not Call Queen a Sausage.' The Duke emphatically denied that he had ever used the word 'sausage' as a term of endearment.

And then the Royal Visit was over and it was like the aftermath of eating too much fairy floss – a feeling of hot sweetness but nothing really satisfying. The Elizabethan Theatre Trust was formed in 1954 to commemorate the Royal Visit. Its funds were raised by public subscription. While it was principally devoted to bringing 'top-quality performing arts companies to Australia', it also had the high-minded aim of being 'a theatre of Australians by Australians for Australians', as its director, an Englishman, roundly stated. And so this all-Australian theatre had an English name, and its inaugural production, Terrence Rattigan's *The Sleeping Prince*, had an English author, an English director and an English cast. This felt more or less right for most Australians. Although this was the decade of Ray Lawler's *Summer of the Seventeenth Doll*, which premiered in Melbourne in 1955, and was co-produced with the Elizabethan Theatre Trust, *and* was sensationally acclaimed, there was little other Australian dramatic material taken up. Ray Lawler said, after the opening of his play: 'We will not have first-class Australian actors until we have plenty of first-class Australian plays. We should have characters who can only be interpreted as Australians; then we will not have to import stars from abroad.'

Up to the 1950s the distinctive sound of Australian inner-city streets was the clatter of the electric tram – a whine and a rattle as steel wheels thumped over rail junctions, and an explosive spitting of blue sparks as trolley poles jumped and rejoined the overhead power cables. Small boys in bare feet rode the outside footboards and, when thunderstorms broke, canvas flaps were rolled down to shield passengers from the deluge. While trams were to remain a part of Melbourne's character through the entire century, in Sydney and then Brisbane trams were regarded as indelibly old-fashioned and the lines began to be torn up.

The tram's disappearance from Sydney's eastern suburbs in the mid 1950s coincided with the rise of rock 'n roll, a phenomenon then associated with Sydney Stadium on New South Head Road, Rushcutters Bay, just down from Kings Cross. The Stadium was on the Watsons Bay tramline. It was bad enough on boxing nights when the trams jutted end-to-end disgorging fans across the road. But when the stadium venue changed from holding boxing and wrestling events to being a performance centre for visiting American stars, the traffic jams were horrendous. Frankie Laine, Johnny Ray, Frank Sinatra and, after 1955 (when 'Rock Around the Clock' was the hit of the year), Bill Haley and the Comets, had their names etched across the stadium's facade in huge, hastily erected lettering. The magical shabbiness of the stadium symbolised the intersection of popular and unpopular styles, the past tripping over the present. These names weren't boxers – they were knockouts.

What did the visiting celebrities think of Sydney with its toast-rack trams and old-fashioned styles? Reporters were always on hand to ask the question the moment visitors touched down at the airport, even before they blinked at the unaccustomed harsh sunlight. And what did they think of the stadium, this tin-roofed ramshackle building in a gully below Kings Cross? (Today, where it once sprawled, on a corner near the Sydney Grammar School playing fields, there's a series of concrete stanchions holding up the eastern suburbs railway.) The new use for the stadium gave a feeling of Australia being noticed by the world. But was Australia up to being noticed? We weren't just hammering sportspeople any more, with cut eyebrows and groggy stances. We rocked in the aisles in an Americanised sort of way. We tore up the tramlines. Soon the stadium would go – and also to be destroyed, reflecting an exasperation with the past, were innumerable finer buildings. There were more wrecks offstage than on as the fifties ripened.

Meanwhile, there was a hunger for a small, blurred, conventional picture – a hunger equal to the passion for the Royal Visit. And so when television began with 'test transmissions' in Sydney and Melbourne in September

Edna's Special Moment in a Show

Chockies, to me, was the special moment in a show. You could buy them by the yard. There was a man called Ernest Hillier who made these long, long boxes of chockies that would travel over several laps. And you could rustle them in the quiet bits too! That's what we used to enjoy. If it wasn't something exotic like that, it'd just be old-fashioned Black Magic or an Old Gold assortment – with a chart so you could tell which were the hard ones and which were the soft ones. Sometimes, sitting in the dark with a fiancé, or even my intended husband Norm, you could easily reach out and grab hold of a hard one instead of a soft one by mistake. 👓

Television Comes to Sandy Stone

We procured our first TV set in 1956. Not to watch the Melbourne Olympic Games, because you couldn't, but to view it. We viewed it. We learned to be viewers. It meant, of course, that we had to move the furniture in our lounge room, from pointing at the hearth — because it gets nippy in Melbourne in the winter — towards our new instrument. And it was not just a TV set, it was a piece of furniture. The salesman said — and Beryl herself said it when she saw it — she said: 'Do you know, that is a piece of furniture.' And it was. I rather wished it had some little doors, which would have made it more like a piece of furniture, but as it was, it was the best you could procure. It was an Astor 21-inch console. And it certainly consoled Beryl. Our console brought a lot of consolation to my wife. More than I could bring her sometimes at certain stages in our rather turbulent married life.

So when I think of it now, I think how important that instrument was for us. Because, you know, I saw Lorraine Crapp on it. I saw Lorraine Crapp on that TV set. And Dawn Fraser. So it's a part of our history. 📺

Above: Swimming gold medallists Lorraine Crapp and Dawn Fraser at the Melbourne Olympics.

1956, electrical stores put TV sets in their windows and people took chairs, rugs and thermoses and sat on the footpath watching truncated travel documentaries and fuzzy test patterns. They parked their cars and sat on the roofs, creating a kind of dress-circle viewing platform in the street. When there was no picture being transmitted, people stood staring at the blank screens waiting for an unpredictably timed 'test' to begin. The rest of the country missed out, and had to wait several years for the tide of new technology to reach them. The sets were expensive, costing a big slice of weekly earnings in time repayments. Who in 1956 could afford 20 shillings a week for an Astor 21-inch console?

Bruce Ruxton, monarchist and outspoken member of the Returned Services League, could. 'I was one of the first to buy a television set. It changed everything. All of a sudden, people didn't visit any more. You know, Saturday night, carting four bottles of beer around to some party. That all started to go by the wayside because people were getting television sets and just locking themselves in their own home and watching TV. It was an antisocial device.'

Despite this, television was where the money was to be made and commercial radio personalities joined the queue to make their mark on the screen. The products they pushed — Colgate, Lux, Rinso, Ampol, Dulux — translated to television with ease. Not so the majority of the stars themselves. The older ones retired with as much dignity as they could muster, while some made separate, often dismal, accommodations with the one-eyed monster. Bob Dyer, an American resident in Australia, switched his 'Pick-A-Box' formula intact from microphone to camera; a few, like the young Graham Kennedy, had phenomenal success as TV performers; Reg Grundy and Hector Crawford went from behind the microphone to behind the desk and became wealthy production-house bosses – while the rest receded in popular memory until now their names register like a rollcall of forgotten heroes: Allen Toohey, John Harper, Willie Fennell, 'Ada and Elsie' (Rita Pauncefort and Dorothy 'Dilly' Foster), Hal Lashwood, John Dease and his 'Quiz Kids'.

I had a friend with the first colour set in New Zealand. I went and I watched, and what he had done was to tint the upper glass of the screen blue, the bottom of it green and the middle of it orange. When sky appeared it was blue – otherwise actors' foreheads were blue, their noses were orange and their chins were green.

There were improvisations behind the screen, too. David McNicoll, columnist on the *Bulletin* magazine, was present at a dinner party held at home by Sir Frank Packer, then the owner of Channel 9. It so happened that, at the time, Channel 9 was showing a John Wayne film. McNicoll recounts what happened: 'The conversation at dinner was about Frank's horse, which the day before had won a race at Randwick. And somebody at the table said: "Oh, I thought it was going to fade in the last stretch." So Frank picked up the phone and he said: "Put on Forsythe running the third race at Randwick." So the poor fellow at Channel 9 – bonk, John Wayne goes off the screen. The next thing, Forsythe's galloping.

'But those were the early days of television. Of course, there would be hell to pay now if anything like that happened. It was a bit rough and ready in those days.'

TELEVISION BEGAN IN 1956 BUT MANY FAMILIES COULDN'T AFFORD THE EXPENSIVE SETS. INSTEAD, THEY WOULD GATHER OUTSIDE ELECTRICAL STORES, WITH THE KIDS DRESSED READY FOR BED, JUST TO GET A SOUNDLESS GLIMPSE OF THE BROADCASTS.

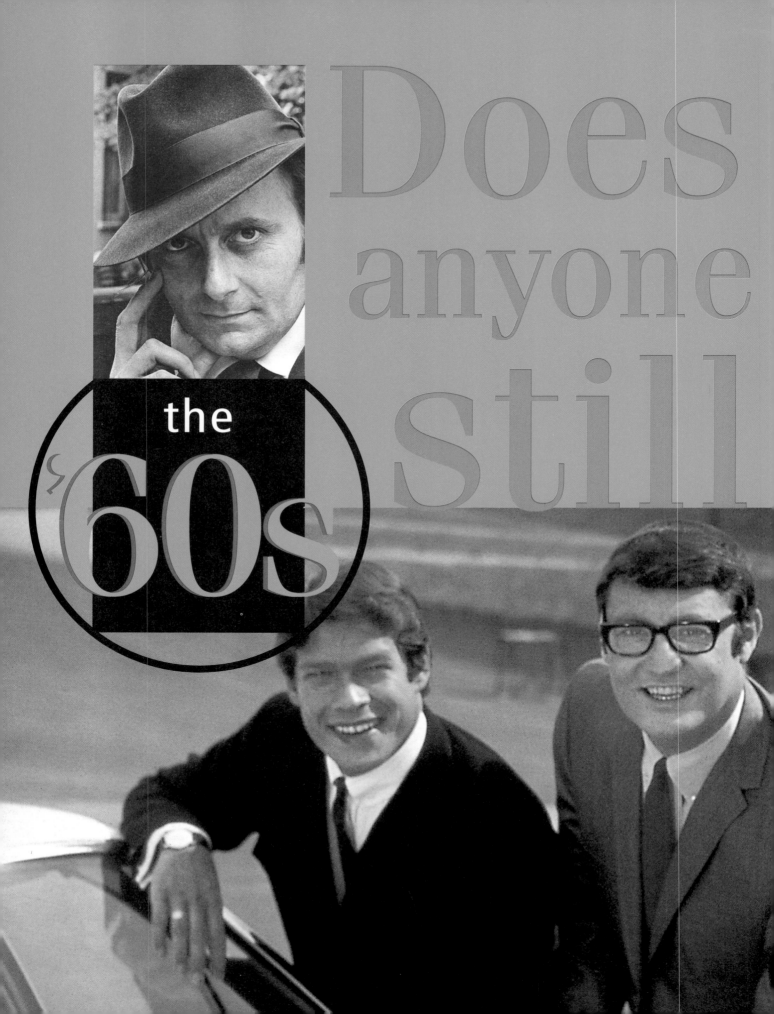

the '60s

Does anyone still

wear
a hat?

GO NORTH TO ADVENTURE!
ALICE SPRINGS / DARWIN
GO BY FAST TAA JETLINER

You're in a house of the 1960s

but it's still the 1950s in here – the smarter end of the fifties, that is. A picture on the wall shows a girl with a big straw hat; her eyes are impossibly green, her skin dusky emerald, her ambience Eurasian. A reproduction Dargie portrait of the young Queen hangs nearby. There's a nest of tables, a chair by Grant Featherstone – very smart, curvaceous, pert. There's crazy stonework around the fireplace. There are ducks on the wall. There are venetian blinds in cream aluminium and duck-egg blue, alternating in a colour combo that makes a feature of the blinds.

This was the great idea, as recommended by *Home Beautiful* magazine – a style the architect Robin Boyd called 'featurism'. It meant everything clamouring for attention.

Featurism was an invention of the 1950s shot forward from stylistic isolation into a popular style. Nobody expected, however, the degree to which the 1960s would usher in an entirely new generation of attention-getters – and not just in the architectural, home-decorating, feature-creating sense, either. This was because nobody in 1960 expected the new decade to be anything other than the full delivery of the promise of the fifties. More cargo for the cult, more comforts, more novelty, greater convenience. Much that would be cheaper, better, newer – a time when the clunkiness of the fifties would have the rough edges smoothed off.

But it wasn't going to turn out like that. If the 1950s promised more than they delivered, the 1960s would deliver more than they promised. They would clamour for attention with their own definition of what it meant 'to feature'.

In 1958 Robert Gordon Menzies renewed his dominance of Australian politics by getting re-elected with a massive majority over Labor of 35 seats. Thus Mr Menzies' regal, complacent eyebrows were set to figurehead the ship of state into the 1960s. In the dying months of 1959 he travelled to the Snowy Mountains in southern New South Wales and performed the ceremony of closing a valve and starting to fill a hydro-electric dam with water. It was ten years since the first explosive charge had been set off and the Snowy Mountains Scheme began. The kids who had stood open-mouthed listening to the rumble of explosives through their primary-school loudspeakers in 1949 were now part of the workforce – serving at shop-counters, learning to be clerks or operating machinery on the factory floor. A few had grown up to take jobs on the Snowy Scheme which, like the Sydney Opera House, was to provide a near-lifetime career for some.

Right: THIS MAX DUPAIN PHOTOGRAPH ADVERTISING CSR FLOOR TILES SHOWS THE IDEALISED AND SOPHISTICATED HOME SETTING MUCH SOUGHT-AFTER DURING THE SIXTIES. 'FEATURE' WALLS OF EXPOSED BRICK, AND CEILING-TO-FLOOR DRAPES, WERE DE RIGEUR AND WERE PROMOTED BY THE DOMESTIC BIBLES *HOME BEAUTIFUL* AND *HOUSE AND GARDEN*, WHICH PRESUMABLY ALSO GAVE TIPS FOR GETTING PIPE SMOKE OUT OF THE CURTAINS. Previous pages: THE SEEKERS (main photo) WERE AUSTRALIA'S FIRST SUPERGROUP. WHILE THE REST OF THE WORLD WAS ROCKING, THIS SWEET FOLK ENSEMBLE WAS ONE OF OUR MOST POPULAR RECORDING ACTS. THEIR 1965 HIT 'I'LL NEVER FIND ANOTHER YOU' BECAME THE FIRST AUSTRALIAN RECORD TO SELL A MILLION COPIES. THE NOBLE SAVAGE IMAGE (inset centre) WAS USED TO ENTICE FRINGE DWELLERS TO EXPLORE THE VAST, DRY INTERIOR OF THEIR CONTINENT, A PRACTICE WHICH HAD BEEN UNPOPULAR SINCE BURKE AND WILLS' ILL-FATED EXPEDITION 100 YEARS EARLIER. JANTZEN SWIMWEAR MODELS POSE ON THE BEACH (inset right). THE GIRL ON THE RIGHT IS MODELLING THE BIKINI WHICH, LIKE LONG HAIR AND THE PILL, BECAME ONE OF THE HOTLY DEBATED TOPICS OF THE SIXTIES.

A small number (just 5 per cent or so of school leavers) were at university. To save money, some of them still wore their school sweaters and carried their schooldays' Globite suitcases around the campuses (though they weren't called campuses then, they were called 'grounds'). Sartorially they had little to show, but they dreamed of being able to afford a pair of desert boots.

Mr Menzies adopted his headmasterly tone as he closed the massive Snowy Mountains valve: 'Power produced here will find its way into thousands of factories in New South Wales and Victoria,' he said. 'The scheme is teaching everyone in Australia to think in a big way.'

Yet thinking in a big way was not exactly what Menzies meant, unless the listener happened to be a large-scale earthmoving contractor with a range of mountains at his disposal. Thinking in a big way was still the prerogative of government and business. Thinking big was vigorously discouraged among humbler citizens, vocal demands for change being routinely attributed to stirrers, troublemakers, ratbags, and of course to communists, who were all those things by definition. Anyone standing up for himself as an individual was a 'Big Noter'. Standing out from the crowd was not a well-liked Australian characteristic, unless you happened to be a footballer, a cricketer or perhaps a pop star. And even then it had to be done with appropriate modesty.

It was to be several years before a bunch of stirrers, troublemakers and Big Noters of a different sort (somewhat rainbow-hued) took centre stage, demanding legitimacy for themselves by wearing bells around their ankles and flowers in their hair. Their politics would go beyond party divisions into the astral realm. But for now, in the early 1960s, it was still the period of overlap between the decades. Talk of astral realms was a recipe for the birds.

THE MASSIVE SNOWY MOUNTAINS SCHEME SAW THE ERECTION OF TEMPORARY WORKERS' CAMPS LIKE THE ONE AT SEVEN MILE CREEK (above). PRIME MINISTER MENZIES CLAIMED THE SCHEME 'TAUGHT AUSTRALIA TO THINK IN A BIG WAY'. THIS SURFER AND HIS BIKINIED GIRLFRIEND (right) CERTAINLY DID; THE MALIBU SURFBOARD WAS ONLY MARGINALLY SMALLER THAN A SPEEDBOAT. NOTE THE PINTS OF MILK — THE IDEAL THIRST-QUENCHER ON A HOT AUSTRALIAN SUMMER'S DAY!

So the large lumbering shadow of the fifties was to sprawl over the new decade for quite some time. Migration was one good effect of this, and for years it went on happening all around native-born Australians without their realising the full effect of the transformation. Perhaps it was the melting pot at work.

Clive James refers to this migration phenomenon as 'a great world historical event. The people who were essentially refugees from political nightmare were arriving in paradise.' At the time, however, the significance of it passed him by.

'I think a lot of what the migrants did for us crept up on us, starting with things like food and wine, and then gradually percolating through the entire culture. Migration is the thing that matters in postwar Australian cultural history.'

It was hard to tell the new ones from the old ones. Of course the new ones you could generally pick because they didn't speak a word of Australian. With the old ones – and some of them had been around since before the Second World War – we had a Greek greengrocer and an Italian fish-and-chip operative. Or perhaps it was the other way around. I think the Greeks ran the fish-and-chip shop. I never knew the difference, frankly. They both had very hairy arms with black curly hair, which Australians tended not to have. And there was always the Chinese restaurant where we sometimes went on a special occasion – had a nice chop suey and half a bottle of riseling [sic]. However, the newcomers really made a difference because they bought the old slums that we didn't want to live in any more, did them up, and a generation later we had to pay through the nose to live there ourselves. So they were very clever. 👓

THE CONTRACEPTIVE PILL WAS INTRODUCED IN 1961 AND AUSTRALIAN WOMEN TOOK TO IT MORE ENTHUSIASTICALLY THAN WOMEN ANYWHERE ELSE IN THE WORLD. MORAL GUARDIANS DISGUISED AS GENERAL PRACTITIONERS WOULDN'T PRESCRIBE IT TO SINGLE WOMEN, AND THE CATHOLIC CHURCH PRONOUNCED IT A SIN EVEN FOR THOSE IN WEDLOCK TO TAKE THE PILL. THE APPROPRIATELY NAMED POPE PIUS XII CLAIMED ITS USE WAS 'A GRAVE VIOLATION OF THE MORAL LAW'.

A sexual revolution was waiting to happen, too, but its impact would not be widely felt until the decade was almost over.

Before the Pill, contraception meant condoms or Vatican roulette. The much talked about contraceptive pill went on sale in Australia in 1961, but the idea of unmarried women needing it was scandalous. Unwanted pregnancies were held to be better than moral decay, and the spectre of young lives ruined by a 'mistake' seemed a just retribution. If a baby was not born in shame and adopted out, then a hasty marriage took place. Before the Pill, it is believed that as many as 40 per cent of weddings were shotgun style. For single young women with persistence and no taste for the marital yoke, the search for an agreeable general practitioner who would write a prescription for the Pill resembled the furtive search for an abortionist that went on in the shabbier parts of town. Quite commonly the result of the quest would be a moral lecture and a humiliating refusal. It would be another ten years before the veil of propriety was lifted from Pill-use and prescription was regarded as a right, not a privilege.

In suburbia the wrestle in the back seat of the Holden was a rite of passage for the 1960s, just as the 1950s had meant parking the Vauxhall or the Austin A40 on a secluded boulevard at night and tentatively exploring a Braemar twinset and Black Watch tartan skirt. In the sixties young women still ventured forth with bras like Assyrian shields and suspender belts that were just another name for corsets.

Let's go to another house of the 1960s. We are into the decade a bit and the passage of time is starting to make its mark. There's a macramé wall-hanging to one side and an abstract painting by John Coburn, full of splats, swirls and sunbursts. There are lots of reds and oranges in the carpets and curtains. A lava lamp sits on top of the TV. There is a wood-veneer stereogram, in black bean, squared off like an oil-drilling platform. And there's a trailing plant or perhaps a 'mother-in-law's tongue' – a spiky indoor plant.

Is there still a hat-rack in the hall, where men can hang their headgear? There is, but it's bare – or else it holds a few dented items gathering dust. Does *anyone* still wear a hat? In the 1960s a schism occurred in

A SIXTIES HOUSEWIFE PICTURED AMONG HER GLEAMING KITCHEN 'SURFACES'. THIS PERKY HOMEMAKER WAS NO DOUBT ALSO THE PERFECT HOSTESS, EFFORTLESSLY COPING WITH THE DEMANDS OF THE DINNER OR COCKTAIL PARTY. POTENTIAL HOSTESSES WERE TAUGHT THE INTRICACIES OF HOME ENTERTAINING AT CHARM SCHOOLS – FINISHING COLLEGES FOR AUSTRALIAN HOUSEWIVES.

Australia. Since Federation it had been a 'fedora nation'. Australian men and women had not ventured forth from their homes without a hat. Then it all changed. At the beginning of the new decade, the children of the last of the hat-wearers were growing up. They were determined to replace hats with hair. But any revolution takes time in Australia.

In this house a teak dining table has been meticulously laid. There is to be a dinner party instead of a night on the town. Home entertaining has become a theme, rather than just a matter of offering a beer and a sandwich to whoever might drop in. The hostess has opted for the newly fashionable fondue, which for her involves the lengthy process of stirring cheese into almost-boiling white wine and for her guests the new art of transporting strings of melting cheese across an immaculate tablecloth to the mouth. The ritual is guaranteed to blister the tongue and cauterise the tastebuds. The forks used are colour-coded to avoid un-hygienic confusion.

Presiding over the intricacies of the evening is the hostess, the housewife. She has stepped from the demographic of the 1950s into the more widespread marketing opportunity of the 1960s. She may not yet be feeling any dissatisfaction with her role, or, if she is, there are not yet the words to express it, and certainly not any social permission. (Indeed, if she rejects any ruling model of behaviour she may need to have a 'breakdown'.) She is making an effort to be 'nice', and before her marriage went to the June Dally Watkins charm school, mecca of touchingly eager young matrons and aspiring models convinced of their social ineptitude. There she acquired the mystical missing ingredient that had been absent from the repertoire of the Australian homemaker for one hundred and fifty years – poise.

For those still approaching marriage there was always another test to pass, another hoop to jump through. Until a young woman's life reached its peak in marriage, child-bearing and washing-up, she could fill in time by being a shopgirl, a typist or a hairdresser. Every woman in Australia could enter a quest – Apple Picker of the Year, Milkmaid of the Year, Steno-grapher of the Year (with a typewriter as first prize) or Hairdresser of the Year. Or even

JUNE DALLY WATKINS' CHARM SCHOOLS TURNED FRUMPY HOUSEWIVES INTO PERFECT HOSTESSES. HER TOUCHINGLY EAGER YOUNG STUDENTS WERE TAUGHT HOW TO WALK, TALK AND, ABOVE ALL, 'BE NICE'. A 'POISED' MISS DALLY WATKINS (above) BECAME THE CENTRE OF A CONTROVERSY WHEN SHE INSISTED ON WORKING WHILE PREGNANT AT A TIME WHEN SUCH SIGHTS IN THE WORKPLACE WERE CONSIDERED VULGAR. THE PRESSURES ON WOMEN WERE CONSIDERABLE AND THIS HOUSEWIFE (opposite top) APPEARS OVERWHELMED BY HAVING TO CHOOSE FROM THE WIDE VARIETY OF NEWLY MARKETED INSTANT FOODS. IN SIXTIES ADVERTISING, COQUETTISH MODELS AND HOME APPLIANCES (opposite bottom) COMBINED TO EMPHASISE THE IDEAL OF THE PERFECT HOMEMAKER.

Sandy Claus

On Christmas Day Beryl and my good self usually make a point of having a few folk around for the midday dinner. It's only once a year, so we like to go to a certain amount of trouble.

Beryl could go on cooking till the cows come home; and as she always says, she doesn't mind how much she cooks so long as people eat it up. Waste not want not, as they say in the classics. Anyway, last year she went crazy. My wife is known for her puff pastry and she turned out a batch of five dozen little mince pies and one big one to keep her hand in. She always gets her plum pudding over and done with early in the piece these days too, ever since the year she fell ill. I did my bit too, boiling the sixpences – wouldn't want the kiddies to get tummy trouble – but my main department was the tree and the decorations et cetera.

We always get our tree from Bob May, a very nice chappie I know who runs his conveyance up to the Dandies at night every Christmas and procures them from one of the new reforestation plantations in the vicinity of the Sylvan Dam. Naturally I don't quibble. I just say thank you very much and leave it at that. Mind you, if I'd known where he got them it'd be an entirely different proposition altogether.

Checker of the Year, celebrating the birth of the supermarket – frenziedly toting up a trolley-load of goods at a cash register set up in some hotel ballroom. And once she entered the married state there was still the opportunity to become House-wife of the Year.

I adore quests of this kind, because I am the very, very proud possessor of a trophy: winner of the Lovely Mother Quest. And that was an Australia-wide competition. They didn't just judge you on beauty, on being a glamour puss. It was bone structure, it was cleanliness, it was niceness. And above all it was poise. What's happened to poise? Do you ever hear a young woman praised these days for her poise? I was poised – I think from birth. My mother told me that when I was born the doctor came in and she said to the doctor, 'What is it? What is it?' And the doctor said, 'Well whatever it is, it's poised.' And I was. Thirsty little Edna was poised to clamp my greedy bubba gums over one of my mother's top tummies.

In the early years of the decade the dusty plain of the fifties still showed through in the array of Bri-nylon, Terylene and

BRINGING THE HAIRDRESSING SALON INTO THE HOME. HAIR BECAME A FASHION ACCESSORY IN THE SIXTIES AS HATS WERE CAST ASIDE. LATER IN THE DECADE A CONTROVERSIAL MUSICAL CALLED *HAIR* WOULD BE DEVOTED TO THE SUBJECT AND HAIR LENGTH WOULD BECOME A POTENT POLITICAL SYMBOL.

Crimplene garments – a style that would remain until around mid-decade when the first colourful invasion of Indian cottons and lightweight, bell-bottomed trousers arrived.

Hemlines still fell below the knee, and woe betide their being lifted any higher. Women still went shopping 'in town' wearing hats and gloves. Coffee lounges abounded for the drinking of milky hot drinks and the eating of cinnamon toast, but there were very few places where women could meet a friend for an alcoholic drink without eyebrows being raised.

The pub was very much men's domain. The public bars were still like urinals – bare, cream-tiled and easy to hose down in the morning. If a woman wanted to drink in a hotel she had to do it in the 'ladies lounge'. When husband and wife went out together another alternative was for her to sit outside in the car and have a drink brought to her by her husband. Things would go on that way until the building of a licensed club in the neighbourhood, where women could become 'associate members'.

Whenever there was a ladies' night on at our local Returned Servicemen's League, Beryl and I would toddle along. It was only a short toddle from where we lived. It was rough and ready, but it was clean. You'd have a nice glass of whatever it was. And there was some very nice food laid on. They had sandwiches. You could have toasted sandwiches if you wanted, if you were prepared to wait. Or pasties. They tried experimenting with continental food – didn't work. Tried the open sandwiches, but people complained they weren't finished. 'Where's the other bit of bread?', they said. There was no smorgabord … smorgonbord. Didn't have them, didn't need them.

But sometimes they'd have a comedian along. Not too blue, on account of the womenfolk. So that altogether it was a very nice night's entertainment. Took you out of yourself.

ALTHOUGH BANNED FROM THE PUB, WOMEN WERE ALLOWED TO JOIN REGISTERED CLUBS IN NEW SOUTH WALES AS 'ASSOCIATE MEMBERS'. THESE ENTERTAINMENT MECCAS OFFERED A WHOLE NEW SOCIAL LIFE WITH ONE VITAL ADDED INGREDIENT: GAMBLING.

It was poker machines that made clubs in New South Wales entertainment meccas – large, luxurious and gaudy. Other states had to wait many years before the resistance to gambling in this form was overtaken by the wish to raise government revenue. Returned Servicemen's Clubs, Rugby League Clubs and Workingmen's Clubs led the way in splendour, and so while middle-class theatregoers were congratulating themselves that they had secured tickets to a second-rate musical with a third-rate cast, working-class clubgoers were enjoying performers like Sammy Davis Jnr, Shirley Bassey, Howard Keel and Kay Starr.

Entertainer and eponymous star of the celebrated *Barry McKenzie* films, Barry Crocker remembers the halcyon days of the club circuit. 'It was money for jam. People flocked to the clubs. You could work around Sydney as an artist for six months of the year. They put on all sorts of entertainment – everything from plays and production shows to guest stars and stars from overseas. People could sit down with a beer at the table or play the poker machines. Gambling was very exciting then. I think the machines were probably a little looser, so more jackpots were won.'

Meanwhile, the pub remained the place for a man to meet his mates and solve the problems of the world, which in a time-honoured Australian way meant expressing a prejudiced point of view and looking around for confirmation from a series of red-faced nods and belches. Almost certainly, every man in the place would be smoking a cigarette or a pipe, and those few that weren't would be inhaling the fumes at a poisonous level anyway. In the 1960s, nicotine-stained fingers, and homes that smelled like ashtrays, were the rule. While the men were in the public bar and the women in the ladies lounge or having a special night at the club, their teenage children were out on a rampage somewhere else, guzzling Brandyvino and engaging in beer-drinking contests called chugg-a-lugging. (Marijuana was only a word, and hard to pronounce at that – a strange cigarette mentioned in B-grade movies set somewhere down Mexico way.)

As clubs grew in scale, pubs became scruffier. There were stories in the papers about a bunch of women in Brisbane who chained themselves to bars and demanded service in an attempt to gain equal drinking rights with men. But why would they want to? What were women up to?

The answer was, nothing much – if the mentors of public morality had anything to do with it. The vast majority of women were still happily preparing for marriage, where their sexual identity belonged. Their virginity was a prized possession to be delivered up to their husbands on their wedding night. They were positively a danger outside that role. Female university students were lectured on the dangers of wearing red, a colour said to inflame male propensities. Certain males were a problem in this respect, too. In the more provincial capitals, male university students were warned off wearing crepe-soled suede shoes unless they wanted the sexual attentions of other males. In distant Tasmania the carrying of an umbrella by men (even in the rain) meant suspicion of homosexuality. Combined with suede shoes the umbrella was an absolute indicator of 'the other track', a cause of public ridicule and not-so-muffled cries of 'poofter'. The only exception to the suede shoe rule was the desert boot, which had become fashionable footwear for the avant-garde male undergraduate in 1960. A sandy-coloured desert boot worn

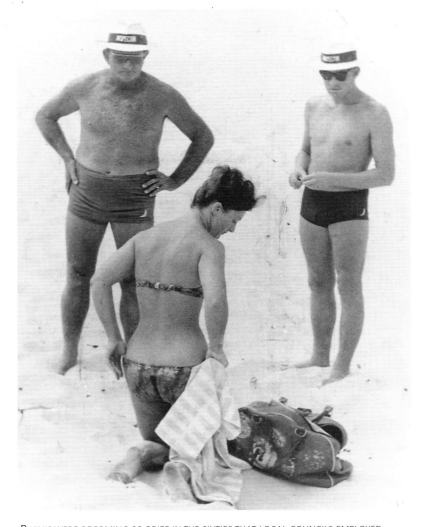

BIKINIS WERE BECOMING SO BRIEF IN THE SIXTIES THAT LOCAL COUNCILS EMPLOYED BEACH INSPECTORS TO GUARD AGAINST THE THREAT TO PUBLIC DECENCY. HERE THEY ORDER A BIKINI-CLAD BATHER TO COVER UP OR LEAVE. IRONICALLY, THE BEACH INSPECTORS THEMSELVES WERE OFTEN THE MOST INDECENTLY DRESSED PEOPLE ON AUSTRALIAN BEACHES.

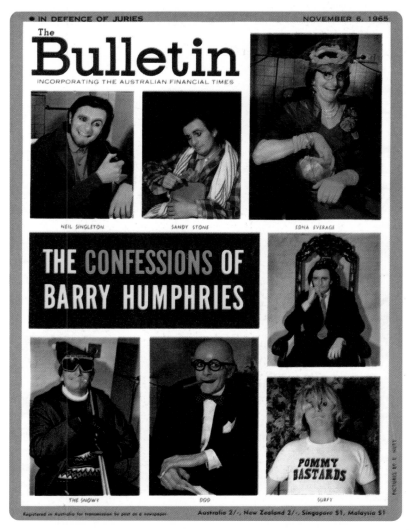

● IN DEFENCE OF JURIES   NOVEMBER 6, 1965

The

Bulletin

INCORPORATING THE AUSTRALIAN FINANCIAL TIMES

NEIL SINGLETON   SANDY STONE   EDNA EVERAGE

THE CONFESSIONS OF BARRY HUMPHRIES

THE SNOWY   DOD   SURFY

Registered in Australia for transmission by post as a newspaper   Australia 2/-, New Zealand 2/-, Singapore $1, Malaysia $1

BARRY HUMPHRIES CAPTURED THE MANY FACES OF AUSTRALIA WITH HIS GALLERY OF
CHARACTERS, CELEBRATED HERE ON THIS 1965 *BULLETIN* COVER. **Clockwise from top left:**
THE PRETENTIOUS INTELLECTUAL, NEIL SINGLETON, WAS A SYDNEY LEFT-WING ACADEMIC
FOND OF KAFKA AND MILES DAVIS. THE 'RETURNED MAN' SANDY STONE EMERGED AFTER
BARRY MET A WIRY OLD FELLOW WITH ILL-FITTING TEETH ON BONDI BEACH WHO TOLD HIM
THE TIME WAS 'APPROXIMATELY IN THE VICINITY OF 5.30'. BEFORE PASSING AWAY IN THE
EIGHTIES, SANDY COULD USUALLY BE FOUND IN HIS MOTH-EATEN GENOA-VELVET ARMCHAIR
WEARING PYJAMAS AND CLUTCHING A HOTTIE. EDNA EVERAGE WAS BORN IN WAGGA
WAGGA, NEW SOUTH WALES, BUT MOVED TO THE MELBOURNE SUBURB OF MOONEE
PONDS AT A YOUNG AGE. SHE WON A LOVELY MOTHER CONTEST IN THE FIFTIES AND LATER
WENT ON TO INTERNATIONAL FAME. LESSER-KNOWN BARRY HUMPHRIES CREATIONS
INCLUDED THE PEROXIDE-HAIRED SYDNEY SURFIE WHO SPOKE 'SURFESE' IN A MONOLOGUE
WITH PIONEERING REFERENCES TO 'TUBES' AND 'ICE-COLD TINNIES', DOD THE CIGAR-PUFFING
GOVERNMENT BUREAUCRAT WHOSE DUTIES INCLUDED THE PROMOTION OF AUSTRALIA'S
IMAGE OVERSEAS, AND SNOWY, THE TRENDY MELBOURNE SKIER. **Opposite page:** THE SIXTIES
FAMILY UNIT: NEAT, COMPLETE AND WITHOUT ANOTHER SOUL IN SIGHT. EVEN CLOSE TO THE
CAPITAL CITIES IT WAS STILL POSSIBLE TO DRIVE TO A DESERTED STRETCH OF BEACH, BOIL THE
BILLY AND BARBECUE SAUSAGES FOR A PICNIC LUNCH.

with a dark blue suit and a narrow tie was the mark of the racy scholar.

Bikinis were the special domain of beach inspectors, a curious profession in which beachfront councils paid middle-aged men to ogle young women and escort them from the beaches to the accompaniment of catcalls, wolf-whistles and tabloid photographers. Everywhere, bikinis were seen getting smaller and smaller, the fascination in how far they would go being reflected in a popular song: 'Itsy Bitsy Teeny Weeny Yellow Polka Dot Bikini'. The guardians of public morality were spiflicated at the brazen cheek of it all. In the early 1960s the June Dally Watkins school of deportment issued strict measurements relating to the size of bikinis. The allowable inches were spelt out to the hotly breathing press: the bikini bottom must have a side measurement of at least 5 inches, and the two sides of the bra should be separated by material at least 2 inches in depth.

The doyen of Australian beach inspectors was a Bondi legend, Aub Laidlaw, who had been operating in Sydney's eastern suburbs since the start of the

1950s and who at all times carried a measuring tape in his pocket. As hundreds of women were ordered off beaches, Laidlaw looked increasingly ridiculous, but acts of censorship such as his continued across society. Anyone quick to strip – nudist, freethinker, so-called libertarian or just plain fun-loving gal – was quickly hustled from public sight. June Dally Watkins herself came up against the guardians of public morality when she insisted on continuing working well into her pregnancy. She received the disapproval of men and women alike, getting anonymous phone calls from women after they'd been out for a long lunch – from midday to 5.30, some of them. Miss Dally Watkins was told that no self-respecting woman should be in an office pregnant. She was accused of neglecting her children, and to go home where she belonged.

The idea of any of this being 'political' was still over the horizon. There was nothing doctrinaire in the revealing of flesh, but a pressure-cooker head of steam was building up around issues of morality. A time was coming when the impulse to bare it all as a political statement, together with 'Make Love Not War', would turn the Bondi Beach bikini-girl and her beer-bellied beach inspector escort into something laughably dated. Aub Laidlaw got it in the teeth from a spirited young dancer, Joan Barry, who called him a fool, with reporters present, when he estimated that the top of her bikini pants started more than five inches below her navel. This from a man whose chest, arms and back were covered in grizzled grey hairs, who went everywhere in a Jacky Howe singlet (a dark navy working vest) frizzling his skin in the sun, and on whose hips sat a pair of floppy white shorts. Meanwhile, the easygoing naked were the lunatic fringe of society, the subject of sensationalist articles in *Pix* and *People* magazines – along with crime reports of unclothed female corpses and the Americanisation of crime in a country where by and large front doors could be left unlocked or cars parked without fear of their being stolen.

This safe sense of openness extended to making free and easy with people's privacy, and to publishing the names and addresses of lottery winners. In October 1960 this led to the kidnapping of Graeme Thorne, an eight-year-old Scots College boy whose parents had won the Opera House Lottery a few months before. A ransom demand was made but no contact with the kidnapper established. The win of £100 000, so widely announced, had attracted the greed of Stephen Bradley, a Hungarian migrant who snatched Thorne from the street and later smothered him and dumped his body. Bradley, a suspect early on, fled Australia by ship but was arrested in Ceylon. Sydney looked over its shoulder more nervously after that, and stopped believing that kidnapping was just an American film theme.

But Adelaide kept its innocence intact and allowed its children to roam free until as late as 1966, when three children from the Beaumont family, aged nine, seven, and four, disappeared in full daylight from a popular Adelaide beach. The suspected perpetrator was described as a tall, blond 'surfie'. The suspect description was very 1960s, but it was a late-lingering 1950s feel that was lost that day at suburban Glenelg, where doors were always open and people swept through each other's houses with an easy trust. The identikit photo of the surfie became familiar in newspapers and on television, but the Beaumont case remained unsolved. In desperation, the family agreed to have a clairvoyant called in. Gerard Croiset, a Dutchman, expressed his intuitions in clear, firm detail. He believed at first that the children were not murdered but killed in some sort of cave-in or avalanche. At several locations around Glenelg he experienced visions. All led to nothing except the taunting of the distraught parents with cruel hope. Eventually the seer's feelings centred on a rubble-filled site, where a grocery warehouse had recently been built. A hole was excavated and nothing found. Nor has anything ever been found.

Murder mysteries provided a powerful focus for omens of social change: styles of killing reflected a decade's mood according to what sent the shivers running deepest. Were murders rarer back then? No – but when they involved titillating details they branded themselves on starved sexual imaginations. The image of a husband and wife attending a New Year's Eve party, and each leaving the party with a different person of the opposite sex, each with the knowledge and approval of their spouse, was the scenario of the night of the Bogle–Chandler murders in 1963 (if indeed they were truly murders and not the accidental result of pioneer LSD-taking or some other libertarian-scientist–concocted brew). This was libertarian wife-swapping come to a gory end. Early on New Year's Day, on a bushy slope above Sydney's Lane Cove River, Mrs Margaret Chandler was found by a youth searching for golf balls. She was shockingly exposed, with her floral party frock draped over her naked body by a person or persons unknown. Dr Gilbert Bogle lay nearby, partly naked, and covered with sheets of cardboard. Their tryst had come to a terrible end. Both had been hideously ill. They were obviously poisoned. But no poison was ever identified or found. The contrast, so extreme, between the excitement of stolen pleasure and the vicious punishment of fate was a perfect framing for a decade of conflicting moral standpoints.

BY 1963 NEARLY 1.5 MILLION AUSTRALIANS WERE LICENSED TO 'VIEW THE INSTRUMENT'. AWA'S REMOTE-CONTROL TV NOW MEANT THAT VIEWERS DIDN'T EVEN HAVE TO GET UP FROM THEIR CHAIRS TO CHANGE CHANNELS. BREATHLESS TELEVISION NEWS REPORTS OF KIDNAPPINGS AND CHILD MURDERS CONFIRMED AUDIENCES' GOOD SENSE AT STAYING INDOORS.

The Menzies election victory catapulting Ming into the 1960s was aided by a Red Scare campaign orchestrated by the Roman Catholic Archbishop of Melbourne, Dr Daniel Mannix, who did Menzies's best electioneering for him on the day by issuing a stirring slander immediately before the poll, giving Labor no chance to answer back. 'Amid the turmoil of the election one thing seems clear,' thundered the elderly Archbishop Mannix, whose taste for politics stretched back to World War I (when his Irish-Catholic sympathies made his loyalty to Australia a questionable affair). 'Every communist and every communist sympathiser in Australia wants a victory for the Evatt [Labor] party. This is alarming. It should be a significant warning for every Catholic and for every decent Australian.'

Thus were timid, fearful Australians sent out in their thousands to vote for the establishment parties once again. Just a few cracks of the reliable 1950s whip was all it had needed.

But in a short time there came a Red Scare of truly terrifying proportions. The Cuban missile crisis of 1961 happened a long way from Australia, but there was little doubt in Australian minds that if nuclear war was unleashed in the northern hemisphere then surely and inexorably the fate imagined in Neville Shute's *On the Beach* would overtake all Australians. A nuclear cloud would spiral its way south, and the whole world would have its death sentence. Australians might have to wait a few weeks longer, but that would be all.

The nuclear threat had its effect on a generation still in its teens. The young asked themselves, would they never be given their chance to live? The effect was impatience, irritation, despair – feelings that built up over the decade and demanded an escape valve. A taste of stark, helpless fear entered the souls of many young Australians that night as Russian ships steamed towards Cuba and President Kennedy issued his ultimatum, playing nuclear poker on a world stage. Glued to the radio, or partying in an end-of-the-world frenzy (this was a night when many girls relinquished their prized possessions), the young felt joined to the vulnerabilities of the world in a way that no previous generation of Australians, isolated on the island continent, had ever been able to feel.

By the early 1960s it was routine, rather than just a novelty, for most Australian households in the state capitals to centre their homelife on a corner of the living room. Nobody ever carried food to a radio, but to eat in front of 'the box' was another matter, a social rite. It was equivalent to the primitive satisfaction you got sitting in front of a fire and watching the flickering flames. Often there was more to ponder in the flames. And when the night's programming ended there was always the test pattern.

Despite the talk of the time it was hardly the Global Village, with that notion's implication of boundless interaction. News and commentary programmes tended to be stiff, pompous and pronouncement-orientated. They resembled public relations releases from businesses or propaganda statements from a benevolent dictatorship. Current-affairs programmes were typically bland, formal debates between preselected representatives of opposing views. On the ABC, two-sided formal debate was conducted with stopwatch exactitude and rigidity. It was an attempt to make choices clear to the viewer, but the effect was a gabble of jargon and an incoherent clash of personalities.

BROTHERS MAURICE, ROBIN AND BARRY GIBB (THE BEE GEES) MIGRATED WITH THEIR PARENTS FROM MANCHESTER TO BRISBANE IN THE LATE FIFTIES AND LITERALLY GREW UP ON AUSTRALIAN TELEVISION, WITH REGULAR APPEARANCES ON SHOWS SUCH AS 'BANDSTAND'. IT WOULD BE ANOTHER DECADE, A CHANGE OF TAILOR AND MANY TRIPS TO THE ORTHODONTIST BEFORE THE BEE GEES WOULD RE-EMERGE AS THE INTERNATIONAL STARS OF SEVENTIES DISCO WITH THE SOUNDTRACK TO THE FILM *SATURDAY NIGHT FEVER*.

Australia had its own rock 'n roll stars feeding through – on commercial television's 'Bandstand' and national television's 'Six O'Clock Rock'. The Americanisation of Australian pop music was almost total even before the Beatles sprang to fame. There were the slightly puzzled and somewhat homely Col Joye and the Joy Boys, and the nuggety, high-speed rabble-rouser Johnny O'Keefe. Between them they covered Elvis Presley territory for the home crowd, with something of Elvis's sexual suggestivity, a lot of his rousingness, some of his melancholy, and all of his American music roots.

But Australia's isolation meant it was hard for local rock 'n rollers to keep up with the latest trends. Col Joye remembers the time-lag. 'I found we were about six years behind America. We even made our own guitars because we didn't think we could import them and get the proper Fender guitars. We were isolated. Johnny O'Keefe had a friend who was a Qantas steward who could bring in all the latest releases each week.'

Onstage at Sydney Stadium with Chubby Checker and three toothy 13-year-old child stars from Brisbane named the Bee Gees, Johnny O'Keefe was a special case. He was 'The Wild One'. Episodes of manic depression drove him onstage and off. Just as the decade started, O'Keefe, driving at high speed, slammed his red Plymouth sedan into a gravel truck somewhere north of Sydney and reduced both vehicles to crumpled metal. He was lucky to escape with his life and innumerable stitches. From then on O'Keefe was like a man possessed, in and out of hospital for treatment including the suspect deep sleep therapy, up on assault charges, divorced, and entirely dependent on prescribed pharmaceuticals. (He kept it up for another 18 years, dying in 1978 at the age

A World of Cosy Certainties

I was taking a vacation in Cornwall in the sixties, at a cottage near Zennor. I took with me a suitcase full of Australian newspapers and magazines which I had got from a friend in Fleet Street. There were copies of the *Women's Weekly*, filled with tips for the fashion-conscious Australian housewife, and illustrated recipes, mostly in the colours of brown and orange with splashes of yellow, since every Australian dish of this period was garnished with pineapple chunks. The *Women's Weekly* also contained an interesting illustrated fashion section called 'What people are wearing Overseas', candid snaps of movie stars in their first-night finery, and a sprinkling of bedizened Sydney socialites photographed on the way to a Royal Garden Party in London. There was a strong bias towards Thai silk, which was the textile of the period.

Leafing through those pages, as we huddled beside a wood stove in a Cornish farm cottage in February, I felt instantly transported back home to a world of cosy certainties; a land of sponge cakes and pavlovas and curried Hawaiian spag hoops, and gingham, seersucker and Thai silk. ✍

of 43. By then his antics seemed child's play in the tally of bodily self-abuse registered by international stars.)

Television was an inspiration for the laying of a coaxial cable between Sydney and Melbourne, completed in 1962. The cable was dug in at the rate of 30 miles (48 kilometres) a month, and was filled with pressurised dry air. It had detectors equipped to automatically pick up leaks for immediate repair and, with the extension of television, would allow live pictures to be transmitted, as well as increase the number of simultaneous telephone calls between Melbourne and Sydney to more than a thousand. This was the technology of a time when the buzz-word was Global Village – a coinage presented to the world by the Canadian theorist of communication, Marshall McLuhan. Telephone lines were still strung overhead across most of Australia, as they had been since the start of telegraphy. The all-knowing exchange operator – part angel, part witch, part voyeur and part bored enabler of joining the great Australian emptiness with words – had her job secure for at least another decade. As for the Global Village – the idea of people seeing and speaking back to each other wherever they were – it was much spoken about but remained a fantasy in the early television years.

With elections over, politics was off the agenda and 1960s men could go back to sport, money and cars, and women to babies, kitchens and household appliances. That was what was expected of them. But changes were coming in a flood, and for some they couldn't come fast enough. So the thing to do was to leave Australia, for that mythological, paradisiacal place where every self-respecting middle-class person would rather be. It was their Utopia, their Shangri-la. It was 'Overseas'.

When I first considered going to England I was advised – in the catchphrase of the period – to 'see Australia first'. I made some preliminary enquiries, but found out that it cost more to go to Alice Springs than to Greece. ✍

Everyone was saving for 'the trip'. Everyone under the age of 25, it seemed, had plans to travel and to work away from Australia. The great white liners that delivered migrants from Europe returned there with shiploads of physios and dental nurses all desperate to 'do the Continent' before settling down.

AN EXCITED MRS NORM EVERAGE POSES IN FRONT OF TOWER BRIDGE ON HER FIRST TRIP 'OVERSEAS' IN 1962, A PRIZE FOR HAVING WON THE LOVELY MOTHER QUEST IN THE SAME YEAR. THIS PICTURE WAS ONE OF MANY HUNDREDS THAT EDNA WOULD LATER SCREEN TO HER LESS FORTUNATE FRIENDS DURING SLIDE EVENINGS AT HOME IN MOONEE PONDS.

Expatriate writer and broadcaster Clive James remembers his experience of travelling to London and how it differed from that of the majority of Australians who had taken the Great White Liner north to explore the motherland. 'There was a tendency for Australians to hang around in Earls Court and do nothing except knock the Poms. And I didn't really want to be part of that. I didn't come away to be an individual in order to hang together with other people and talk about old times or about how I wasn't getting anywhere. So I became isolated and I didn't see all that many Australians, except a few close friends, for years. And in fact I almost died of loneliness, and I would have come home if I could. But I was broke. Fortunately, I'd burnt my boats in every way. I'd certainly burnt the boat I'd come on – it burnt *itself* out, actually, on the way back to Australia on the following voyage. And so I never could get away until much later on. And by then I didn't want to, so much. I was lucky. I pulled a few wires, got into Cambridge, did another degree, got myself into the network. And it could be said that without that I probably would have crashed and burned. To be

THE P & O LINER *ORCADES* ABOUT TO SET SAIL ON THE FIRST *AUSTRALIAN WOMEN'S WEEKLY* WORLD DISCOVERY TOUR. SAFETY LAY IN NUMBERS FOR THE 700 'MEMBERS' OF THE TOUR AS THEY VENTURED FORTH TO ENCOUNTER 17 COUNTRIES IN FOUR MONTHS.

clannish would have been a mistake. And those of my friends who have actually done things in the arts abroad – like, in my generation, Barry Humphries, Germaine Greer, Bruce Beresford, Brett Whiteley, and so on – tended not to spend all that much time together as Australians. They had their own row to hoe. And they got on with it.'

There were others, of course, who preferred to enjoy 'the Continent' from the comfort of an Australian lounge room.

Beryl and I used to love going to slide evenings, because we hadn't travelled very much and we didn't have any inclination to do so. But a lot of our neighbours and friends had itchy feet. And whenever they came back from a big trip, they'd have a slide evening. When the slides came back from the chemist, we'd get a phone call. They'd say: 'Come round on Thursday night and we'll show you the Lowlands.' Or Switzerland, or something like that. Mostly it was the clean countries our friends liked to visit. And I don't blame them, personally. Generally speaking, a slide evening took about three hours. That would mean you'd see about half a country. But over a period of time you'd feel you'd gone on the trip with them. You really would. Mostly they were pictures of Vi and Alan Chapman standing against shrubs in various countries. And sometimes, too, of the floral clock in the gardens of some place or other. It was all very informative. One night, however, Vi Chapman, who loved to serve savouries during the slide evening, nipped out to the kitchen because she thought she could smell the devils-on-horseback burning. She tried to sneak out in the dark. And unfortunately she tripped over the flex attached to the slide projector and we lost half of Scandinavia. 📷

As a reward for maintaining the reach of the 1950s beyond their use-by date, Mr Menzies was knighted and became Sir Robert Menzies, being graced at regular intervals through the 1960s with additions to his gongs. When Elizabeth II made her second Royal Visit in 1963, Sir Robert greeted her with the dizzy devotion of an ageing man for a wisp of a thing: 'Remember that every man, woman and child who sees you will remember it with joy – remember it in the words of that seventeenth-century poet who wrote, "I did but see her passing by, and yet I'll love her 'til I die."'

It was reported that the Queen responded with a gracious speech and later conferred upon the prime minister the Most Noble Order of the Thistle, an honour accorded to only 16 people outside the Royal Family. In 1965 Sir Robert was made Lord Warden of the Cinque Ports, an obscure custodianship of five ancient English coastal towns, requiring no duties at all except the ceremonial. The previous holder was Sir Winston Churchill, whose voice Menzies sometimes echoed in his antipodean oratory. Menzies' appointment started rumours that Sir Robert was about to retire and live in Britain. Indeed, there was a feeling that the whole country, not just the deputies in his own party, was being held back from a looser expression of the times by Menzies-era fustiness.

A slow fuse was burning and getting faster. What had been minority enthusiasm in the 1950s started to spread into the beginnings of a widespread

WHILE MANY SET OUT FOR NEW EXPERIENCES IN LONDON, MENZIES CREATED A HAVEN FOR MONARCHISTS AT HOME. THE OBSEQUIOUS PRIME MINISTER OVERSAW A COUNTRY WHICH PLAYED 'GOD SAVE THE QUEEN' BEFORE CONCERTS AND MOVIES. WHEN ELIZABETH II VISITED IN 1963 (above), MENZIES GUSHED, 'I DID BUT SEE HER PASSING BY, AND YET I'LL LOVE HER 'TIL I DIE.'

youth culture. The national anthem was 'God Save the Queen' and it was played at the start of every concert and every showing of movies (still called films), with the face of the young Elizabeth II superimposed over a windblown national flag. There were those who refused to stand when her tune came on; they endured the hisses of loyalists, and grew in number. Those with a further taste for nonconformity could dress up in black, attend films with subtitles, and pretend to be French intellectuals or American beatniks.

At the beginning of the 1960s, Australian cities boasted a handful of beatniks. These hobbledehoys were usually art students from the East Sydney Technical College or the Royal Melbourne Institute of Technology, who strove to resemble characters in the romances of Jack Kerouac. They wore a uniform of black duffle coat, stove-pipe jeans, Roman sandals and guitars. Before the age of pot they experimented with alcohol and slimming tablets with an amphetamine constituent. Their 'hip' talk was superimposed upon their mournful Aussie inflections in a painfully self-conscious way. They were also fond of speaking very sententiously indeed about light dance music. ✍

Clive James also recalls the scene: 'I knew both of Sydney's beatniks in the late fifties. I'm only mildly exaggerating. They hung out in a pub called the Royal George Hotel downtown. Originality, first of all, tended to be copied from overseas. And those who were deemed to be original, and publicised as such, would hang out in very, very small groups, in very, very tight enclaves. Rosaleen Norton, for example, was the entire bohemian movement of Kings Cross. And the bohemian movement of Kings Cross, i.e. Rosaleen Norton, was chiefly famous for appearing on the streets in heavy mascara, sometimes as late as eleven-thirty in the evening.'

Counteracting the dominance of rock 'n roll was a folk music revival centred on folk clubs in every city. Folkies had republican sentiments before such an idea was ever aired. Their clubs were dim places with an air of earnest righteousness, the home of banjos, guitars, mouth organs and the more arcane instruments of bush bands, giving a scatter of fans a feeling of belonging to a select crowd. 'Folk' to these fans never meant the folk in general, the

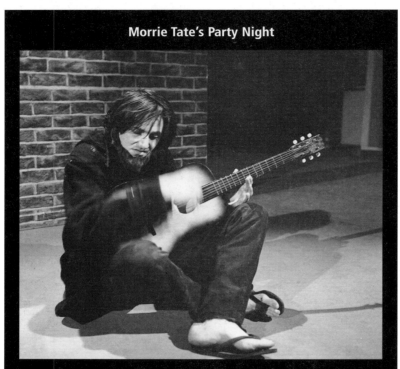

Morrie Tate's Party Night

Was anyone down the Cézanne Coffee Bar last night? It was a real swinging scene, man. There was a group of cats that had hitched over from Adelaide for the Snake's big farewell party and the place was stacked with guitars and sleeping bags and empty packets of No-Doz. Crazy, man. Big Sonia and me and the Mouse and a real cool little raver from the Teachers Training College went up to the Greek's for a blowout, and we ended up at the Mouse's pad imbibing the old marsala and listening to a few really swinging Ella Fitzgerald sides with Clark Terry very interesting as usual on trumpet. ✍

Above: MORRIE TATE WAS A 1962 HUMPHRIES CREATION: AN ARCHETYPAL BEATNIK, COMPLETE WITH ROMAN SANDALS, DUFFLE COAT AND GUITAR ON WHICH HE WOULD STRUM OUT AN ACCOMPANIMENT TO MOURNFUL FOLKSY LYRICS ABOUT HOW 'SUBURBAN CONFORMITY GIVES ME THE SHITS'.

Martin Agrippa: Down Underground

Hi there! Yes, my name is Martin Agrippa and it was my motion picture which ran off with the big prize in Helsinki this year for the best Australian entry in the experimental film section.

A lot of people have asked me *why* I made this film and the answer is a simple one: it had to be made.

I knew I was trying to say something in this motion picture which no young Australian filmmaker had had the guts to say before, and I guess I kind of knew deep down that I'd have to invent a new kind of cinema to say these things.

The story kind of happened like the best modern jazz music. I just took myself off to Bilgola Beach with a tape recorder and talked. God, how I talked!

I talked about my childhood, my attitudes to my parents, to women, my responses to hallucinatory drugs, to the finest in modern jazz music and towards the place of creative people such as myself in antipodean society. I even talked about myself.

I talked of images, too: the surfrider poised on a green wall of water, the curious splendour of old-age pensioners eating, the ageless symmetry of an egg, the statuesque beauty of a newborn child, and the timeless quality of my own reflection.

I poured all of myself, all of my consciousness and creativity, into those reels and reels of tape in the house at Bilgola Beach, and these tapes have been distilled into the motion picture you are about to see.

MARTIN AGRIPPA, ANOTHER OF HUMPHRIES' CREATIONS, WAS A HISPID AUSTRALIAN UNDERGROUND FILMMAKER OF THE SIXTIES. THE TRANSCRIPT IS PART OF AN AGRIPPA SKETCH MADE INTO A SHORT FILM BY DIRECTOR BRUCE BERESFORD. IRONICALLY, IT WAS SHOWN AT SEVERAL INTERNATIONAL FESTIVALS OF UNDERGROUND CINEMA WHERE IT WAS ACCLAIMED AS A MASTERPIECE OF THE GENRE.

Australian music-loving public who were making a hit of The Wild One's 'Shake, Rattle and Roll' or of Aboriginal country singer Jimmy Little's 'Royal Telephone', first recorded by Burl Ives, or of Lucky Starr's 'I've Been Everywhere', a recitation of innumerable Australian place-names.

Folk clubs were mostly left-wing in orientation, at one with the progressive working classes and almost invariably favoured by middle-class university students. Their emphasis was on Australianness in the music, which mostly meant Irish-Australianness – songs of convict ships, the cruel deeds of gaolers, misunderstood bushrangers, and songs of union men. In 1963 a group called the Seekers (two guitars, cello and female vocalist) was formed, playing a kind of sweet folk sound – rather apolitical, much to the annoyance of devoted folkies. Australia's international folk singer and zither-girl, Shirley Abicair, returned from London to show the motherland just how modern Australia had become. Lefties glowered at their TVs, watching her interview such nation-builders as the property developer L. J. Hooker. Until Bob Dylan gave the folk movement an international pop blessing later in the decade there was a bunker mentality among folk fans – they wanted their music loved by all, but its wider popularity would detract from its secret power, the inner-circle feel, and so a folk singer

A 1960s Creation: Neil Singleton

Some people insisted they knew Neil Singleton. He was a left-wing academic, not very high up in his department, but an identity at the Newcastle Hotel in George Street, Sydney, or the Windsor Castle in Paddington. Long hair and the fringe of beard around the chin, sans moustache, identified him very precisely, according to my 1965 audience at the Theatre Royal, Sydney. Someone else, in Melbourne, was positive Neil was inspired by an annoyingly successful Sydney art critic, while the art critic in question asked me confidentially if a tall, bearded Melbourne radio playwright had recognised himself or was going to sue.

In adding this new class of character to the gallery, I had no idea how many real Neil Singletons would emerge from the woodwork. Until the mid sixties, Neil's class of puritan, leftist, querulous, turtle-necked, elbow-patched, pipe-sucking, wife-cheating, wine-buffing, abstract-art–digging highbrow had been among my most enthusiastic fans, eager for a chuckle at the middle-class effusions of Edna, Sandy and the other Australians they never met at their own parties. But deep chagrin greeted this impersonation; it was only after the birth of Neil Singleton that the arty periodicals began hinting that I lacked 'relevance'.

appearing on television was a mixed blessing. Was folk music likely to be the next craze? If so, how would it keep its exclusivity?

This Australian folk singer was one of my more masculine roles. Big Sonia wore Roman sandals, a long black wig and a micro-skirt. She entered with a guitar and concluded her monologue with a song. Folk music, fortunately less popular today, enjoyed a great vogue in the late 1960s, probably because its composition and performance required no talent whatsoever. Australian cities boasted innumerable imitators of Bob Dylan and Joan Baez.
Rereading my delightfully dated piece from 'Just a Show' (1968), I notice that Big Sonia doubted whether the Gallipoli campaign ever took place, in much the same way as in 1980 the swimmer Dawn Fraser challenged the multinational media to prove that Russians had really invaded Afghanistan. Here and there in remote communities the simple-hearted, ever-questioning spirit of Big Sonia lives on.

Australia had no established film industry at this time, but Bolexes – hand-held, clockwork-operated 16 mm cameras – were quite reasonably priced. The so-called 'student film' made its debut at intense, breathless screenings. The most extreme filmmakers were prototype Fellinis. The most extreme poets were Ginsbergs. The most extreme novelists remained unpublished. The nursery for film and television talent was the ABC, which had a system of specialist trainees who joined the organisation and worked in Talks, Drama, Education or Rural, honing skills that in a later generation would be taught in film schools.

Except for small magazines there were few outlets for new writers. Even good, new young writers remained largely unpublished in the 1960s, thanks to the dominance of literary publishing by the old-guard publishing house, Angus & Robertson. Every so often the A & R editors would choose an up-and-coming new 'voice' – but mostly in the 1960s they gave prominence to writers who had emerged in the 1940s. The absolute pick of the youth crop (the outstanding debuts of Randolph Stow and Christopher Koch, for example) and new work by older writers (such as Patrick White and George Johnston) were snapped up by English and American publishing houses. There was a truculence in Australia's cultural self-assessment, a defensive pride in the home-grown product. It was a pride that needed the heavy reinforcement of 'overseas' approval, particularly from the cultural taste-makers of London. In 1960 Sir Macfarlane Burnet of Melbourne won the Nobel Prize for Medicine, but the idea that an Australian might win the Literature prize, for a depiction of how Australians lived at an ordinary level of life, was a far-fetched fantasy – something else for the birds or the astral plane.

Even so, there were signs. The literary publishing event of the year in 1959 was *The Penguin Book of Australian Verse*. This immediately gave authority and a widespread readership to writers with feeling for the Australian landscape, like Judith Wright and David Campbell. It made something very old in Australia feel very modern, bringing a feeling to writing that Nolan, Boyd and Tucker had already brought to painting. Yet, except for the poets, a great part of the artistic push of the time came from writers, painters and performers who had exiled themselves in order to make their names.

In 1960 the first Adelaide Arts Festival was held. It was in effect a cultural crowning of the 1950s. The patron was the governor-general, an Englishman, Viscount Dunrossil. A massed symphony orchestra played European and English compositions. Sir Donald Wolfit, an English Shakespearian actor, played scenes from a tragedy. Dave Brubeck, an American musician, played jazz. Meanwhile, Hugh Hunt, the Englishman who ran the Australian Elizabethan Theatre Trust, directed the Anglo-American T. S. Eliot's *Murder in the Cathedral*. But 'many visitors from interstate and abroad,' reported a newspaper of the day, 'commented on the archaic liquor laws which meant pubs closed on Sundays and at 6 p.m. on weekdays. The lack of good restaurants was also a sore point for the gastronomically inclined.' The festival was attended by an estimated 398 000 people – two-thirds the population of Adelaide – over its two-week duration. They revelled in the 'recognition' accorded by overseas visitors.

These were the 1960s but they were not yet 'the Sixties'. *Their* moment was waiting for a defining point in time, which might come very soon or might not occur until the decade was well advanced. Meanwhile, the 1950s had a few paroxysms left. In 1961 Sydneysiders took their last tram ride, to La Perouse on Botany Bay, and then there were no trams any more. It was a tense year for Bob Menzies, who was returned in the December election by a narrow majority of one member (proving to be Labor's closest brush with power in

'C'MON, LET'S TWIST AGAIN, LIKE WE DID LAST SUMMER' – AUSTRALIAN TEENAGERS DUTIFULLY APED THE AMERICAN DANCE CRAZE, THE TWIST.

23 years). Even so, Menzies had confidence enough for a majority of 100. A few days before the elections Frank Sinatra was in town and sang 35 songs to a packed house at Sydney Stadium. In 1962 a standard-gauge rail link joined Sydney and Melbourne – until then, passengers had had to change trains in Albury. In 1962, also, it was pronounced that all Aborigines were entitled to vote (with the exception of some 30 000 deemed 'not ready to vote'), but even those entitled to vote were not entitled to full citizenship. In the same year, talk of possible war with Indonesia stopped when Indonesia was granted Dutch New Guinea (Irian Barat; now Irian Jaya). A team of 30 Australian soldiers left for Saigon to train South Vietnamese troops. And the Twist became a dance craze.

There had been end-of-the-world parties for the Cuban missile crisis, but no parties occurred late in 1963 when J. F. Kennedy was assassinated. A new music was starting to be played, though, and later memories of the two events – the death of an American president and the arrival of the Beatles – somehow went together. Nobody quite realised what strange, inner hope had been invested in the bodily shape, voice and charming air of President Kennedy. His death made people feel as if a black hole had opened up. It was personal and shocking, even when there hadn't been much feeling before. There seemed a loosening of anarchy in the world, a crack in the facade of accepted authority as well as a shocked reminder of mortality. The Beatles came harmonising through that mood with a humorous, flip and existential whimsy.

Everyone from the 1960s is said to remember where they were when they heard the news from Dallas that Kennedy was dead. It was early morning in the eastern states of Australia. People still half asleep wandered around looking dazed, repeating the words, 'JFK's been shot'. America was a democracy, and Australia was associated with America in a number of traditions, and it couldn't have happened, could it? What hope was there for us all?

With the Beatles it was a lighter matter; people remembering the first time they heard them recall a mood rather than a place. Later it would be called a 'headspace', as the 1960s threw in more and more extreme rock developments. But not for a while yet, because the Beatles when they first appeared were the music of shaking something off, a loosening that gave a light-limbed variation to rock 'n roll and came with an offhand reflection of north-of-England humour that struck a chord with Australians. There was a lot of the BBC's 'The Goon Show' in the Beatles' press-conference and film antics. Late 1950s teenagers who revered the Goons arrived in their first year of university able to repeat whole episodes off by heart. Hardly into their twenties, they found their mood of being was an international fad.

The Beatles gave the opportunity to turn hair into a symbol of attitude just by letting it grow

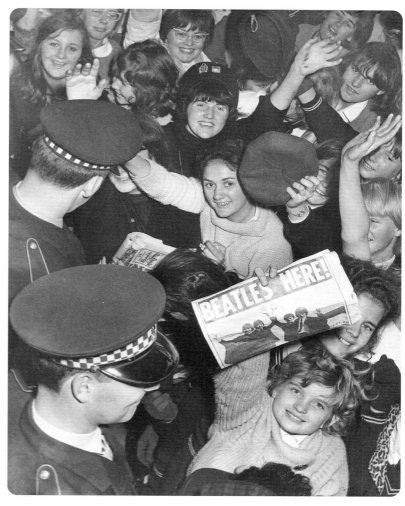

IN 1964 THE BEATLES TOURED AUSTRALIA AND MAYHEM ENSUED. IN SYDNEY, ADELAIDE AND MELBOURNE TEENAGERS RIOTED IN THE STREETS. HITHERTO RESPONSIBLE YOUNG GIRLS TURNED INTO SCREAMING FANS LIKE THESE ABOVE, WHILE YOUNG MALES GREW THEIR HAIR IN AN ATTEMPT TO WIN THE SEXUAL FAVOURS GIRLS SEEMED SO KEEN TO OFFER THE FOURSOME.

out into a modified helmet shape. Beatle haircuts did not so much get styled as *happen*. Long hair before this had been a symbol of foppishness or outrageous bohemianism, or the mark of the oddball artist. Now it was lengthening everywhere, although so-called 'official Beatle suits' – collarless, grey, as worn by John, Paul, George and Ringo – did not have the same impact. The Beatles were called the 'Four Hairmen of the Apocalypse' by older journalists made slightly fearful of what the group might mean to their daughters. Younger journos were called 'official Beatles reporters' and if they were female they had an inside track as groupies.

In some quarters there were violent reactions to the new mood of young people. George Young and Harry Vanda of the Easybeats remember their own experiences on stage: 'Brisbane Festival Hall! There were shows up there that were absolute pandemonium – and the *cops* up there! In those days Brisbane was regarded as "Dodge City" and the cops looked at the music business and us, the people that got up there, as being pansies

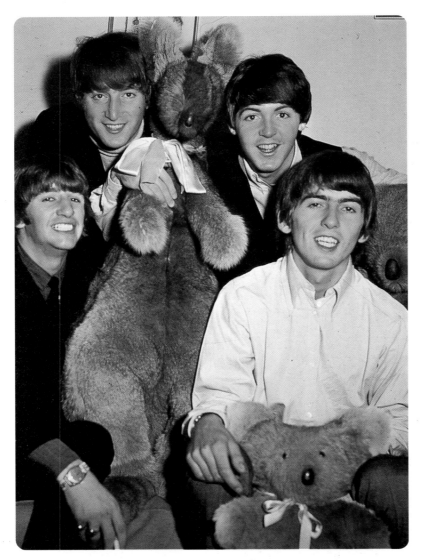

Above: THE BEATLES (PICTURED DURING THEIR 1964 AUSTRALIAN TOUR) PROVIDED A SOUNDTRACK FOR LOCAL TEENAGERS IN SEARCH OF AN IDENTITY. HORRIFIED PARENTS WATCHED AS A GULF, LATER DUBBED THE 'GENERATION GAP', GREW BETWEEN THEMSELVES AND THEIR FORMERLY COMPLIANT OFFSPRING. WHEN THE FAB FOUR DEPARTED, AUSTRALIANS CLONED THEIR OWN POP ACTS IN ORDER TO MAINTAIN THE RUSH OF OESTROGEN IN ADOLESCENT GIRLS. THE EASYBEATS **(opposite top)** HAD A HUGE INTERNATIONAL HIT WITH 'FRIDAY ON MY MIND', AND ARE PICTURED, ALONG WITH THE MODELS **(opposite below)**, WEARING THE LATEST FASHIONS FROM SWINGING LONDON.

or whatever. So if there was an opportunity for them to let rip and show their authority and shut the show down, or shove the bands around, or shove the kids around, they took the opportunity. And there were quite a few times we would be standing on stage and see kids being dragged out of the audience and given a thump – and some of it looked pretty gruesome as well.'

These days, the notion of 'the Sixties' is inextricably linked with sex, drugs and rock 'n roll. It is as if no one did anything else. But those who were there can assure you that people went to the movies, listened to classical music, created works of art, baked cakes and went fishing. However, it is true that Australians, a little later than the rest of the world, discovered the writing on the wall. They discovered sex, they discovered nudity and they discovered dirty words. They took off their old-style Akubra hats at last, and underneath they discovered hair.

Length of hair became a barometer of social change. It was noticed that, as men's hair got longer, women's skirts were getting shorter. The more radical the opinion expressed by the young male student, the longer his hair. This was particularly so after 1968, when the rhetoric of the 'student revolution' started taking hold. Other sorts of hair made contrary points. A surfie's bleached hair spoke of the endless summer and following the waves up to Byron or Noosa. The precise length of a male employee's hair was of obsessive interest to the employer. Hair told parents when their children were growing apart from them. Hair in this sense was as welcome in a Returned Servicemen's Club as a party of Japanese tourists.

Teenagers wondered at the fuss. Little Pattie, the singer, remarks: 'Children weren't children any more – we ceased to be just seen and not heard, we weren't mindless any more and we started to think. We were called ratbags and hippies and communists. I was one of those kids, and I was OK. We thought and we felt. Older people were putting labels on kids because they didn't understand what we were starting to understand. I know that out of that came drugs and lots of ugly things. But lots of great things came out of it too – and the fact that teenagers started to think and form opinions that were pretty deep, and that feelings went deep, that was great, and I was really proud to have been a part of it.'

The Beatles were jamming the Australian pop music airwaves by early 1964 and the Rolling Stones, with their bad-boy, lip-curling image, were not far behind. So were other teams of four (or five) like the home-grown Billy Thorpe and the Aztecs. And so too the 26-year-old American, P. J. Proby, who had grown up singing Elvis Presley covers and who wore

velvet pants, with ribbons in his matted hair, and played an even more frankly sexual game with his fans than most – mopping his face with girls' discarded knickers and craftily arranging to split his trousers as a climax to every show.

The Beatles arrived on their first Australian tour in June 1964. According to estimates, more than half the population of Adelaide turned out on the streets to greet them. In other cities the Beatles' hotels were besieged by up to 10 000 screaming girls. In Melbourne 150 were injured rushing at barricades erected by police; and then the army was called in to reinforce police ranks. There hadn't been crowds like these since the 1954 Royal Visit, and the hysteria then had been a quite proper and sometimes orchestrated excitement – hardly to be compared with under-age girls bribing, conniving, hiding and then doing their best to burst into the rooms of the Fab Four (the rooms of any *one* of the Fab Four) and there to indulge, if they could, in what their mothers had reserved until marriage.

Oz MAGAZINE WAS FOUNDED IN 1963 OUT OF A SENSE OF FRUSTRATION AND BOREDOM IN A COUNTRY STILL RULED BY THE 'GENT-OCRACY'. ITS YOUNG EDITORS APPEARED ON THE COVER OF AN EARLY ISSUE 'PEEING' INTO A URINAL-LIKE SCULPTURE IN DOWNTOWN SYDNEY.

Sometime in the 1960s there came a day when Australians woke with a queasy, worrying feeling. Under the pie-crust of respectability it was still the 1950s, wasn't it? But cracks were showing.

They were the defining moments. They were when the 1960s began truly defining themselves – yet at the same time, paradoxically, they were when the 1960s started leaving themselves behind. For those hating change, the cracks were worrisome. For those wanting change the cracks weren't coming fast enough. In 1963 a student magazine called *Oz* had begun publishing, splashing out with four-letter words like bullets in a guerrilla war against pomposity and wowserism. On Cape York, police had evicted Aborigines from the Mapoon community and razed their buildings to allow bauxite mining to start. It was done with the connivance of church missions, but such actions wouldn't go unchallenged much longer. In 1964 Menzies (by then Sir Robert) was re-elected with a huge majority after yet another scare campaign, characterising his Labor opponents as being controlled by the 'faceless men' of the Labor caucus.

In the same year a young Aboriginal leader, Charles Perkins, travelled by bus with a crowd of white, mostly middle-class students and supporters, taking a US-style freedom ride through the most racist towns of northwestern New South Wales. Aborigines were not yet citizens in their own country and they were demanding to know why not. When the Aboriginal poet Kath Walker went as part of a deputation to Sir Robert to ask for a referendum on citizenship, he refused. He wasn't going to risk his political career. But he poured himself an enormous Scotch whisky and offered drinks to the deputation, who reminded him that in several parts of Australia it was against the law to serve drinks to Aborigines. Slightly taken aback, he thumped his chest and said: 'I'm the boss here.'

The adolescent rampaging called Beatlemania doubtless raised Bob Menzies' ageing eyebrows, but only for the duration of what was seen as a passing fad, and not the door opening on a new set of expectations in society. What interested Menzies most keenly was a mechanism for channelling youth into the Australian army, getting them 'short-back-and-sides' haircuts, and transporting them to the battlefields of Vietnam. So, at the end of 1964, conscription was introduced.

'The measures have been prompted,' said a government spokesman, 'by the perceived threat of Indonesian aggression in Papua New Guinea and Malaysia, and the spread of communist military insurgency throughout South-East Asia, particularly in Laos and South Vietnam.'

Call-up was made by ballot, the aim being to increase the regular army's strength from 22 000 to 37 000. Men turning 20 were required to register. The idea of harvesting youth in a lottery, gathering them in by birthdate in any given year, and then, when enough dates had been chosen, of ceasing the ballot and making no demands on others who turned 20 in that year, appealed (for a while) to the Australian sense of fair play.

But not to everyone. Harry Vanda and his mates were among those who saw it differently. 'For us to have gone into the army at that time was completely inconceivable. This was another one of the Establishment things, the upper class, call it what you will – it was part and parcel of that whole thing. The very idea of going into the army, where you get your hair cut and stand to attention and say "Yes sir, no sir, three bags full, sir" – forget it! That really wasn't what we were all about. We weren't anti-Establishment, but there had to be better things, there had to be a better way.'

MENZIES' AUSTRALIA HAD BOWED BEFORE THE QUEEN. UNDER NEW PRIME MINISTER HAROLD HOLT WE BOWED BEFORE THE MIGHTY UNITED STATES. HOLT ANNOUNCED THAT AUSTRALIA WOULD GO 'ALL THE WAY WITH LBJ' – ALL THE WAY TO VIETNAM, THAT WAS. PHOTOGRAPHER DAVID MOORE WAS APPALLED BY HOLT'S OBSEQUIOUSNESS, AND CAPTURED THIS PORTRAIT OF CRAVEN SUBMISSION DURING PRESIDENT LYNDON JOHNSON'S CONTROVERSIAL VISIT TO AUSTRALIA IN 1966.

WHILE PRIME MINISTER HOLT HAD VOWED AUSTRALIA WOULD GO 'ALL THE WAY' IN VIETNAM, THOSE WHO HAD TO ACTUALLY DO THE FIGHTING THOUGHT OTHERWISE. DEMONSTRATIONS DURING PRESIDENT JOHNSON'S VISIT IN 1966 SHOWED JUST HOW DIVIDED AND PASSIONATE AUSTRALIANS HAD BECOME ABOUT THEIR INVOLVEMENT IN VIETNAM. NSW PREMIER ROBERT ASKIN WAS SO ANNOYED WITH THE PROTESTERS THAT HE REPORTEDLY TOLD LBJ'S DRIVER TO 'RUN OVER THE BASTARDS'.

The Australian people had voted Menzies in repeatedly, and had recently increased his majority to the point of overweening complacency. And so, just before the next election, he stepped down from the leadership and his loyal lieutenant, Harold Holt, took over. Mr Holt went to Washington in mid 1966 and promised the Americans that Australia would go 'all the way with LBJ' in the escalating Vietnam War. Then, within a few short months, the country found itself divided. When President Johnson visited Australia amid anti-war street demonstrations, the New South Wales premier Robert Askin told LBJ's driver to 'run over the bastards'. Fortunately the police chose not to comply. (Ordinary Australians didn't approve of Askin's suggestion, either – mostly on the grounds of unseemly language.)

In the federal election of November 1966, a campaign based almost entirely on the issue of the Vietnam War, the Holt Government won by a landslide, with a majority of 40 seats over Labor.

Despite this show of wide popular support, anti-government protest continued to be a feature of city street life – an edgy counterpoint to suburban dreaming.

The voter of the Menzies and Holt era remained a demographic norm beloved of advertising agencies – secure with his block of land, his patch of lawn, his Victa motor mower, his Holden car, his flutter on the horses, his licensed club, and his television set dominating the household routine absolutely. His wife still had her place in the home, and had her hand on the purse strings when it came to choice of washing powder, cleaning agents, furnishings, bedding and drapes. The 1960s were when the great majority of Australian homes attained refrigerator and washing machine ownership. (The dishwasher boom awaited the 1970s and 1980s.) Mum and dad listened to Cole Porter and Frank Sinatra, booked their seats for *Hello, Dolly* and waited for the Beatles to pass along. If the music got too loud, dad could always give an extra twist to the throttle of the Victa, couldn't he? And if sonny's hair grew too long he could always join the army.

The Victa mower had been on the market since 1952 and become immensely popular with its irresistible slogan, 'Turns Grass Into Lawn'. By 1960 it was changing Australia, with specially designed

DATSUN CARS (above) WERE FIRST
IMPORTED IN 1960 AND, DESPITE
MURMURS ABOUT 'JAP CRAP' AND
DISQUIET AMONG RETURNED
SERVICEMEN, SEXY MARKETING
CAMPAIGNS SET AGAINST AUSTRALIAN
ICONS GAVE THE LOCAL HOLDEN A
SERIOUS RUN FOR ITS MONEY.

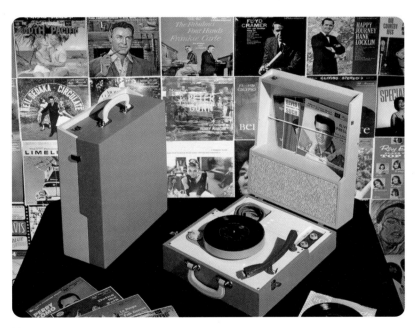

THE PORTABLE STEREO (above) TRANSFORMED SUBURBAN BEDROOMS INTO HOTBEDS
OF MUSICAL DISCONTENT. WHILE COLE PORTER PLAYED IN THE LIVING ROOM, TEENS
GROOVED TO NEW SOUNDS FROM THE LIKES OF NORMIE ROWE (left) FROM BEHIND
CLOSED DOORS. BY THE AGE OF 19 NORMIE HAD SELLOUT CONCERTS, NUMBER-ONE
RECORDS, AND EVEN NOTCHED UP AN ACQUITTAL ON CARNAL KNOWLEDGE CHARGES.
HE WAS HAVING FAR TOO MUCH FUN, SO THE GOVERNMENT CALLED HIM TO GREATER
THINGS: HE WAS CONSCRIPTED TO FIGHT IN THE VIETNAM WAR.

models available for tougher, tropical conditions. 'Shredder' was a better word than mower for the early Victa. Wielded by men wearing a backyard uniform of terry-towelling hat, short-sleeved shirt, khaki shorts and rubber thongs, it was responsible for innumerable toe-amputations. It was a solid piece, with short steel blades attached to a spinning steel disc beneath a cast-metal cover. It had a chunky two-stroke motor that snarled, moaned, and sometimes stopped dead as it was rammed into the wiry undergrowth of semi-tropical backyards.

The Victa mower was responsible for the loss of a scruffy, turn-of-the-century look that had been maintained in tropical Australian towns well past World War II. Such towns loomed over the horizon in a timeless colonial haze of entangled grasses and seedheads, like tombstones in a municipal cemetery. The houses in these towns were on stilts, and the main gardening occupation was cutting down any trees (except for mango trees, which flourished) in the belief that trees stopped breezes and so made things hotter. But with the advent of the Victa the wild unkemptness changed – another part of Australia became suburbanised, and the houses, obeying this instinct, started to be built at ground level. Queenslanders had a special knack for knowing when the Victa had struck a cane toad in the grass – as distinct, say, from striking a mango. There was a subtle alteration in the sound of the engine's snarl.

In the wake of the Beatles' first Australian tour, home-grown idols emerged to soak up the available supply of hysteria. The chief of these was 17-year-old Normie Rowe, whose first hit was based on the refrain: 'The things that you're liable, to read in the Bible, ain't necessarily so.' It was hardly an attack on organised religion, although certain radio stations refused to give it air-time. The song was a mere wink at social conventions and was delivered, in Rowe's case, with a hugely engaging smile that had the singer's young female fans desperate for anything. One of them carved Rowe's name into her flesh and stated her reasons: 'I just wanted to do it because I love him so much. He's gorgeous. I always cry when I see him and I screamed so much when he was at the stadium that I lost my voice and couldn't talk for two days.'

What could a boy do except bow to the blandishments of such passionate souls, and take

IN A PRECURSOR TO THE LOTTO DRAW OF THE EIGHTIES, MR McKINNON, MP, HOLDS ALOFT A MARBLE IN THE FIRST NATIONAL SERVICE LOTTERY IN 1965. IF YOU WERE A YOUNG AUSTRALIAN MALE AND YOUR BIRTH DATE MATCHED THE NUMBER ON THE MARBLE, YOU WON AND WENT TO FIGHT IN VIETNAM. THERE WERE NO SECOND PRIZES.

what came to him? Normie Rowe was told by a 15-year-old girl: 'I am available any night of the week you want. Every night, if that suits you.'

A charge of carnal knowledge was brought against the 19-year-old Normie Rowe in 1965, over an incident with a 13-year-old girl at Double Bay (just along the road from the Sydney Stadium), but it was dismissed on the grounds of lack of evidence. Following the case, Rowe's popularity kept on increasing. He was popular without being hip, a middle-of-the-road Australian when the novelty of idolisation was stripped away. There was a touch of the genial digger about Normie Rowe. In 1968, when others in his generation were rioting against the idea of military service, he accepted his call-up, having his long hair shorn by an army barber and his loose body shirts

replaced by scratchy khakis. He had to wear a tie, too – but then even at rock concerts it was still possible to see fans wearing white shirts, tweed sports-coats and Wool Board ties. Normie Rowe went from being one kind of symbol to being another. What's more, he went willingly.

Of the call-up method, Normie Rowe has said: 'The ballot to go to Vietnam was a weird way of doing it. They used the Tattersalls (lottery) barrel in Melbourne. Inside were wooden marbles with numbers on them – like a Lotto type of deal. And each one of these numbers corresponded with a day. For example, say the number that came out was 31, then everyone born on January 31st was going into the army, and then off to Vietnam. I'd registered in all good faith and was called up. But I found out – ten years after I got back – that there were a whole bunch of people born on my birthday who weren't called up.' It has been suggested that because of Normie's great popularity with

Les Patterson Does Wool

In the sixties I played a part, small but significant, in the popularisation of Australia's national fibre – wool. It was my idea to make wool sexy. Oh, it was marvellous! I got the idea of getting old Pierre Cardigan to come out to Australia – a distinguished Frog couturier if ever there was one. We whipped him into the bush and we got him into a shearing shed. He had the time of his life staring at them young sheep-shearers stripped to the waist and sweating like buggery. He couldn't wait to get his fingers into the short and curlies and do a bit of fleece fondling!

Then out in the paddock a bit later on, a whole bunch of ewes charged straight past him. They sensed old Pierre wasn't a particular threat to them. No New Zealand blood there, they reckoned! Besides, most of them had pretty well passed their ewe's-by date … you with me?

Above: PIERRE CARDIN (RIGHT) PICTURED AT A MELBOURNE TRAM STOP IN 1967 WITH THE PRIZE-WINNING RAM DADDY-OH AND ITS OWNER RICHARD NORTHCOTT.

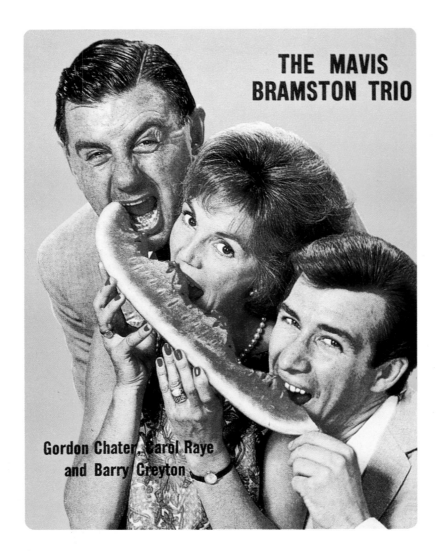

THE MAVIS BRAMSTON TRIO

Gordon Chater, Carol Raye and Barry Creyton

TELEVISION WAS STARTING TO BECOME ADVENTUROUS IN THE SIXTIES. 'THE MAVIS BRAMSTON SHOW' (above) WAS A HIGHLY POPULAR SERIES THAT SPECIALISED IN 'SEND-UPS'. THE BATTERY-POWERED TRANSISTOR RADIO (left) HELPED RADIO SURVIVE THE IMPACT OF TELEVISION, BUT SERIOUS MUSIC DIDN'T SOUND TOO GOOD ON A TRANNIE, SO THE GOVERNMENT COMMISSIONED DANISH ARCHITECT JOERN UTZON TO DESIGN SYDNEY'S OPERA HOUSE (opposite page). CONSTRUCTION WAS HAMPERED BY BUREAUCRATIC MEDDLING AND UTZON RESIGNED IN FRUSTRATION BEFORE IT WAS FINISHED.

the youth at the time, the authorities felt that he would make a fine example to other young men less willing to go.

Far from the hysterical concert halls of the cities were the rickety dance halls of rural Australia. Here it was possible to see young men wearing shorts and sporting rubber thongs on their lumpy-toed feet, learning awkward dance steps with despairing, perspiring female partners. The ritual was preparation for the annual Debutantes Ball. The idea of the Australian Debs Ball was always hard to explain, even in the 1960s, even to those participating. Yet it was a tribal ritual across the whole of country society, encompassing Aboriginal advancement organisations through to Rural Youth and any number of church groups from Catholic to Presbyterian. The Debs Ball was said to be an entry into society – but what sort of society, it now began to be widely asked, and how were Debs to be different afterwards from the way they were before?

By the mid 1960s, even in the remoter parts of the country, on the fringes of social change, there were ground-shifts. Once the town councillor or visiting

My Fair Lady continued its successful run in the early sixties. The tale of a young woman who came from nowhere, aspiring to be somebody, matched the aspirations of Australia itself at the time. It played to sellout audiences in beautiful old theatres, some of which would become the target of developers and be demolished before the end of the decade.

parliamentarian had stifled his yawns and 'received the Debs', and when the obligatory awkward waltzes and old-fashioned dances were done to the tune of snare drum and piano, the floor was cleared and a record player brought in and something wilder started up. A young man bellowing the Rolling Stones' refrain 'I Can't Get No Satisfaction' was expressing something so close to the bone that he might have been ostracised for it a generation earlier. Now it was just a wildness released, and the Debs Ball was in accord with a widening social mood of revolt.

At the end of the decade the chief Stone, Mick Jagger, came to the town of Braidwood, New South Wales, to play the bushranger Ned Kelly in English director Tony Richardson's movie of the same name. Locals wanted to show Mick a good time but he barely socialised at all, and his girlfriend Marianne Faithful overdosed on barbiturates, almost died, and the party went on without him.

Mick was unable to get a handle on Australian country life, but Australians themselves were constantly kept aware of the importance of rural earnings to their economy. Practically all a schoolchild needed to know was that Australia had almost unlimited natural resources, with iron ore and bauxite added to the export side of the ledger in vast shiploads taken from Western Australia's Pilbara and from Cape York in Queensland. In the 1960s new railways were built across Queensland, and coal was shipped nonstop to Japan in an export wave that cushioned national expenditure.

The country still 'rode on the sheep's back' and advertising copywriters were paid handsomely to make wool sexy. The Wool Board devised a symbol intended to be internationally recognised, but when Australians were asked what it meant they reacted with mental confusion. Was it the World Council of Churches? The ABC? The Boy Scouts?

This was the dawn of corporate symbolism, with graphic designers kept busy inventing logos for banks, airlines, insurance companies and broadcasting services as a way of symbolising the holding together of institutions starting to feel the pressure of change.

The rage to demolish anything old-looking reached its peak in the 1960s, and Australian cities began to resemble Dresden after the Allied bombing. At the beginning of the decade the Australian theatre-going public was still under the spell of *My Fair Lady*. Its appeal was not surprising: it gave hope to a nation of Eliza Doolittles that, if they learned to speak nicely, they'd all be duchesses. But later on the *Hello, Dolly*s and the *Mame*s failed to generate the old magic. Developers had pulverised many of the beautiful old theatres. Television had scooped up most of the audiences and locked them in their homes. Those who had paid to see the English-born Stuart Wagstaff as Professor Higgins could stay at home and watch him smoke Benson & Hedges for nothing.

Intimations of provincial paranoia began to occur. Was Australia behind the times? Old-fashioned? Retrograde? Demolition was the answer.

The erection of the Sydney Opera House and the usual farcical compromises that attended its construction gave the authorities a perfect excuse to demolish every theatre in Sydney. The finished Opera House, after endless bureaucratic tinkering, might never be perfect for opera, but at least it would look good on a stamp.

Within ten years, Melbourne's opulent Victorian architecture suffered a fate that Goering had failed to inflict on Glasgow. Cream brick, the preferred fabric of suburbia, engulfed the rural environs of our cities and the colours we loved were burgundy and duck-egg blue. ✏

Small theatres sprang up in old pram factories, churches, stables and penitentiaries, and a more or less authentic Australian voice began to be heard in experimental plays. Local theatrical pundits got overexcited with all this creative activity, and the emerging cultural boom (which was to be more a mark of the 1970s) reduced its advocates to ecstatic explanation – as when the young journalist Tony Morphett (in his maturity to become a no-nonsense scriptwriter) talked on ABC-TV about new-wave theatre. 'It's a sphere thing, it's a dig, it's a groove,' he said, 'an all-round head experience. You go there not to see it but to *be* it.'

And as for the written word, a novel had to be 'big'.

Just what constituted 'big' in the arts was open to question. A new exhibition of Australian painting, including works by Sidney Nolan and Arthur Boyd, opened at the Adelaide Festival and went on to great acclaim in the Tate Gallery in London. The idea that Australian art could be 'contemporary' (a word synonymous with 'from overseas') and 'Australian' at the same time was difficult to absorb. As the world came closer, Australia looked out of step with itself, and the idea was funny – suddenly everything was worthy of a 'send-up'. Television programmes like 'The Mavis Bramston Show', with Gordon Chater, brought comic revue sketches to a national audience. Chater did old-fashioned burlesque party pieces – squirting himself, breaking eggs on his head and hitting himself in the face with a custard pie. On television, sending up the long-running Kings Cross male revue *Les Girls*, he appeared in drag as a 'Les Men' artiste.

The trannies that made the greatest impact on Australia in the 1960s weren't the transvestites, they were the transistors. With the advent of the 'trannie' the wood-veneered radiogram in the corner of the living room and the dusty-smelling, Bakelite 'feature' radio gained a new lease of life after the early dominance of television. Radio stars rose out of the ashes of the 1950s, creating a new breed called 'disc jockeys'. They were salesmen hitched to the rocket of popular opinion, and their endorsements could make or break a product. This was

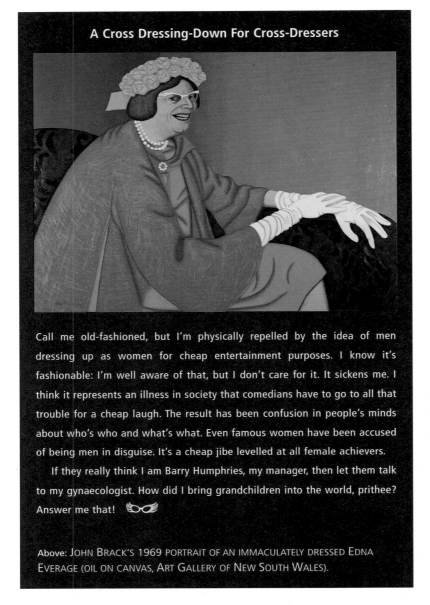

A Cross Dressing-Down For Cross-Dressers

Call me old-fashioned, but I'm physically repelled by the idea of men dressing up as women for cheap entertainment purposes. I know it's fashionable: I'm well aware of that, but I don't care for it. It sickens me. I think it represents an illness in society that comedians have to go to all that trouble for a cheap laugh. The result has been confusion in people's minds about who's who and what's what. Even famous women have been accused of being men in disguise. It's a cheap jibe levelled at all female achievers.

If they really think I am Barry Humphries, my manager, then let them talk to my gynaecologist. How did I bring grandchildren into the world, prithee? Answer me that! 🎭

Above: JOHN BRACK'S 1969 PORTRAIT OF AN IMMACULATELY DRESSED EDNA EVERAGE (OIL ON CANVAS, ART GALLERY OF NEW SOUTH WALES).

particularly so around pop music. It wasn't long before disc jockeys found they could work a quasi-political constituency, and inflate their egos, their bank balances and their sponsors' coffers all at the same time. When it came to working up the rabble, they found a few well-chosen prejudices could light up the switchboard and attract a chorus of agreement followed by a roar of disapproval. When these calls were put to air, it was the birth of talkback radio. So the hat-wearers of the 1950s had their last say in the twilight years of the 1960s.

While Sydney's splendid Queen Victoria Building barely escaped demolition as a tired symbol of the past, the concrete sails of the Opera House started going up as a symbol of an unknown future. The demographic norm of Australia liked neither the past nor the future, and the Sydney Opera House confused him (or her) mightily. In 1958 the building's cost had been estimated at $9.6 million; by 1962 this had more than doubled. Three years later it had doubled again, and by 1969 the estimate had soared to over $85 million. This for a building to house an art form that most Australians had never seen, and cared even less about.

To the advertising and promotional fraternity the Opera House meant putting Australia on to the 'world stage'. The Opera House was a chance for planet-wide boosterism, putting forward the image of a country worth visiting at a time when many Australians considered travelling within Australia as interesting as eating dirt. So even before architect Joern Utzon's Opera House sails took shape, when the site was still a broad lump of concrete with steel reinforcing rods poking up, the Utzon look was adopted as an Australian promotional icon. A new model of the Holden car adopted an echo of the idea in its fins, and 'town houses of the future' were modelled, although never built, with roofs sweeping to the sky like cockatoos' beaks.

A driving force in the 'boosterism' process was Captain Hugh Birch, image-maker for Qantas, who was one of the first to realise that bristling skylines and tall buildings weren't going to entice American tourists to visit Australia. If taste-makers overseas (meaning Britons and Americans – still not Asians) could be persuaded there was something interesting and original going on in Australia, even if Australians knew there wasn't, then maybe Australia could strengthen its belief in

THE SYDNEY OPERA HOUSE MIGHT HAVE BEEN ONE OF AUSTRALIA'S MOST CONTROVERSIAL BUILDINGS, BUT ITS IMAGE WAS SOON ACCEPTED BY ALL AS A POTENT MARKETING SYMBOL OF DOWN-UNDER CULTURE. SUDDENLY THE NOBLE SAVAGE AND BOOMERANG IMAGES HAD SOME COMPETITION ON OUR SOUVENIR TEA TOWELS AND POSTCARDS. CLEVER HOLDEN CAR DESIGNERS EVEN CREATED FINS FOR THEIR 1961 'EK' MODEL TO REFLECT THE DESIGN OF THE BUILDING'S SAILS.

itself. Cuddly marsupials and spiky Opera House sails joined the international promotional circuit. With this kind of thinking, even Australians themselves might eventually start feeling proud of the Opera House, even if deep down they *knew* it was ugly and useless. Also, they might start travelling in the outback, or at least visit an animal enclosure in a wildlife park.

Or for absolute, unbeatable excitement they might start miniskirt-watching.

When the world's top model, Jean Shrimpton, arrived in Australia for the 1965 Melbourne Cup wearing a skirt 4 inches above her knees, she caused a sensation. No hat, no gloves, no stockings – and the press went into a lascivious frenzy and made sure that every angle was covered. Within moments, it seemed, the 'mini' was everywhere. The youngish Sydney *Daily Mirror* fashion correspondent, Maggie Tabberer, was frankly disappointed. Her biggest problem with the mini was the difficulty for a woman of maintaining poise while sitting down. 'Stockings just have to have tops and exposure of those tops certainly takes away all elegance,' Maggie wrote.

Miniskirts really suited girls like me with lovely legs, but they were particularly popular, especially the micro-skirt, with girls with horrible legs. They really liked to wear them, particularly on escalators standing right in front of you. Often they didn't shave their legs as well as they might have, and they'd wear sheer stockings. Not a nice look. 🕶

It must have seemed unfair to socialites that in one blow the hard-earned lessons of charm and deportment schools were worthless. (If stockings were a problem then they needn't be worn, or pantyhose could be tried.)

Studying a girl's way with a mini became a male spectator sport. It was open season for fashion amateurs, as even a long T-shirt could be worn now that knees were revealable. For a while, the scrutinising skills of the beach inspector became widely needed inland as skirt lengths became big news. Even groups of marching girls had modesty-police enforcing the hemline – coaches checked that dresses were the right length and peeked underneath for any frilly underwear. But the barriers were falling. The next lot to fall were not just on definitions of fashion acceptability but on sex itself. 'Don't Forget The Pill' was written on every honeymoon car, and it was starting to be engraved on the minds of single women as well. Older values still greyed the sky, but with the pop-star explosion scattering the ground with flowers it was just a matter of time before the sexual revolution declared itself more in doing than in wishing. Fewer general practitioners bothered giving young un-married women their moral lectures. They rolled their eyes and signed.

ENGLISH MODEL JEAN SHRIMPTON (left) SHOCKED SOCIETY MATRONS BY WEARING AN UNPRECEDENTEDLY SHORT SLEEVELESS DRESS AT THE 1965 MELBOURNE CUP. AMERICAN SERVICEMEN ON REST AND RECREATION LEAVE ('R & R') FROM VIETNAM (above) DESCENDED ON AUSTRALIA IN 1967. LES PATTERSON RECKONS THAT R & R STOOD FOR 'ROOTING AND RANDINESS'. IF THE GOINGS-ON AT THE TIME IN SYDNEY'S KINGS CROSS WERE ANY INDICATION, HE WAS RIGHT.

Australians discovered drugs on television when documentaries on teenage drinking gave way to exposés on the newer drugs from overseas. Viewers were treated to students 'tripping', with footage of a young girl telling the story of being at a party when a friend used LSD and took on the 'expression of an animal' and started to do 'animalistic things to a tree'.

I yield to none in my abhorrence of mind-changing substances. But in this epoch, I was offered everything. You'd go to a party, and horny little chicks – little hippies – oh, they'd try to turn me on left, right and centre. I remember one girl – oh, lovely little thing, smelling of that patchouli – she come up to me and she said: 'Les.' She had a bit of blotting paper. She said: 'Stick this under your tongue and you'll have a mind-expanding experience.' I said to her, I said: 'If you want an expanding experience, why don't you slip this under your tongue?' Then another girl come up to me and she said: 'Like a joint, Les?' I said: 'Call that a joint?' I said: 'THIS is a joint.' 🍺

For a time in the latter part of the 1960s Australia became a crossroads of comings and goings. New ideas flooded in, giving an international or, rather, Americanised style to music, political ideas and anti-war protest. Into this mix came thousands of American servicemen, fresh from the battlefields of Vietnam and ready for R & R. The Americans didn't drink very much (at least, not compared with Australians) but they had smooth manners and perhaps a marijuana cigarette or two, and there was no shortage of young Australian women willing to go with the flow during the week or ten days the Yanks were visiting.

ON THE 14TH OF FEBRUARY 1966, POUNDS WERE REPLACED WITH DOLLARS. BOB DYER, HOST OF THE TELEVISION QUIZ SHOW 'PICK-A-BOX' (above), HELPED LAUNCH THE NEW DECIMAL CURRENCY FOLLOWING A DEBATE OVER WHAT IT SHOULD BE CALLED. THE 'DOLLAR' NARROWLY WON OVER THE 'ROYAL'. BEFORE THE ADVENT OF DOLLARS, BAROSSA PEARL (right) SOLD FOR 8 SHILLINGS AND THREEPENCE A BOTTLE – A SMALL PRICE FOR SUCH SOPHISTICATION. THE WINE WAS LIGHT, SWEET AND SPARKLING AND ESPECIALLY POPULAR AT PARTIES IN THE SIXTIES.

In those days it was called Rest and Recreation, R & R. Personally, I thought it was more like Rooting and Randiness, because that was the name of the game. Oh, I got called a lot of dirty words. Just because I was trying to put people together and have a good time – I was called a pimp. I was called a pander, a ponce. I was called a procurer. A politician, even. There was just one dirty word they didn't dare throw at me, one 'P' word. Pom! 🍺

With the arrival of the Americans the bohemian quarter of Kings Cross changed forever. Once raffish and artistic, after dark it now told a different story. The brothel quarter had formerly been around Palmer Street in East Sydney, but with R & R, Kings Cross became one big brothel. Australians were anxious to please their American friends – in fact, they bent over backwards (or assumed some other position). The nation had switched allegiances over its currency, toying with the idea of replacing pounds with 'royals' but in 1966 adopting 'dollars' and 'cents' to denote the new decimal coinage – and it couldn't wait to throw around the word 'bucks' as its newfound friends did.

Happy **NEW** DESIGN FOR LIVING

The sparkling sunshine of the famous Barossa Valley is in every glass of Barossa Pearl.

On those special occasions — at home or "out" — dine to the joyous accompaniment of Barossa Pearl. What a happy wine it is! Just sweet enough to please all palates, Barossa Pearl is characteristically brisk and refreshing. Its gaiety comes from its pearly, bubbling effervescence. From the first exciting "pop" till the last drop, you'll love Barossa Pearl. It's at its very best served icy cold.

Barossa Pearl

MADE ONLY BY

Orlando WINES

Enter the house of the 1960s towards the end of the decade. Take your bottle of Barossa Pearl from its brown paper bag and present it to the hostess. She'll serve veal with a creamy sauce with a French or Italian name. There'll be garlic in the salad dressing and a plate of salami and olives for starters. (Even in the late 1960s there are still those who say that salami, being made from donkey meat, is fit only for New Australians, but their numbers are declining and will soon go the way of those who believed that spaghetti undermined the Australian way of life unless it came in tins.) What was formerly in the house of the 1960s in the way of 1950s features is gone – the lamps, chairs, tables, trays, vases, bookends. Visit your local op shop if you want to see them. Featurism is dead.

But wait, there are new signs of growth in the air. Youth is coming full on – in the concert halls, clubs and art galleries, in *gatherings* and *happenings*. It is beginning to cluster around words like *commune*, *flower child* and *inner space*. These buds will blossom by 1970. The world is getting its fill of the changes and they are still only just bursting forth – with student riots, booming apocalyptic imagery on the staid old black-and-white TV screens, and everything formerly taken for granted starting to be questioned in every way. Bishops have doubted the existence of God and priests have doubted the justice of America. Youth questions age and asserts that anyone over 30 is effectively dead. The nuclear build-up gets bigger by the hour and the cloud in the back of the mind is vast and unthinkable, yet only as far away as an itchy finger on a button: a very human showdown involving pride or human frailty, or catastrophic accident.

The house of the late 1960s demands clarity and certainty because there isn't any anywhere else. Let's have natural materials, say the architects, rugged and rustic, giving an appearance of sobriety, strength and solidity. Get rid of the frivolous confusion of featurism. Now the indoor rooms are as bare as the exterior. Brick walls that were formerly plastered are left raw. Beams cross rooms below the ceilings. Douglas fir – traded as oregon – is brought in from the United States and either left furry and bare or 'stained' in brown, red or conservationist green.

Have we jumped ahead too fast? Father, we know, left the house: old man Menzies took his silver hair and cantilevered eyebrows and left the prime ministerial mirror to his cheery treasurer. On the box, soothing the mood of the nation, was genial Harold Holt, 59 years old but often portrayed by cartoonists as a schoolboy, and not the brightest of the bunch at that. Holt loved what so many other Australians loved, the sun and the sea. He enjoyed nothing better – though he was not an outstanding swimmer – than hurling himself into the surf at Melbourne's Mornington Peninsula and bodysurfing his way back in through the 'humpies'. So it was not just going all the way with LBJ that he loved, but going all the way beyond the breakers on one of the wildest coasts of Australia and splashing around like a porpoise. Holt's zippy, zany wife Zara enlivened the evening news with her zigzag dress patterns and her openly frank manner. She caught a whiff of the spirit of the times and life was a party.

Holt was part of it too (in the brief time he had), enjoying the contrasts: enlarging Australia's commitment to the Vietnam War, whereas Menzies was more cautious; overseeing the referendum on Aboriginal rights, whereas Menzies was too timid; going to the theatre when he could and applauding send-ups of the society he inhabited, whereas Menzies was mainly above the spirit of the people. Under Harold Holt, thanks to the May 1967 referendum, the Commonwealth Government would at last be able, if it wished, to make laws to benefit Aborigines. Before the referendum the government had established schools to teach migrants in many parts of Australia, but it lacked even the power to establish schools for Aborigines. Now the government would ensure justice and social acceptance for Aborigines, Mr Holt said.

Summing up the decade to date, Harold Holt might have said there were other bright markers for him. There might be riots in the cities, with Brisbane particularly violent as police laid into anti-Vietnam protesters, but that was to one side. What about the $70 million US navy communications base opened at North West Cape, near Exmouth in Western Australia? It was a bond with a great ally. A new government bank, the Australian Resources Development Bank, had been created to fund a minerals boom. The crisp new Australian dollar was firm against the British pound. And in the November 1967 Senate election Holt's conservative Labor allies, the DLP, won the balance of power.

With that, and surely well

LIKE BOB HAWKE 20 YEARS LATER, PRIME MINISTER HAROLD HOLT TRADED ON HIS MALE VIRILITY AND WAS PARTICULARLY FOND OF PITTING IT AGAINST THE PUNISHING SURF. HOLT WAS KNOWN BY SOME AS THE '007 PRIME MINISTER'. UNFORTUNATELY HE PUSHED IT TOO FAR BY ATTEMPTING TO SWIM IN ROUGH SEAS AT VICTORIA'S CHEVIOT BEACH IN DECEMBER 1967. HIS BODY WAS NEVER FOUND, AND WHILE SOME THOUGHT IT WAS SUICIDE, OTHERS SPECULATED THAT HE HAD BEEN PICKED UP BY A CHINESE SUBMARINE.

pleased, Holt went down to his holiday house at Portsea a week before Christmas. It was a Sunday. He drove his car down to Cheviot Beach on the ocean side of the peninsula. A friend who happened to be there saw him from a distance. When Holt entered the surf a king tide was coming off Bass Strait, sending waves up to 30 feet over the rocks. The friend saw Holt dive from a rock – his favourite 'diving board' – and later, after taking a dip himself, saw the prime minister drifting further and further from the shore, until he finally disappeared, never to be seen again. His memory is tastefully preserved in the Melbourne suburb of Malvern where they named a swimming pool after him.

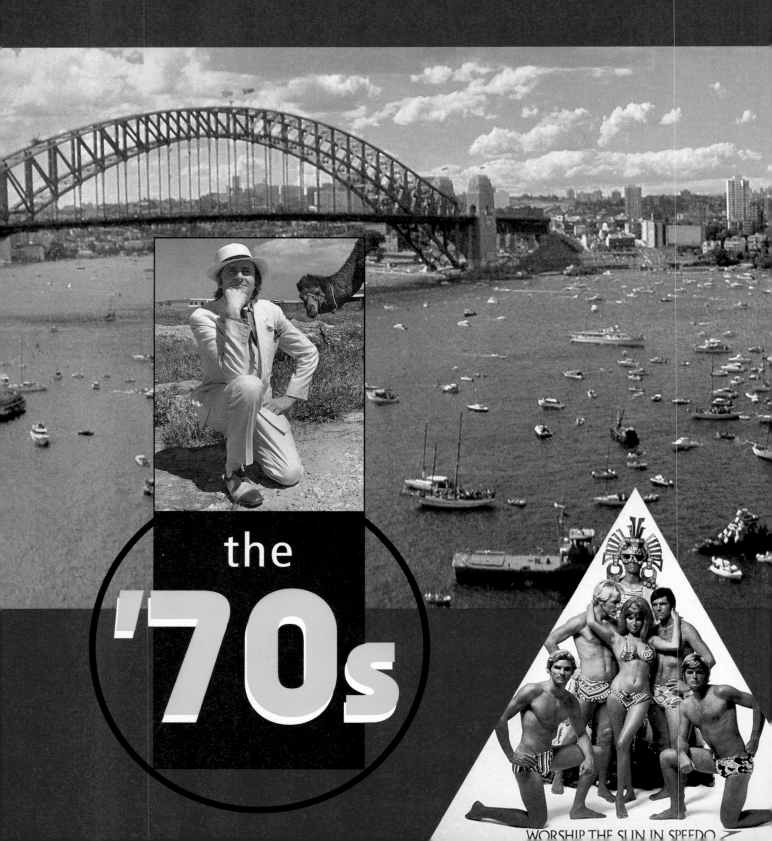

On the
the
'70s

WORSHIP THE SUN IN SPEEDO

map

at last

The sudden collapse

of a huge section of Melbourne's half-finished West Gate Bridge in October 1970, killing 35 men, left a sombre pause as Australia moved into the new decade. But a slower collapse was happening in another structure, one that could not be repaired by the work of brave and gifted engineers. Bob Menzies' retirement and Harold Holt's demise proved to be serious stress fractures in the conservative Liberal–Country Party edifice that had governed the nation since 1949. Holt's successor as Liberal prime minister, John Gorton, lasted just three years before being replaced by one Billy McMahon, whose term in office would be shorter still.

Meanwhile, the poets laureate of the Australian Labor Party were sharpening their pencils and knocking out a few ideas for focusing the national mood. When the time came, Labor would be sold with all the emotional sophistication of a car dealer's sales pitch.

Not a particularly inspiring assembly of words, to say the least – but give them a choir of rousing unisex voices, and in the background the wail of a thousand Mantovani strings, and it might be time.

GOUGH WHITLAM (right) MAY NOT HAVE BEEN POP SINGER LITTLE PATTIE'S 'BLONDE-HEADED STOMPIE WOMPIE REAL GONE SURFER BOY' (HER FIRST HIT IN THE SIXTIES), BUT THE SOON-TO-BE-ELECTED PRIME MINISTER WAS A FAVOURITE WITH THE MUSICIANS AND ARTISTS WHO SANG THE MESSIANIC JINGLE 'IT'S TIME' AT LABOR'S 1972 CAMPAIGN LAUNCH. **Previous pages:** A FLOTILLA OF CRAFT **(main photo)** GATHER IN 1973 FOR THE OPENING OF THE 'EIGHTH WONDER OF THE WORLD' – THE SYDNEY OPERA HOUSE – BY THE QUEEN, WHO WITH PRINCE PHILLIP HAD ARRIVED IN AUSTRALIA BY 'FLYING KANGAROO' **(inset right)**. BARRY HUMPHRIES **(inset left)** IN FULL SEVENTIES REGALIA WITH A CAMEL; AND A SPEEDO AD **(inset centre)** FROM THE 'DECADE THAT TASTE FORGOT'.

Time for freedom
Time for moving
It's time to begin
Yes, it's time.

Time for old folk
Time we loved them
It's time to care
Yes, it's time.

Time for children
Time to teach them
It's time it was free
Yes, it's time.

HOT, STICKY, FATTY FOOD IN THE GUISE OF UP-TO-THE-MINUTE TRENDY DINING REPLACED TRADITIONAL FARE IN THE SEVENTIES. A FONDUE PARTY MEANT SOPHISTICATED FAMILY FUN; THE ADULTS WASHED DOWN MELTED CHEESE WITH ROUGH RED WINE AS CHILDREN BURNT THEIR TONGUES. DUSTY FONDUE SETS CAN NOW BE FOUND ON THE SHELVES OF OPPORTUNITY SHOPS AND AT GARAGE SALES.

Time for what? And was it really time? Well, not quite yet. The decade was still in its infancy. Maybe it was time to just peer tentatively out into a changing world – out through the window of the family home. Or even from that domestic citadel, the kitchen.

Whereas the house of the 1950s and 1960s was a centre of life, with the family meal the centrepiece of the week's entertainment, the house of the 1970s became, tentatively at first, a place to leave in order to eat elsewhere. One alternative venue for meals was that ubiquitous establishment known as 'the club'.

As a child of the 1970s, the writer Kathy Lette, who now lives in London and specialises in excoriating the English, recalls more than just the club meal subsidised by poker machine takings: 'I remember Mum talking about going to the St George Leagues Club [in Sydney] to see Shirley Bassey, Dave Allen and Sammy Davis Jnr. But the performer she loved the best was this creature, Edna Everage. Mum came home one night – I was about nine or ten – and said she'd discovered this woman who satirised her life: all the little coloured cotton-wool balls in the little glass container in the bathroom, the fondue parties, and all that kind of thing.

'Actually I think that Barry Humphries invented me. Dame Edna's daughter is called Valmai, and she lives with Mervyn in a blond brick veneer in the suburbs. And my mother's name is Valmai, and she's married to Mervyn, and they live in a blond brick veneer in Sylvania! You know, this irony was not lost on my parents either. They don't suffer from an irony deficiency. So I feel somehow as though he made me up.'

Another kind of mecca was the Shoppingtown, or the malls. Here too was the novelty of everything seeming to be made from plastic, and of air conditioning under a gigantic roof.

This was a changing Australia, but among the glitzy symbols of a convenient future the past clung on. Next door to the bright new shopping centre with its acres of car park there might well be a row of dilapidated small businesses – a fish-and-chips shop, a seedy disposals store, a down-at-heel hardware retailer. Or perhaps a shop for those for whom the future would not be so convenient.

When my lady wife Beryl and I were finally relocated, our old home, Kia-Ora, 36 Gallipoli Crescent, Glen Iris, was demolished. With a couple of dozen other homes in the immediate vicinity between Gallipoli Crescent and Dardanelles Road, it went to make way for a magnificent new shopping complex and car-parking facility which had been erected by an Asian consortium who had their eye on the area. They had done a feasibility survey to see if this was where the people would really like to have a 24-hour supermarket so they could pop in at four in the morning and buy a bottle of tomato sauce, desiccated coconut or fly spray. So it was that our old living-room area and kitchen is now in breakfast cereals and our bedroom is in frozen foods.

It was indeed a changing Australia, a place where television frontmen now seemingly all had Beatle haircuts and collarless shirts, where they wore flares and platform-soled shoes – and also, curiously, were invariably called Mike. Nineteen-seventy was a year when advertising men wore red bandannas and performed at poetry readings; when university professors wore ponchos and Indian headbands, and seduced their students in the name of free love and got away with it – while everybody else wondered how to recognise other free-lovers when they ran into them. Would it be by the hair? By the patchouli oil? By the use of swearwords formerly taboo in public places?

It wasn't just profanity that became popular. Welcome to the word 'wrinkly' – meaning anyone over 30 and therefore not deserving of a life. Welcome to bra burning – as a political act. Welcome to unisex – meaning men's hair being blow-waved in women's hairdressing salons. Welcome to the decade that was counter-culture the year it started and over-the-counter-culture, a marketed style, well before it ended. Each year there was a new word describing what was going on. One year it was power, the next it was flower, then there was disco, liberate, free, alternative, head and freak. Then the latest was earth.

Richard Neville, the author of *Hippie Hippie Shake*, tells us: 'Boutiques sold earth clothes, clubs played earth music, Danish clogs were renamed earth shoes. And naturally, everyone ate earth food. The word "earth" in a book title doubled its sales.'

THE NEW SUBURBAN SHOPPING MALLS DELIVERED A CAPTIVE MARKET FOR EVENTS SUCH AS THIS 'CARPET DISPLAY' (above) WHERE SCANTILY CLAD 'HOSTESSES' WOULD ENTICE PROPSECTIVE CUSTOMERS WITH THE DELIGHTS OF A LUXURY SHAG-PILE. IN THE SEVENTIES BARE BOARDS WERE COVERED WITH CHRISTO-LIKE ZEAL BY EAGER CARPET-LAYERS. TWO DECADES LATER THE REVERSE HAPPENED AND CARPETS WERE PULLED UP WITH EQUAL FERVOUR. IN THE SEVENTIES THE COUNTER-CULTURE COULD BE PURCHASED OVER THE COUNTER AS 'EARTH' BECAME A SELLING POINT FOR JUST ABOUT ANYTHING. THESE MODELS (opposite page) ARE WEARING DRESSES PRINTED WITH 'EARTH' DESIGNS.

Fashions were very weird at the beginning of the 1970s. I remember I had a pair of hot pants – that was the thing. There was still the hippyish look. Flares. And some of the menfolk wore crushed velvet in purply colours – mulberries, purples and browns, rather like food or like the inside of animals' tummies. I didn't much like the statuary attire that a lot of Australian diplomats, car salesmen and high-fliers wore – the pastel-coloured suits, the big wide lapels and the Englebert Humperdink shoes. I myself am statuesque anyway, so I don't need much of a heel.

Denim was also a big thing in the 1970s and I pioneered it. I wore an Australian-designed denim outfit by JAG which created an absolute sensation because people only associated denim with jeans, and I had a whole frock made of it. But then I've always been at the sharp end of fashion. 👓

If you are too young to remember, you can at least feel the cringe. Next time you walk down the street, check out the over-50 generation – the so-called 'baby boomers', gone to seed. See the reflection of social-protest haircuts in certain ageing shaggy locks. Sense a distant jaunty style in the careworn paisley shirt. Feel a whole decade's political optimism in the trudging, hopeful shuffle of the high-heeled boots. These are the forgotten Australians. Here is somebody still anti-Vietnam almost 25 years after the end of the Vietnam War – as the social commentator Donald Horne remarks – being anti-Vietnam 'could seem to mean a great sharing of all kinds of hopes for a better world; "Vietnam" was seen as a transcendent issue, overriding all others, sorting out good from evil'.

See the tattered flares, the still-proud pouch of the crudely stitched pony-express bag dangling from a bony shoulder

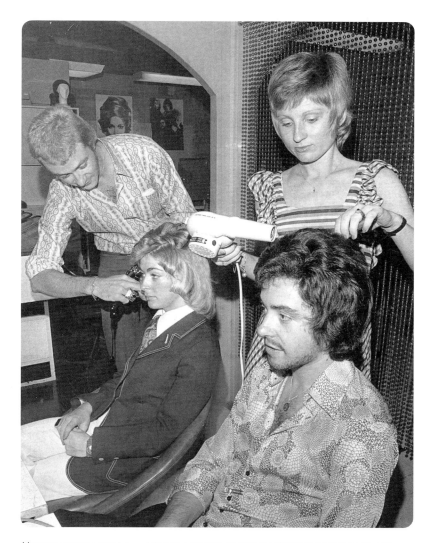

UNISEX HAIR SALONS (above) POSED A THREAT TO THE TRADITIONAL 'SHORT-BACK-AND-SIDES' BARBER SHOPS OF THE FIFTIES AND EARLY SIXTIES. PERMS AND BLOW-WAVES WERE DE RIGUEUR FOR GUYS, WHILE WOMEN ENDURED HOURS IN ROLLERS FOR THE 'CRIMPLED LOOK', HELD IN PLACE BY A LAYER OF OZONE-DESTROYING SPRAY. Opposite page: A HIPPY STUDENT AT A UNIVERSITY FOUNDATION DAY, ALONE WITH HERSELF IN THE SERIOUS BUSINESS OF BEING AT ONE WITH THE UNIVERSE.

IN MAY 1970 OVER 100 000 ANTI-VIETNAM PROTESTERS MARCHED THROUGH THE STREETS OF MELBOURNE. DEMONSTRATIONS AGAINST AUSTRALIA'S INVOLVEMENT IN THE WAR ATTRACTED PEOPLE FROM EVERY WALK OF LIFE – STUDENTS, UNIONISTS, PRIESTS, AND OTHERS FROM THE LOBBY GROUP SAVE OUR SONS (SOS).

– does it hold a book of Rimbaud's poetry? A copy of Hesse's *The Glass Bead Game*? Tolkein's well-thumbed *Lord of the Rings*? You can be sure it does. This is the living ghost of another time, the era of the male purse, the Danish book bag, sheepskin seat covers, natural childbirth, coloured candles, flavoured massage oil, the displaying and storage of pasta in tall glass jars. It is the decade of the sublime to the ridiculous. The 1970s were when the human-potential movement started to grow – transcendental meditation, sensory deprivation, assertiveness training, Sufism, Taoism, Buddhism, yoga. Harold Holt was the precursor, doing his merging with the Infinite at Cheviot Beach.

Now see the head of that 1970s relic turn and the ears twitch at the sound of shouting. Maybe there's a demo happening around the next corner? (The 1970s live on in hope.) The word 'demo' has a special ring to it – a hallelujah for the division of society between those crying for law and order and those out on the political ran-tan-tara – the symbolically hairy, noisy, scornful creatures that others called 'stewed ants'.

Any good cause was worth having a demo over, and if there was a demo then it had to be a good cause.

It was predicted when the 1970s started that demos, 'a rediscovered tool of democracy', would occur more widely as more groups used them. The prediction came true, and the population got into the mood of taking to the streets on other days apart from Anzac Days and Royal Visits. Stewed ants weren't the only ones to demonstrate – there were pensioners demos, mothers groups, farmers, builders, even bikies demos. From the eastern suburbs came the gay libbers, chanting: 'Two-four-six-eight, gay is twice as good as straight.'

From the western suburbs came the women's libbers. From the south came peaceniks, including splinter groups such as 'perverts for peace'. There were republicans to the left, Nazis to the right.

Australia's original demonstrators, however, were the Aborigines who hurled their spears at the invading white man – and Aboriginal demonstrators remained the avant-garde of protestors. Back in 1966, hundreds of Gurindji walked off their jobs on stations at Newcastle Waters and Wave Hill in the Northern Territory appealing for legal control of their own land. They weren't getting heard by the Australian government and so they were

THE SEVENTIES WERE THE 'DECADE OF THE DEMO'. AUSTRALIANS USUALLY ONLY TOOK TO THE STREETS FOR ANZAC DAY OR A ROYAL VISIT, BUT NOW PEOPLE PICKED UP BANNERS AND MARCHED FOR GAY RIGHTS, GREEN BANS, WORKERS' CONDITIONS AND ABORIGINAL RIGHTS. WRITER/ACADEMIC DONALD HORNE (CENTRE) AND NOVELIST PATRICK WHITE (RIGHT) ARE SEEN HERE LEADING A REPUBLICAN RALLY IN SYDNEY LONG BEFORE REPUBLICANISM BECAME FASHIONABLE.

forced to appeal to the United Nations. Working on cattle stations they received $6.60 a week, while the poorest white man earned seven times that figure and usually lived in a modest, cramped, yet comfortable house – not a galvanised iron shelter, not a humpy in the dirt.

Two years later, in 1968, Australians witnessed a cavalry charge when mounted police galloped into some 2000 anti-Vietnam War demonstrators in Melbourne. They weren't just students in that crowd but trade unionists, interested citizens, women's libbers, and priests and ministers of religion. In the Menzies era, only just finished, the industrial strike had been the national form of public street protest, an affair for paid-up wharfies, miners and shearers. The demo, however, was unlike the more exclusivist union event, becoming an instant expression of the emotions for all who wanted to try it out. The demo was where the office worker became a hippy. It was the roadway version of talkback radio – shout-back, fist-clenching, face-to-face confrontation. It was an end in itself, quite often. Demonstrators went home feeling fired and cleansed.

By the time the seventies rolled around everyone had the knack of the demo down pat, and long-accepted stratifications in society began blurring. A Morgan Gallup poll found that half of all Australians wanted their military involvement in Vietnam ended. And in 1971 a group of housewives at Hunters Hill, a classy Sydney suburb, enlisted the aid of the rough-and-tumble Builders' Labourers Federation and their charismatic communist secretary, frizzy-haired Jack Mundey, to save a piece of urban bushland from the bulldozers of a housing developer, A. V. Jennings. The bush was saved by this unholy but exceedingly happy and somewhat titillating alliance of rough and smooth – work singlets and silvertails.

GURU OF THE 'GREEN BANS', BUILDERS' LABOURERS FEDERATION SECRETARY JACK MUNDEY IS CARRIED BUDDHA-LIKE FROM ANOTHER PROTEST. MUNDEY AND THE BLF FOUND SOME UNUSUAL BEDFELLOWS IN THEIR ATTEMPTS TO PRESERVE PARKS AND HISTORICAL BUILDINGS. AT ONE STAGE THE FRIZZY-HAIRED COMMUNIST AND HIS MEN WERE CALLED IN TO JOIN THE WELL-HEELED HOUSEWIVES OF SYDNEY'S HUNTERS HILL IN THEIR BATTLE TO SAVE A SLICE OF URBAN BUSHLAND.

Mundey was a new-style Prague Spring commo rather than an old-style Aussie Stalinist. He had the rare power of breaking stereotypes. Likewise, when the first-ever Aboriginal member of the national parliament was elected in 1971, it was difficult to absorb the fact that Neville Bonner was actually a thoroughgoing conservative. 'I want to see Aborigines succeed,' the newfound Queensland politician said, 'but I want to prove to my people that the only way of doing this is through proper channels – through the party and Parliament.' He was branded an Uncle Tom.

Senator Bonner arrived to take up his seat wearing a 1950s suit and tie, a 1960s smile, and a good head of 1970s hair. A year later a rather wilder-looking group of his compatriots arrived in front of Parliament House and set up a tent embassy on the lawns. The tents were regularly pulled down by police, but remained there for seven months, the most noticeable, succinct and embarrassing demo Australia had ever had. Parliamentarians had to face it arriving at the House each morning and tourists made the embassy a feature of their visits to Canberra. The condition of the tents reflected the contrast in living conditions between Aboriginal and white Australians. It was 'fringe-dwelling' at the heart of the nation. But these tent ambassadors weren't the passive fringe-dwellers of the 1950s. They were no longer shutting up.

Perhaps to appease them and to thumb the conservative nose at Labor (which, elected three weeks later, would abandon Imperial Honours) Pastor Doug Nicholls of Victoria was made the first Aboriginal knight, in November 1972. Pastor Nicholls travelled to London and met the Queen, whom he found very sympathetic. One of the first acts of Gough Whitlam's Labor Government was to establish a Federal Ministry of Aboriginal Affairs; and the tent embassy was dismantled, having made its point.

THE ABORIGINAL 'TENT EMBASSY' AT PARLIAMENT HOUSE IN 1972. THE TENTS WERE REGULARLY PULLED DOWN BY POLICE, ONLY TO BE STUBBORNLY RE-ERECTED BY PROTESTORS. THE TENT EMBASSY REPRESENTED AN INTERNATIONALLY EMBARRASSING PROTEST AGAINST THE CONSERVATIVE GOVERNMENT'S ABORIGINAL POLICIES. THE 'EMBASSY' WAS DISMANTLED AFTER THE ELECTION OF THE WHITLAM LABOR GOVERNMENT LATER THAT YEAR AND THE ESTABLISHMENT OF A DEPARTMENT OF ABORIGINAL AFFAIRS.

And so, welcome to a time when everything went wide and shot wider – barricades, trouser-bottoms, smiles, loudhailers, hair, opinions. Certain words still hadn't reached their use-by date, and others hadn't surfaced into daylight as yet. The word 'lesbian' was up for grabs as comedians went around asking if they could join lesbian action groups. On TV's 'The Naked Vicar Show' a medallion-wearing male on the make (known in Australia as a lounge-lizard) sidled up to a woman in a bar and asked what star sign she was. He guessed incorrectly ('Taurean? Piscean?') until finally she said, 'I'm a lesbian.' Laughs aplenty.

A whole new world of permissiveness began to open up, but not without hiccups of resistance. Australians rushed to climb aboard the newly fashionable waterbed, but all the rhythmic pulsation above and below the rubber membrane – as seen on TV, and in colour after 1975 – caused horror within the ranks of the clergy. Tough as rubber himself, the Reverend Fred Nile was one of Australia's most convinced social critics when it came to matters of the sexual thermometer. Whatever it was he feared back then, it was not of being wrong. Back in the early seventies he complained about the crisis in civilisation due to falling standards of morality. When asked how long civilisation had left if the moral decline continued he replied with confidence: 'Ten years.'

The background to it all remained the spreading suburbia. The 'brick venereal disease of suburbia', Kathy Lette says of it. She then becomes reflective – sort of: 'It was hideous where I grew up. I hated it. It was the most sexist place in the world, the Australian suburbs. The boys – they were all surfies, you know – used to get us to cut holes in paper in the shape of their name, sticky-tape the paper to our stomach and then sunbake, so we'd get a tan tattoo of the name. Which I suppose was vaguely amusing until I realised a few years ago that, if I ever get cancer, I'm going to have a melanoma called Bruce. And I'm going to have to have a Brucsectomy to get rid of it.

OLD TIMES CONFRONTING THE NEW. NOTHING SYMBOLISES THE PACE OF SOCIAL CHANGE BETTER THAN THE AIR OF MYSTIFICATION THAT EMANATES FROM THIS IMAGE. THE ELDERLY COUPLE DO NOT SEEM DISMISSIVE OF WHAT THEY SEE STARING AT THEM FROM THE WALL, RATHER THEY APPEAR STUNNED, ROCKED ON THEIR FEET, BY THE ATTEMPT TO ASSIMILATE A WORLD AS ALIEN TO THEM AS A MARS INVASION. THIS WAS THE 'GENERATION GAP', A CHASM OF POLITICS, STYLE AND UNDERSTANDING.

'So we lived vicariously through the boys. We folded their towels, we ran and got their chiko rolls. We had no life of our own, no identity. For example, their terms for women, in Sydney, were bush pigs, swamp hogs or maggots. And if you were good-looking they called you a glamour maggot, or a glam mag. The terms for sex were rooting, tooling, plugging, stabbing, poking and meat injecting. It's not exactly a Shakespearian love sonnet, is it? So it was a very difficult place to grow up in. Which is why I ran away from home really early – I left the suburbs when I was 15. You know, the only examination I've ever passed is my pap smear! But you can understand why I had to get out of there.'

Is that a faintly malicious glint in Kathy Lette's eye? 'Those boys – they actually disproved the theory of evolution. They were sort of evolving into apes.'

It was 1970, a year whose footnotes of history would linger in the mind. In March nine young Australians were killed by landmines, and another 29 were injured in Phuoc Tuy province, South Vietnam. In April a Western Australian wheat farmer declared himself independent of Australia, calling himself Prince Leonard of Hutt River, a district with a population of 30. In May the notorious 'escape artist' Darcy Dugan was once again sentenced to gaol after making six successful escape bids from custody. In the same month hundreds of thousands of Australians called for peace while 200 000 protesters marched through cities across the nation.

The cry for law and order was

'PROFESSIONAL DANCER' CHERIE AMOUR HAD LITTLE TO HIDE WHEN SHE FACED THE COURT OVER THE CHARGE OF RIDING TOPLESS ON A HORSE ALONG A SYDNEY BEACH. NUDITY WAS A MOVEMENT UNTO ITSELF IN THE SEVENTIES. STREAKERS MADE REGULAR APPEARANCES AT SPORTING EVENTS, AND NUDIST BEACHES WERE BECOMING POPULAR.

loud in the land. Television gave huge publicity to demos and also to so-called crime waves that criminologists pointed out were an American phenomenon and not reflected in local statistics at all, despite the occasional TAB (betting agency) robbery and a few service-station hold-ups. Television made gullible Australians think crime was worse than it was, and television was blamed for affecting the Australian pattern of life. It was observed by the actor Leonard Teale, whose early fame lay in his playing Superman on radio, that before 1956 (the year TV started) police cars were unmarked but that by 1970 police officers were visibly armed, even when directing traffic.

As the better sort of journalist plaintively pointed out, anyone could see that Australians didn't have guns always to hand, except for shooting rabbits, 'roos and wild pigs for target practice in school cadet units – or when settling the national honour in Vietnam. Admittedly, the time-honoured Aussie rural philosophy was: If it moves, shoot it. If it doesn't, chop it down. Yet, while pub brawls might have been settled with fists, it was hardly likely that anyone was going to whip out their 'Wyatt Earp mail-order pistol' and start pumping bullets. There were drug addicts but they weren't roaming the streets crazed and ready to kill for funds for the next fix. They were more likely to be from good schools, to have well-off parents, and to be in the vanguard of radical styles from elsewhere.

For the time being the word 'camp' still served for indicating homosexuals, and 'gay', though appropriated by gays, was not a word that most people were comfortable with. To most citizens it still meant being in a happy mood (something to do with good vibes). And policemen were still apt to set traps for homosexuals: '… at the time of the year when cicadas shed their crisp, brown corsets and abandon themselves to pleasure … the time when constables doff their blue uniforms to feign homosexuality, in the hope of bringing deviates to justice. Overnight the long arm of the law (or "lily law" as homosexuals affectionately dub its custodians) becomes limp-wristed while its heavy tread feigns the characteristic and coquettish mince. The lads then loll around the lintels of leading loos or disport themselves upon our beaches, poised to pounce upon the flirtatious poof.' Thus observed Phillip Adams, advertising man and columnist.

By 1972 it was still possible to invite a 1960s-style arrest, not just through a male-to-male encounter in a public place, but by riding a horse topless on a Sydney beach where scores of young women were undoing their bra straps and leaving their backs naked while lying on the sand. This new, eye-catching facet of women's lib suited the afternoon tabloids perfectly – a blurry photograph was just the thing – and so every nuance of social-sexual change was written up by horny male journos in the afternoon press. When it came to a court appearance, as it did with Miss Cherie Amour, 26, a dancer, then the upper body remained the proper focus of journalistic attention: 'Miss Amour appeared in court wearing an open pants-suit coat and no bra', reported the Brisbane *Sunday Mail*, its eyes out on stalks.

Changing standards went past each other like trains on opposite tracks. The official guardians of public morality stayed dressed in hot navy serge and removed their metal numbers while walloping members of the general public. For others it was the age of a little loosening-up – purple shirts and orange trousers; the vogue for safari suits; terry-towelling hats, long socks and grey shorts north of the Queensland border; and the long socks and pink shorts worn by the premier of South Australia, a state hitherto described as having the best seventeenth-century government in the world. Welcome, though, to the gradual easing of 1960s excitement over bare-breasted women until topless models could appear in Shoppingtown promotions and hardly raise a protest. Welcome to the term 'free love', which to a woman meant staying in charge of her choices – but to a man meant getting lucky.

Beach culture is central to an understanding of Australia in any decade. The growth of youth unemployment in the 1970s meant that the beach became the habitat of the breed that used to be known as the 'beachcomber', then the 'beach bum', then the 'surfie', and finally the 'dole bludger'. Young people confessed that they would rather surf than work. A new definition of genuine Aussie attitudes became possible: not the capable, ready-for-anything young bronzed Anzac, but the defiant, ready-for-nothing young bronzed bludger. Some declined to go on the dole because they were too lazy to queue up. They would rather surf. Others believed they were unemployable because employers thought that all they did was surf. Well, small wonder! That's all they were going to do, surf.

You can bet on it. Who could blame anyone languidly enjoying themselves at the taxpayers' expense? Not in the 1970s, anyway.

The concept of the nude beach in Australia is, I'm proud to say, my idea. From an early age I would look at our beaches and I'd say, what's wrong with them? The women are wearing too many clothes – simple as that. They'd look much better in the altogether. Well, some of them would – not all of them. I also had a mate in Adelaide, where we'd kicked off the nude beach concept. He was a taxi driver whose wife had taken him to the cleaners. He didn't have a razoo, he was broke to the wire. So I thought, if we get a beach as an experimental nude beach a long way from town this bloke could pick up a few quid running people to and fro, hiring out binoculars – that kind of thing. So we created Maslin's Beach, down the coast from Adelaide.

Well, this fella, his name was Syd, he told me a very funny story. He said to me on one

ALMOST EVERY CONCEIVABLE SYMBOL OF RAMPANT AUSTRALIANA IS INCLUDED IN THIS DEPICTION BY BARRY CROCKER OF THE HUMPHRIES CHARACTER BAZZA MCKENZIE: THE TOPLESS, SEXUALLY PREDATORY WOMAN, THE BOOMERANG, THE CUDDLY KOALA, THE CLASSIC AKUBRA HAT, THE CAN OF FOSTER'S LAGER, AND THE BAGGY SHORTS OF YESTERYEAR.

particular occasion he was running a nude sheila down to the beach. She was sitting in the back of the cab, starkers. Starkers! He said, 'Les, would you believe, starkers – in the back of my cab!' And he was looking at her in the rear-vision mirror, checking her out. 'And when we finally got there,' he said, 'she turns out not to have any money.' She said, 'I've left my pocket behind,' she said. 'I don't have any money.' 'Oh', he said, 'just my luck.' She said, 'But would you accept this?' And she flashed the old map of Tasmania at him. Quick as a flash he turned around and said, 'Haven't you got anything smaller?' 🐛

There were other cultural changes, apart from those on the beach. In books, matters became noticeably more explicit – the equivalent of 'no bra' in literature being the four-letter word. The anti-censorship movement focused on getting through as many four-letter words as possible, the terms not used as swearwords so much but as 'appropriate and sensitive' language in detailed descriptions of physical love. None of this impressed the Victorian Vice Squad who destroyed 414 copies of *Portnoy's Complaint*. They were seized from the publisher's

ONE OF AUSTRALIA'S FIRST TOPLESS BEACHES WAS AT SANDRINGHAM, IN MELBOURNE. IN THE SEVENTIES FREE LOVE AND THE SEXUAL REVOLUTION LED TO MANY STRANGE PRACTICES, INCLUDING A REVIVAL OF THE MUSLIM PRACTICE OF TAKING MULTIPLE WIVES. AUSTRALIAN ACTOR JACK THOMPSON LED THE WAY BY SHACKING UP WITH TWO SISTERS, BUT FOR THE AVERAGE AUSTRALIAN THE PRACTICE PROVED RATHER TAXING AND SOON PASSED.

warehouse (this was still 1972) and treated as viciously as a dangerous snake, with a magistrate ruling that 'anybody who does not think this book is filthy is not in step with the community as far as decency is concerned'.

And if you were a student orator and wanted to sear the hide of a confused old vice-chancellor (or even a youngish one) in the name of Maoist revolution, it helped to use the staccato words for fornication and female genitalia as often as possible.

It was a time when striking an attitude was believed to be the same as the real thing. A trip, for example, didn't have to mean you were going anywhere. When Patrick White was awarded the Nobel Prize for Literature in 1973 his citation said he had wrestled with the English language in order to take its expressive powers to the verge of the unattainable. And he had done it by staying at home. He also declined to travel to the awards ceremony and stayed close to his native soil, in his house at Centennial Park in Sydney.

In the same year that White got his prize the Australian-made drama series 'Boney', based on the novels of Arthur Upfield (an Australian who spent all his writing life in America), was being filmed on location in Western Australia with a white New Zealand actor playing the Aboriginal detective Napoleon. Other popular series were 'Frost Over Australia' and 'On the Buses'. Australians got to love British television even as they shook off the Pommy yoke with their own creations. Indeed when it came to art the dominant theme was Australian.

In the early 1970s art became repulsively popular. Most university students wished to become artists and the Whitlam Government encouraged as many people as possible in this foolish delusion by bestowing enormous sums of tax-free money upon anyone skilled enough to complete an application form. The price of Australian paintings soared. I decided to depict one of the new breed of Australian art dealers in my 1974 show, At Least You Can Say You've Seen It.

To get across to a general audience the image of some high-pressure huckstering picture-salesman I decked the stage with multicoloured plastic pennants and suspended three large canvases in which the mannerisms of the Australian painters Nolan, French and Olsen were parodied. Wearing a sky-blue suit with flared trousers and straw-coloured pageboy haircut, this fanciful hybrid – Parramatta Road spruiker-cum-aesthete – proved to be less fanciful than I thought. Several of Australia's most successful art dealers, I later heard, were fugitives from the used-car lot. 🖎

The early 1970s were when the Ugh boot, an Australian invention dating from 1965, had its glory as a fashion statement, although it never reached the mania proportions of the built-up shoe sometimes called a wedgie (and often completely hidden under long, flared trousers). The Ugh boot was a crumpled elephant's foot in style, while its opposite number was a hard, high, cork or leather block. The latter style gained fame when a young schoolteacher, kidnapped in Victoria with her class of students, kicked her way to freedom through the side of a panel van using her wedgies. She later appeared in newspaper photos wearing a short miniskirt and a flowered hat, making her resemble a lolly on a stick. It was how many young primary schoolteachers looked then.

It was a time when living naturally, close to the earth, in harmony with nature, could be equated with a visit for a few days to a muddy, overcrowded cow-town in rural New South Wales, where it was possible to sit on the roadside murmuring 'Om' and to feel what it was like to be a child of Aquarius. The badge of commitment was a magic mushroom eaten on the way through Nimbin, a bout of topless dancing, and a skinny-dip in a muddy, leech-infested creek.

To Kathy Lette, child of the time, it was hardly an ecstatic experience: 'When I ran away from home at 15, I went and lived on a commune. We all did. And actually I secretly hated it. We grew hairy legs and sprouted mohair armpits and got stuck in the upside-down lotus position and everything. But being a middle-class girl from the suburbs, to me it was incredibly sort of, dirty, and I really didn't like it. I had to fake it, of course. But the trouble with all those communes – I mean, by the time you find yourself, there's nobody home. You've done so many drugs by then, you know. But I did try that.

'And then I ricocheted into town and became a punk. At the end of the seventies we were just getting into the punk stuff. We lived in Woolloomooloo in a squat and ate cockroach sandwiches and I had a band called the Salami Sisters. We used to follow Spike Milligan all around the place – he was coming out to Australia a lot then, because his mum lived in Woy Woy. We used to hitchhike round the country, following him. And he was fantastically generous. He used to put us up in hotel rooms and restaurants and I used to try and

BEFORE HARE KRISHNAS AND THE ORANGE-CLAD DEVOTEES OF RAJNEESH GAVE THE COLOUR A BAD NAME, ORANGE WAS THE *HUE DE JOUR* IN AUSTRALIA. THE SUNBURNT COUNTRY WENT ORANGE MAD IN THE SEVENTIES: CLOTHES, KITCHENS, CARS, FURNITURE AND FOOD ALL CAME OUT IN THIS MOST UNSUBTLE SHADE. NOTE THE COLOUR OF THIS FASHIONABLE DUO'S COUCH **(above)** AND THE PHALLIC-LIKE ARRANGEMENT OF FRESHWATER YABBIES **(opposite)**, WHICH TOOK PRIDE OF PLACE AT MELBOURNE'S FASHIONABLE JARDINS RESTAURANT.

seduce him all the time. But you know, he's very Catholic, very good. He wouldn't have a bar of it. It was like having a sugar daddy but no sex.'

Somewhere along this road we're travelling on were the first serious encounters with drugs, when children who were in school the year Harold Holt drowned were dead from overdoses before Gough Whitlam was jostled from the political stage in mid-decade. Television images of the 'alternative lifestyles' that were starting to become a feature of society only served to inflame the vast majority of Australians who weren't chanting, nude bathing or joining crypto-lesbian co-ops or Nimbin communes.

Make no mistake – a job, marriage, a home and a mortgage were still top priorities in the 1970s. Banks were willing to lend, and in the days before machines dispensed the cash they actually used people. Whimsical, perhaps, but it seemed to work. Human staff entered into conversation even with the humblest of customers.

It was enough to turn the face orange with pride.

Despite the decade's tacky newness, the 1970s were still a time when most adults had memories of an older, simpler Australia. Even in 1979 many adults had memories stretching back to the 1920s. It was for these – the decent law-abiding majority; church-going, God-fearing, change-resistant – that the 1970s hardly existed at all, except as a long series of incomprehensible coloured images projected on their television screens. They gritted their teeth and waited for the decade to be over. They prayed that when some day someone brought them the news, that person would be of determinate sex and would not be wearing a rainbow-coloured kaftan.

In the world of colour, Australia, the sunburnt country, discovered its indigenous hue for the times. Everything seemed given over to orange. Men wore orange suits tailored from hessian and lined with orange silk. Kitchens were done in orange, casserole dishes were orange, and if duck l'orange seemed excessive for the home cook then chook l'orange was a possibility. The wine accompaniment was of course 'Cold Duck', a sparkling red. The sparkling wine of the 1960s, 'Chateau Gay', would no longer do. Orange Chryslers came off the production lines and cruised the cities. The first girl massaged at the opening of the first of the lifestyle gyms was rubbed down with an orange towel. Thirst could be quenched at the Orange Spot. When the Whitlam Government chose a new growth area it was declared centred on the town of Orange, New South Wales. The benevolent authorities insisted that as many objects as humanly possible should adopt an orange hue or related shades of rust, shrimp, mango, ochre, pumpkin, mustard, pawpaw, mimosa, earwax or marmalade. The equipment and uniforms of the telecommunications system (formerly the Postmaster General's Department) went over to orange. When it was renamed Telecom the logo resembled an orange. It was difficult to make an orange wine, but a sparkling wine called Blue Rhapsody was attempted. When it was withdrawn from sale, desperate Blue Rhapsody afficionados would tint spumanti with Harpic Flushmatic.

It was in this decade that the leaders of the Labor Party discovered chardonnay, a wine with subtle orange aromas. Wine had always been made in Australia but the invention of the wine cask, a cardboard box enclosing a silverfoil bladder typically holding 4 litres, brought serious alcoholism within reach of the leanest budgets.

Other Australian inventions of the 1970s included the Café-Bar, the child car seat, the Sebel chair, and also the electrically heated toilet seat (which failed to take off in this hot, dry continent despite being promoted by a highly entrepreneurial store owner called Dick Smith – nicknamed 'The Electronic Dick' in view of the high-tech electrical products he sold). Even when products originated elsewhere, Australians liked to feel they had perfected them. Pantyhose was an example. Australian women took to pantyhose with relish. One manufacturer, claiming the country led the world in pantyhose construction, elected to sell them as 'Sleekies'. And resourceful Aussies found a way to make the most of them: it was discovered that wearing pantyhose made a surfer or swimmer far safer from the sting of the deadly box jellyfish.

Australian pantyhose really came in in the 1960s, and I went for them hook, line and sinker. Particularly when I went for a swim, because when you're wearing pantyhose the box jellyfish can't sting you to death. They used to be called sea wasps, by the way. But swimmers, when they heard the cry 'Look out for the sea wasps!' would look up expecting a wasp and get stung to death below water level. The pantyhose, too, has a double gusset very often, and its so easy to rub through. Give it a rub through and it's as good as new. And when your pantyhose are worn-out that gusset comes in very handy, ladies, for the straining of soups, preservatives and jellies. Waste not want not, as my mother used to say. We would have called it recycling if that term had been invented. 🕶

Orange was also subversive or threatening to established religious practices. This was the case with the Hare Krishnas, a movement involving nice middle-class children going over to the ultimate niceness of Nirvana, all donning orange robes. When a Hare got married the whole commune was on hand, as well as the cameras, once again. Even the neighbours were curious. But the parents of the bride, like most Australians confronted with an alternative to the way things were, had a look of being under sedation. It was the stunned-mullet look of the incomprehending postwar Aussie confronted with change of almost any kind.

Maybe the blankness came from being expected to be shocked. Everyone watched TV, but then nothing could be done normally when a TV reporter was around. Find a woman in one of those transforming sub-tropical cow-towns weeding her garden and two things could be guaranteed: one, she would be weeding the marijuana patch; two, she would be topless. Otherwise, no story.

So this was the 1970s, a time when the 1960s had ripened into the last years of their decade and had stayed around to ripen even further. Their freshness became decadent, slightly 'off', in retrospect slightly mouldy, and looking quite unbelievable as excess always does in hindsight. Yet they held the core of the changing national psyche within.

EDNA EVERAGE WASHING HER UNDER-DRAWS IN A FOREIGN HOTEL IN THE EARLY SEVENTIES – BEFORE HER ELEVATION TO DAME-HOOD. AUSTRALIANS WERE INGENIOUS WITH SUCH GARMENTS, EVEN USING PANTYHOSE AS A MARINE SAFETY AID FOR PROTECTION AGAINST THE STING OF THE DEADLY BOX JELLYFISH.

It was time to change attitudes to foreigners. In the years since World War II, European foreigners – 'migrants' or 'New Australians' – had become much more widely accepted. But just as that came about the question of those former enemies, the Japanese, raised itself for consideration. This was difficult because of Australia's paranoia about Asia. Australian farmers and graziers did good business with the Yellow Hordes over wool and wheat, but rarely had to meet them face to face.

We didn't have a lot of time for the Japanese then. Little did we dream that they would be coming to Melbourne in their thousands to play golf with the penguins. They come to Melbourne and go all the way to Phillip Island to watch the penguins coming in, then they play golf and then they go back. And apparently it's cheaper for the Japanese tourists to watch the penguins in Melbourne than to see them in their own country. To see them in their own country apparently costs an arm and a leg. Whereas they can save up all year and come to Melbourne. It's an amazing thing. And they're apparently quite delightful. 📞

The paranoia wasn't just leftover bits of White Australia policy but had its basis in the reality of recent history. A whole generation of Australian children had grown up being refused rubber thongs by their fathers who had fought in the islands, men who crossed the road if they ever saw a Japanese coming their way, and who would not consider buying one of the new, and increasingly popular, Japanese cars. On television, footage was shown of an Aboriginal boy saying that he longed for the day Australia would be taken over by the Japanese so that white Australians would know how it felt.

So how was Australia to deal with closer relations with the potential invaders from the north? The answer was a skyhook. No one knew what a real skyhook looked like until they saw the Australian Pavilion at Japan's Osaka Expo. Formerly this was a joke played on army recruits when they were sent to the quartermaster's store in search of 'a left-handed hammer and half a dozen skyhooks'. Later they would hear a band called the Skyhooks singing 'Living in the Seventies' and maybe meet young Japanese people disco-dancing in the Rocky Horror Café in Sydney or The Love Machine in Melbourne. But not just yet. In Osaka, Japanese visiting the Australian exhibit were carried along by 'travelators' and stared at images of the great Australian lifestyle, as represented by gigantic transparencies of Ayers Rock and artists' impressions of the about-to-be-completed

THE APPEAL OF EASTERN RELIGIONS WAS TOO MUCH FOR THE SEVENTIES GENERATION TO RESIST. YOUNG LAPSED CHRISTIANS WERE TAUGHT TO LOSE THEIR ATTACHMENT TO THE PHYSICAL WORLD BY GURUS WHO GLADLY TOOK CONTROL OF THEIR IMPRESSIONABLE DISCIPLES' POSSESSIONS, WHICH THEY CARTED OFF IN FLEETS OF ROLLS ROYCES – A WIN–WIN SITUATION.

SHERBET WAS *THE* TEEN-BAND OF THE DECADE, WITH HITS LIKE 'SUMMER LOVE' AND REGULAR APPEARANCES ON ABC-TV'S 'COUNTDOWN' BEFORE A SEA OF ARM-WAVING TEENAGE GIRLS. WHEN NOT POSING NUDE FOR THE CAMERA, THE BAND MEMBERS WERE USUALLY OUTFITTED IN A TYPICALLY SEVENTIES ENSEMBLE OF SATIN VESTS, SATIN BAGGIES, BOMBER JACKETS AND SCARVES.

Sydney Opera House. Was giving them a good look by way of the Skyhook pavilion going too far? In Australia, citizens stared at television images of the event and wondered how the Japanese takeover was to happen. For happen it would, although in a far more benign way than imagined.

Meanwhile, there were some expatriate Australian intellectuals who said they would never return to Australia until there was a change of government. As the conservative Liberals had been in power for over 20 years, they could say this without much risk of having to come back. Germaine Greer had other reasons for not coming back. She said she was afraid she'd be shouted at in the streets for wearing red stockings and not shaving her armpits. (This led to television panels debating hairy legs and armpits for women. They knew she was right.) These expatriates were the self-styled Spirits of the Time to Come in Australia – the ones who had left Australia in the forties, fifties, and sixties. They were sworn not to return until the society showed a capacity to 'advance'. Those who had left in the 1960s were particularly scathing about their homeland. They had grown up with censorship and it bothered them hugely. To them Australia was still full of wowsers and khaki-coloured conformity and a rejection of anything exciting and new in art and literature. The political inertia of Australia under Menzies produced a cultural inertia that for some was unbearable. It took a particular kind of stomach, like Patrick White's, to reject almost totally the cultural pretensions of Australia and still draw art from the very limited social attitudes found to hand. But then White always delighted in acidly etching Australian limitations, and only in the seventies came to attack its implications in the public arena.

Richard Neville, the then editor of *Oz* magazine, recalls the 'Australian contingent' of the late sixties and early seventies: 'Australians in London at that time were kind of brash. They were a self-elected people because they'd got there and they'd decided to stay. I think they were looking for things to do and they were quite confident. Some of them – I mean, you know, there were all sorts of little snobberies within the Australian contingent. I personally was very snooty about the Earls Court Australians. Earls Court was an el cheapo district in London, much favoured by large numbers of Aussies. And I was absolutely thrilled when the *New Statesman* said that our new magazine, *Oz*, was coming out and that it would not be written in Earls Court strine. Now I'm rather embarrassed by that, but at the time I was strutting down the street thinking yes, yes, we're a different breed of Australians.'

He continues: 'The Barry McKenzie archetype, if you like, grew out of Earls Court. And yes, in a way, Barry McKenzie was the person we were running away from. That's who we tried to leave behind in Sydney. The guy that was always going to tease you about your hair at the pub and then vomit all over you. And to our absolute horror, we woke up in London and there he and all his mates were, living in Earls Court. And if that wasn't enough, bloody Barry Humphries came along and started doing a comic strip about him in *Private Eye*. But the truth is that, inside all of us, there was a little bit of Barry Humphries – oops, a little bit of Barry McKenzie.'

At least it was no longer possible for the Australian to be mistaken for a New Zealander or a South African.

I feel partly responsible for all this. In the late 1960s I had invented the crude and loutish stereotype of the Australian innocent abroad whom I named Barry or (Bazza) McKenzie. He had begun as a comic strip and became the star of a successful film. We were given a government grant, and I recall the official who'd given us the money rushing across the tarmac as we flew off to London to make the film. His final words to me were: 'By the way, Barry, I hope there won't be too many colloquialisms in the film.'

Actually, the colloquialisms seemed to improve the picture. It was as if, through each colourful euphemism for urination, copulation and regurgitation, the island continent was coming into sharp focus for the world at large, who had previously only viewed us from a distance. ✍

Right: GERMAINE GREER GETTING INTO THE SPIRIT OF THE COMING DECADE, IN A SHOT TAKEN IN 1969 FOR *OZ* MAGAZINE. THE LONDON-BASED WRITER AND FEMINIST IS PICTURED HERE WITH VIV STANSHALL OF THE BONZO DOG DOO DAH BAND IN WHAT SHE CALLED A 'POP CONSPIRACY TO BLOW THE MINDS OF MY GENERATION'. A FEW YEARS LATER, FELLOW FEMINISTS BEGAN TO UNDERSTAND JUST HOW MUCH THEY'D BEEN EXPLOITED BY FREE LOVE. THEY REALISED THAT WHAT HAD BEEN CONSIDERED 'EXPRESSION' WAS ACTUALLY EXPLOITATION.

AUSTRALIA'S FIRST WORKING-CLASS HERO EVOLVED FROM A *PRIVATE EYE* COMIC STRIP, WRITTEN BY BARRY HUMPHRIES AND DRAWN BY NICHOLAS GARLAND, TO THE FEATURE FILMS *THE ADVENTURES OF BARRY MCKENZIE* (1972) AND *BARRY MCKENZIE HOLDS HIS OWN* (1974), DIRECTED BY BRUCE BERESFORD AND STARRING BARRY CROCKER. DESPITE ITS BOX-OFFICE SUCCESS, THE CRITIC MAX HARRIS DUBBED THE FIRST MOVIE 'THE WORST AUSTRALIAN FILM EVER MADE' AND FOSTER'S WAS HORRIFIED BY THE DEPICTION OF ITS SOPHISTICATED BEVERAGE.

The aforementioned *Oz* magazine had been published in Australia from 1963 to 1968, and had seen its editors Richard Walsh and Richard Neville given prison sentences for obscenity in 1964. At their Sydney trial elderly men in grey suits argued obscure points of law, discussing for days on end in a stuffy courtroom the precise meaning of the term 'get folked'. A defence witness argued that 'get folked' was a common phrase among folk singers. They'd all say, 'Let's go out and get folked', and pick up their guitars and be off.

With *Oz* being published in England from the end of the 1960s, Richard Neville was again at the helm, but now offending British moral standards with Australian brashness. For this he was to face another obscenity trial – from which, with the assistance of the now famous lawyers Geoffrey Robertson and John Mortimer, he emerged victorious.

So when *were* these 1970s for the rest of Australia? Were they to stay trapped like a stale air pocket of the 1960s? Was their true and proper start in counter-culture 'happenings' – or when Harold Holt surged seawards in 1967, giving Australia a push onto the front pages of the world's newspapers? The 1970s were the decade when recklessness was celebrated, after all, and Harold Holt himself had come across in the way that a good many people viewed Australia – and why they had left Australia and gone to live somewhere else … as Don Whitington puts it: 'lonely, dependent entirely on his own resources, with a dogged determination not reinforced by outstanding ability, and a desire always to be in a position where he could attract admiring or approving attention and congratulations.'

In his own modest way Harold Holt entered the celebrity hall of fame of international ghosts. He would be joined exactly ten years later by Elvis Presley and exactly 30 years later by Lady Di. It was said that he had been whisked away in a Red Chinese submarine. This was a rather more prescient rumour than the story that he was eaten by a shark – because history records that Harold Holt, for all his bumbling, boring ordinariness and his penchant for increasing the number of Australian troops sent to Vietnam, was a key figure in inaugurating a changing Australian view of Asia. It was no longer just the Red Peril bogeyman and communist playground, but a place where people – fellow human beings and not just

Having been convicted in Australia of 'publishing rude undergraduate humour', Richard Neville travelled overland on the hippy trail in the late sixties and set up *Oz* magazine in London. The 'schoolkids issue' (above) was at the centre of an obscenity trial at the Old Bailey in 1971.

King Arthur and the Round Table

I'm proud to say that I, Les Patterson, was an integral part of the Whitlam Camelot. If you think of Gough as King Arthur and the Round Table with old Margaret there as Queen Gwena ... Gonna ... Gonorrhoea ... Gwenervere, I was Merlin. I was the think tank – I was the ideas man. And I came to him one day and he locked the door and he said, 'What is it this time, Les?' And I said, 'I need money, Gough. Because this is for a special project: it's the disabled black lesbian puppet workshop.' He looked a bit strange when I said that. 'You need big bickies for that, Les?' 'Yes,' I replied, 'The black disabled lesbian women's puppet workshop.' As he started to write the cheque he said to me, 'Now look, Les, who's this really for?' 'Ha, ha, Gough!' I said. 'It's for me.' At that he said, 'What are you going to do with it?' and I replied, 'I'm going to piss it up against the wall.' 'Les,' says Gough, 'You're an honest man – I'll double it.'

Above: PRIME MINISTER WHITLAM HOLDING COURT IN HIS PARLIAMENT HOUSE OFFICE.

mysterious Chinamen and other small brown races – might actually aspire to the standard of living enjoyed by middle-class Australians. Holt achieved this connection by regular visits to Asian capitals followed by a jaunt to Washington, which from then on became the route followed by all Australian prime ministers. No longer was the trek to London such a key expedition.

The split-personality factor in Australian society began to exercise itself like the death throes of a de-fanged old snake. If Australia was a flower child at the end of the 1960s it was a swaggering adolescent in the 1970s. After Harold Holt the nation's new Liberal prime minister was a larrikin ex-fighter pilot named John Grey Gorton. He had a face like a mashed pear from reconstructive surgery. When told of his extensive plastic surgery, one Hollywood matron exclaimed, 'You mean he *paid* for that face?!' But he had a twinkle in his eye and a liking for a late-night party with a pretty secretary in tow. Australia was in the mood for change and Gorton would do as an image for that change until Labor came along – a boozer, a bungler, a chortler, a charmer. London's *Private Eye* magazine had him having an affair with the singer Liza Minnelli, but the only time they met, apparently, Minnelli's mother-in-law (mother of the Australian singer Peter Allen) was present. It has never been possible in Australia for a sexual scandal among parliamentarians to be taken quite as seriously as in Britain.

Baiting Gorton from the Labor side of the House as the 1960s dragged to an end was the tall, large-boned, and quip-ready Gough Whitlam, a Canberra-born lawyer and member for the outer-Sydney working-class seat of Werriwa. He had become party leader early in 1967 and from that time on gained a huge following among younger voters, as well as getting the Labor Party back together. He became a winning force, always looking at new turning points in foreign policy and at ideas for recovering Australia's independence as a nation. Like Gorton, Whitlam was a former Royal Australian Air Force officer. With his equally statuesque wife Margaret, the silver-tongued Gough was a regular theatregoer, and one of the first national leaders to elevate the shadow arts portfolio to the highest levels. Whitlam and the arts would bring politics and the Yartz together when the time came; the tone of Australian culture would never be the same again. When he spoke, he fixed his interlocutor with a sharp, glassy gaze and the silver hairs at the nape of his neck seemed to fluff out a bit. Cartoonists liked to depict him as a chook.

Date: Saturday, 3 December 1972. **Place:** the Royal Albert Hall, London. **Event:** the crowning of Miss World, 1972. **The winner:** Belinda Green of Australia, wearing silver platform shoes.

Date: Saturday 3 December 1972. **Place:** the Sunnybrook Hotel in western Sydney. **Event:** celebration of the Labor Party victory in national elections. **The winner:** Gough Whitlam, campaigning under the slogan 'It's Time'.

3 DECEMBER 1972 WAS A MOMENTOUS DAY FOR AUSTRALIA: GOUGH WHITLAM SNATCHED THE THRONE FROM THE LIBERALS' BILLY MCMAHON TO BECOME THE FIRST LABOR PRIME MINISTER SINCE 1949, BUT, MORE IMPORTANTLY, AT LEAST TO THE READERS OF THE *AUSTRALIAN WOMEN'S WEEKLY*, BELINDA GREEN WAS CROWNED MISS WORLD IN LONDON.

Same week, same historic events. **Place:** Consolidated Press headquarters in Sydney. The dilemma at *Women's Weekly* magazine: who would get the cover story? Mrs Whitlam or Miss World?

The solution: Miss World.

This was another victory for Australia, a cultural one. When Belinda Green finally came home she was borne to the steps of Parliament House in Canberra in a Cobb and Co. coach. Caesar himself was on the steps of the Senate to welcome his generals with the spoils of their victories. It was a great honour for Miss Green to meet Gough Whitlam in this way, but by then it was her eleventh month of being Miss World. 'I was very tired,' she was reported as saying, 'and once again it was an experience of having lots of cameras shoved in my face. By that stage I was tired of smiling and tired of chitchat.'

PIERRE CARDIN POSED WITH A PRIZE-WINNING SHEEP IN THE SIXTIES, SO IT SHOULDN'T SEEM STRANGE THAT AUSTRALIA'S MISS WORLD, BELINDA GREEN (AT LEFT, WEARING FASHIONABLE HOT PANTS), GOT TO POSE WITH A CHAMPION GREYHOUND – OR 'DISH-LICKER', AS THEY ARE MORE COMMONLY KNOWN IN AUSTRALIA.

Barry Crocker, who played the film role of Bazza McKenzie, recalls a special scene in *Barry McKenzie Holds His Own* in which Gough and Margaret Whitlam, press-ganged into taking part, appeared: 'We dressed on the plane, actually, flying in from London. I dressed as Barry McKenzie, and Humphries dressed as Edna. We got off the plane, went through customs, and the doors opened and there were 500 people all dressed as Barry McKenzie fans. And in the centre of them, Gough and Margaret were standing there. Of course, we had five cameras rolling and it was all captured on film. Then Edna Everage knelt before Gough Whitlam, who said: "Arise, Dame Edna!" And so from that moment Edna was a Dame, which was a great turning point in her career.'

When Gough Whitlam QC, 56, defeated the Liberals' Billy McMahon and was sworn in as Australia's eighth Labor prime minister, he was the first since Ben Chifley lost office in 1949. It had been a long wait for the party that was the most natural inheritor of Australia's egalitarian traditions. Now it was allied with an intellectual and artistic panache, somewhat variable except at the top. Whitlam had style, learning, wit, vision, and stood tall above the heads of his fellow Australians both intellectually and physically. Brilliant compared with Menzies and his lesser cohorts (both the drowned and the saved), he was seen as Australia's best bid for international statesmanship. Inevitably he was seen as lacking the common touch, too, although nobody doubted the depth of his

An historic moment as Dame Edna receives a bouquet of flowers following her investiture by Labor prime minister Gough Whitlam (here accompanied by wife Margaret). The moving ceremony took place during the filming of *Barry McKenzie Holds His Own* at Sydney's Mascot Airport in 1974.

compassion – it was just that he seemed a little lofty at times. Ready with a Latin epigram, an etymological quip, a quote from Gibbon or holy scripture, he was hardly a reincarnation of Harold Holt or out of the same stable, even remotely, as Australians in the Barry McKenzie mould. His wife Margaret had a political heart all her own, and the two of them, regarded nationally with a mixture of wonder, disbelief and awe (intermingled in some quarters, with the vicious hatred reserved for the envied and superior), brought the Lodge in Canberra to the nearest equivalent of the White House that Australia had ever known. Gough and Margaret were Presidential quality.

I will never forget the day when I knelt before Gough (Fellow Socialist) Whitlam and he said 'Arise, Dame Edna' in that inimitable way of his. It was one of the most thrilling moments of my life – a life full of thrills and excitements. I'm not sure why he made me a Dame. It could have been for political reasons – because we see eye to eye on most topics. But it could have been for my services to Australian culture. After all, I pretty well put Australian women on the map. And my services to conservation are well known. In fact the United Nations has just given me special mention. Not just for the Australian landscape I've conserved, but our wildlife, particularly our lovely old marsupials. 👓

The Whitlam years were pockmarked with a disastrous sartorial clutter – shoulder-bags for men, spinnaker-sized ties, ponchos, Greek fisherman's caps, long sideburns, wide hair, droopy moustaches. Add to the list Che Guevara berets, peace-and-love belt buckles, embroidered jeans and platform-soled shoes – a feelgood cargo with an almost religious overlay of social signals. It was an era when people with

Les Patterson on Sartorial Matters

SOUTH AUSTRALIAN PREMIER DON DUNSTAN STEPS OUT IN HIS SAFARI SUIT.

I pioneered the wearing of white shoes for men in Australia. I can say without fear of successful contradiction I was the first Australian diplomat to wear white shoes. And it's a brave thing for a drinking man to do, considering what very frequently follows. I also pioneered the long white socks and the shorts which became universal. I've always been at the sharp end of Australian men's fashions. Little wonder that I should have notched up about 12 or 13 nominations for the best-dressed man in Australia through the seventies. I'm very proud of that record.

But my biggest triumph in the clothing department was the fashion statement that is the safari suit. Ever since I seen Stewart Grainger, and people often mistake me for him, in *The Snows of Kilimanjaro* wearing that safari suit, I thought, that is for me. Well, I bought one and they all copied me — Jim Cairns, Al Grassby, Don Dunstan, Andrew Peacock. They all started strutting out in their safari suits.

bad physiques wore skin-tight clothes — pop stars squeezed into white leather, portly intellectuals poured themselves into black leather, and leading ladies of the feminist vanguard, fake-fur-fringed and flared, flung off their tops of stiff, unmanageable fabrics and went bare-breasted.

'You are only liberated when you realise just how awful you are,' announced Germaine Greer, launching her book, *The Female Eunuch*.

If that was the definition, then 1970s Australia would come to be very liberated indeed.

The Female Eunuch set off a fevered examination of the role of women in Australian society, especially after the author claimed that women were the true proletariat, which appealed to the Australian sense of fair play and the myth of the working-class society. Germaine Greer also said that if women left their husbands because of her book, it wasn't her fault. All this sparked off a flurry of quasi-scientific investigations. How far did a housewife walk in a day? Attach a pedometer to her foot and find out! How good a lover was a housewife? A good titillating question, especially if posed to a background of 'Wives and Lovers' disco music. It seemed as if, from all this, the traditional woman who baked and cleaned was becoming a curiosity. Young girls gathered around their tribal elders in amazement and disbelief while the latter extolled the benefits of keeping surfaces clean.

There were pockets of resistance to the new ideas, of course. One such redoubt was Rockhampton, Queensland, where the rough old mayor, Rex Pilbeam — on the assumption that one family didn't need two incomes and that a wife's place was in the home — sacked women staff who got married. Sexy Rexy was the judge of it all. Meanwhile, women marched the streets of Sydney while reporters asked them what they had to complain about — after all, they weren't barefoot and pregnant in the kitchen any more!

Germaine used to live near us – Germaine Greer, that is, now Dr Greer – and she used to come to my kitchen, about once a day, and she'd sit there on a chair looking at me as I went about my duties, cleaning surfaces. She used to love watching me working on my surfaces, and she'd say: 'Teach me to make cakes, Edna, teach me to wash up. Teach me to scrub the floor.' Do you know what I'd say to her? I'd say, 'Germaine, you're a clever girl – you've got your head screwed on the right way. You're bright. Don't learn these domestic skills. Like me, you're not going to need them. You're not a canary bred for captivity. You'll come out of your cage and horrible birds will peck you to death and you'll have no defences against them.'

Well, she looked at me with total incomprehension and said: 'What a silly metaphor, Edna.' 🎭

Under Gough Whitlam the White Australia Policy was finally abandoned and Australians began to see not just visitors but migrants arriving from Asia. The frontman for the new Australian ethnic stir-fry was to be the flamboyant immigration minister, Al Grassby. With his pencil-thin 'greaser' moustache, heavy-lidded eyes and shiny black combed-back hair, Grassby looked like an extra from *The Godfather*, although he was actually born in Brisbane to an Irish-Australian family. He was the member for Griffith, in the Murrumbidgee irrigation area, and had many honest Calabrians and just a couple of slightly crooked and infamous ones in his electorate. (All of the latter happened to be out of town, and with cast-iron alibis, on the day in 1977 when the Griffith anti-drugs campaigner Donald Mackay was murdered. It was a famous case and led to the acceptance into common use of the term 'grass castles' to describe the outrageously self-indulgent mansions, featuring Graeco-Roman columns, built in the Griffith area by several land-holders.)

Striped jackets, silk ties, spotted shirts, white belts, white shoes – these were standard choices for the genial, enthusiastic Grassby, who had an organ-grinder's cheekiness as he sold the idea of multiculturalism to an Australian public only just starting to trust salami or the newer kinds of pasta. Grassby attracted more hate mail than any other Australian politician of the time – not just for his dress sense, which he conveyed to other parliamentarians, who began slipping into white shoes, but because he dared to suggest that the composition of Australian society was changing and that it wasn't such a bad thing. Horse-breeders weighed in to the debate, suggesting that British breeding was as necessary among people as it was in animals. It kept up the strength of the stock.

Supporters of the Whitlam Government have scattered to the four winds after more than 20 years, but a few true believers still hold to their faith. For one who was much maligned at the time, the ministerial secretary Junie Morosi, the Whitlam era represented 'the birth of Australian soul and identity'. Miss Morosi was principal private secretary and close friend to the left-leaning treasurer, Dr Jim Cairns. She saw the Whitlam Government, and the 1970s decade as a whole, as a time of visions and dreams. But she was heading for a downfall. By 1975 there had already been much speculation about the nature of her private life when a chance remark, 'Of course I love Jim Cairns', led to intense press speculation over whether they had a sexual relationship. Junie Morosi's beautiful smile, her Filipina grace, her feminist forthrightness and her long, dark, glossy braid of hair were just too much for the rampant libidos of Australia's boiled-dry journos. They needed a scandal and had found an easy target.

Dr Cairns had a bumbling, boyish, heartful foolishness about him, and his mistakes, like those of other Labor ministers, were building up into a long list. But Miss Morosi believes she served the last truly idealistic government Australia has had. She loved not just Dr Cairns but Mr Whitlam and his dreams, his ministers and their dreams – they all had dreams. She didn't think a dream was ever really naive. She thought a dream led to an ideal, that the ideal became an ideal only because of the power of the dream. She was, in a way, the quintessence of the moment.

For better or for worse, Australia first appeared on the world map in the early 1970s. Until then it had lurked obscurely on the underside of the globe. And it was Gough

JUNIE MOROSI (above) WAS PRIVATE SECRETARY TO THE IDEALISTIC BUT NAIVE WHITLAM GOVERNMENT TREASURER, JIM CAIRNS. UNFORTUNATELY JUNIE BECAME IMMERSED IN ONE OF THE GOVERNMENT'S MORE SALACIOUS SCANDALS AS THE MEDIA SPECULATED ON WHETHER SHE AND CAIRNS WERE LOVERS.

Whitlam's prime ministership (1972–75) that brought it to the rest of the world's notice. Here was a news story worth following: Australia with a patrician, polymath PM? In the Whitlam era the British papers upped their accounts of life under the southern stars. In this they were greatly assisted by the efforts of a distinguished Australian.

At the moment I am holding down an enormous incumbency. I think I can say without fear of successful contradiction that it is one of the biggest incumbencies I have ever held down in my political career. I am the Australian Cultural Attaché to the Court of St James. It wasn't always thus, I can tell you. Back in the sixties I was a politico and I held a very important portfolio – I was the Minister for Shark Conservation.

Under the Whitlam regime I too believed in Camelot built upon this brown unpleasant land in Australia … I copped the Cinderella appointment in London as Australian Cultural Attaché, spearheading our penetration of the European artistic community, working my arse off for Australia, sometimes a 24-, 25-, 26-, even a 27-hour week! Not bad for an Australian civil servant, I can tell you.

A lot of people probably forgot about old Les slaving his arse off for Australia; but someone up there must have been thinking about me. I refer to the Queen, little Betty Windsor. She must have been thinking about old Les, because the time came for me to present my very sizeable credentials to the Sovereign and I found myself with my lady wife Gwen – you'd like Gwen; I wish I did for Christ's sake – strolling along to Buckminster Castle, the Queen's delightful colonial-style town house set as it is in 5.4 hectares of lush British bushland a stone's throw from Piccadilly Shopping Mall. And all of a sudden it was a bend of the knee and a tap on the shoulder and it was 'Arise, Sir Les and Lady Gwen'. And stuff socialism! Are you with me?

But I'm a maverick, I'm a wag, I'm a hard-nosed carpet-bagging troubleshooter, and if ever there is any strife in the world that needs a bit of finesse, a little savoir faire – what has become known in diplomatic circles as the 'Patterson touch' – they send for old Les.

In Australia, national pride reached epidemic proportions. The new assertiveness produced aggressive advertising methods. Hitherto, television commercials had been fronted by nice people, polite to the point of gentility. They were now purged and replaced by the ocker, the loud-mouthed yobbo. Barry McKenzie had been a vulgar embarrassment. Those who came later were to become heroes.

THE CAST OF 'NUMBER 96', A NIGHTLY TV SERIAL ABOUT THE GOINGS-ON IN A FAR-FROM-TYPICAL SUBURBAN BLOCK OF FLATS. IT RAN FOR OVER 1000 EPISODES, RESCUING THE AILING TEN NETWORK AND OPENING THE FLOODGATES FOR AUSTRALIAN SOAPIES.

Down from the Sydney Harbour Bridge clambered an amiable rigger, Paul Hogan, to make his name – initially in advertising – with the persona of a dry, cheerful, ordinary bloke with a clown's cunning. With Hogan, all the high talk of artistic elites was replaced by the image of the Aussie battler, the working-class hero getting the better of all comers. While Whitlam and his proconsuls on the Australia Council made their lofty judgments, two extremes of Australian culture were fought out over two cigarette brands. Benson & Hedges was represented by the urbane, English-born Stuart Wagstaff. He symbolised cultural knowingness, snobbishness, connoisseurship. Winfield was represented by the football-shirted, ropy-necked, sun-frizzled Hogan. In a television advertisement for Winfield, Hogan walked on to a stage with a symphony orchestra in the background. He said to the conductor, 'Let 'er rip, Boris', and the orchestra played Tchaikovsky. It was no contest.

The Australian accent became fashionable at last. Women were encouraged to be ocker. Singing commercials developed a fiercely patriotic style to sell margarine, cricket or even personal hygiene. International conductor Sir Charles Mackerras counted an Australian accent a boon to the opera – suggesting that Australia had so many top-flight singers because of their accent. The voices that had thrilled Covent Garden audiences in the 1950s were still there in the 1970s, but now on a brand new stage somewhere beneath the conch-roofed Sydney Opera House. (Journalists quizzed the soprano June Bronhill about her voice. 'Is it still there?' She attempted an answer by trilling.)

The 'Eighth Wonder of the World' was opened by the Queen in 1973. Vast as the roof was, the stage turned out to be roughly the size of a large bus shelter, proving frustrating for set designers. Meanwhile, on the rooftop an Aboriginal actor, Ben Blakeney, proclaimed: 'I am Bennelong ... Two hundred years ago fires burned on this point – the fires of my people. And into the light of the flames, from the shadows all about, our warriors danced.' Neither Utzon, the designer, nor Goossens, the ill-fated conductor who was an early inspirer of a building on the site, were present at the opening. One had fallen out with the government; something nasty had fallen out of the other's travel bag.

Through the residents of 'Number 96' and other television soaps, Australians were getting to meet a cross-section of their own society – not least nymphomaniac virgins, lesbian witches, knicker-snippers and even (and this was revolutionary) sympathetically portrayed homosexual characters. The opening-out in people's acceptance of divergence of various kinds was real, to the point where what was once called 'deviance' (and that was the educated person's term) would become more or less mainstream. The Whitlam Government did much the same job on the Australian public, in the sense that it took action and made changes that had been overdue for public recognition. Certain rifts in society were healed by this, while others were opened wider.

The moment Gough Whitlam was elected, his government ended conscription and brought the last few Australian servicemen back from Vietnam. East Germany and the People's Republic of China

Opposite: A RIGGER ON SYDNEY HARBOUR BRIDGE IN THE SEVENTIES, PAUL HOGAN FIRST APPEARED ON TELEVISION IN THE TALENT SHOW 'NEW FACES', WHERE HE LOST OUT TO A 15-YEAR-OLD CELLIST. BUT HIS DRY-HUMOURED, CHEEKY 'OCKER' STYLE WAS SOON PICKED UP BY ADVERTISERS WHO CHOSE HIM AS THE FACE OF WINFIELD CIGARETTES. IN THE EIGHTIES HOGAN WOULD FIND FAME AND FORTUNE WITH THE *CROCODILE DUNDEE* MOVIES.

THE OPENING OF THE CONCH-ROOFED SYDNEY OPERA HOUSE IN 1973 PROVIDED INSPIRATION FOR TALENTED (AND NOT-SO-TALENTED) AUSTRALIAN CRAFTSPEOPLE.

were recognised. A young ambassador to China was appointed and he actually spoke the language. Miss Elizabeth Evatt, aged 39, became the first woman appointed to the bench of the Commonwealth Conciliation and Arbitration Commission. She came back to Australia after 14 years in England to take the job. The voting age was reduced from 21 to 18. The national security organisation, ASIO, was raided by its own governmental masters, and held accountable to the will of the majority, even if ASIO operatives considered their own government dangerously leftist. Maternity/paternity leave was extended to all Commonwealth employees. A supporting mothers benefit was introduced, and extended to single mothers. The catchcry 'the environment' became an issue in politics beyond matters like the flooding of valleys and relief for bushfires and droughts. Gough Whitlam visited China, the first Australian prime minister to do so.

In 1975 the Australia Council was reconstituted under special legislation. Whenever some of its grants went to individual artists rather than to arts organisations a great deal of criticism was voiced in the press. There was a lot of room at the bottom of the pyramid in the crafts and in film – but in some areas, such as fiction and poetry, the small amount spent went a long way. Not that the afternoon press or much of the public ever agreed. It was somehow honourable to be on the dole or to lean on the shovel in a government job, but to get money for a year or two to write a book, compose music or set up a painting studio was nothing but a wank. But then, when was the pretension to make something from nothing ever a reality to anyone except the creator of it?

As well as spawning an industry of professional ockers, *The Adventures of Barry McKenzie* and its profits begat a whole Australian film industry. Australians could see David Williamson's *The Removalists* on stage one night, and the next night see it as a movie. While Prime Minister John Gorton had got the film industry going, the Honourable Gough was there at the film festivals to take the credit. With Labor largesse, directors were literally running projectors in a film co-op one week and attending the Cannes Film Festival the next. For years, actors had had to go overseas to work and then agonise about coming back. Now they agonised over having to leave at all.

Piss-up at Hanging Rock

A SCENE FROM PETER WEIR'S *PICNIC AT HANGING ROCK*.

I am extremely, very extremely proud to say that I kick-started the Australian fillum industry with a brilliant idea of mine which I sold to Gough Whitlam. The idea of mine, the concept, was a group of Australian Rules footballers, all good masculine blokes, having a picnic on a hill in the middle of the outback. It was called 'Piss-up at Hanging Rock'. Boy was that a ripper concept! Well, the fillum industry, of course, got hold of that and the poofta mafia who runs it, or 'poofia' as we call them, turned it into some arty crafty thing about a whole bunch of sheilas in see-through nighties drifting around and in the end they disappear. Disappear! Eaten by Abos or something. However, I took a beautiful little actress to the world premiere of this fillum. Oh, she was beautiful. But she got a bit sceptical halfway through and she nudged me and she said, 'Aw, come off it, Les,' she said. 'Whose leg are they pulling? Things just don't disappear like that.' I said, 'Well, darling, watch this thing disappear.' Are you with me? Oh, she was nice. She could have had a picnic on my outcrop any day of the week. And it wouldn't be hanging, I can tell you.

After a time, the Whitlam-esque changes – hardly dangerous or world-shattering by any outside standard – came a little too fast for many Australians. They whinged and complained at record levels. There was a tremendous controversy when the Federal Government purchased Jackson Pollock's 'Blue Poles' for a then vast sum. The national anthem was changed from 'God Save the Queen' to something worse – 'Advance Australia Fair' – not after a referendum but after a public opinion survey conducted by the Bureau of Census and Statistics. In 1974 Sir John Kerr, 59, was sworn in as governor-general. (He used strangely distancing language in accepting this high office, describing it as an 'exercise'.) The Gurindji people in the Northern Territory were given rights to 3250 square kilometres of their tribal land, in the final chapter of a long-running dispute.

And yet, according to our own publicity, we were continually coming of age. And like any truculent teenager we rebelled against a parent. Until Whitlam, Australians were still described as 'British Subjects' on their passports and they chafed at the attachment, even if it was only traditional, sentimental and legalistic. When would they be allowed out as world citizens? Like anyone not quite grown, but feeling they ought to be, they took their rawness for the ripe article. As in any family there was constant bickering about when the growing started and when the misbehaving child was likely to become an adult. Many, though, felt they had arrived and that others around them had to do the catching up.

On Christmas Eve 1974 Cyclone Tracy roared in from the northwest and flattened Darwin under winds of more than 200 kilometres per hour. Houses and other structures were wrecked over a wide area and 50 or

THE AFTERMATH OF CYCLONE TRACY, WHICH STRUCK DARWIN ON CHRISTMAS EVE 1974, KILLING OVER 50 PEOPLE AND LEAVING 25 000 HOMELESS.

more people lost their lives. It was an omen, of a sort, for Labor. The party had less than a year to go in office.

Unlike President Kennedy, there was no assassin's bullet, although notions of a CIA plot to undermine Whitlam and his 'dangerous' government persisted in the minds of conspiracy theorists. Things got worse when news leaked that Gough had despatched a senior minister, Rex Connor, to the Middle East to borrow $4000 million in petro-dollars. Covert deals with Saddam Hussein and Colonel Gaddafi were reliably rumoured. They were needed, the government said, 'to buy back Australia's natural resources from its overseas investors, to establish transcontinental pipelines and chemical complexes to convert coal into oil and gas into gasoline, and to enter the field of uranium enrichment'.

The new leader of the Opposition, Malcolm Fraser, sharpened his teeth. He planned moves to block Supply in the Senate (where the Opposition had the numbers) in order to force an early election over the scandal. The broker in one of Rex Connor's deals was a Pakistani financier with a shady background. He was brought to Australia to set the record straight, but said nothing. The Senate cut off funds to the administration, the government was unable to pay its bills, and yet Labor refused to go to an election on the issue. It would get its funds from somewhere, it said, and there was a feeling that Whitlam might end up embattled in the chamber like Allende in Chile, though being attacked by gibes and insults rather than bullets. Then, on 11 November 1975, the governor-general, Sir John Kerr – formerly Whitlam's man but now Malcolm Fraser's 'cur' – sacked Gough Whitlam as Prime Minister of Australia.

Shameful, shabby, humiliating, predictable and yet at the same time dramatic, this was the defining event of the embarrassing decade.

Oddly enough, there were hints of the 1980s in the way the 1970s lived themselves out. Could it all be attributed to Malcolm Fraser and the Dismissal of '75? – Fraser being the politician who couldn't wait for an election to roll around and so demanded his day of power. Fraser 'wanted it now', and that was when he got it. He was ably assisted by the actions of the long-ago Laborite governor-general, whose silvery locks and taste for the pleasures of the table made him a worthy harbinger of times to come. After the sacking of Whitlam, Sir John Kerr went to the Melbourne Cup, wearing his vice-regal top hat and tails, and looking like a lord.

GOUGH WHITLAM (RIGHT) MADE MANY MISTAKES DURING HIS TIME IN GOVERNMENT BUT THE BIGGEST WAS APPOINTING SIR JOHN KERR (LEFT) AS GOVERNOR-GENERAL IN 1974. THE MAN BOB HAWKE DESCRIBED AS THE 'LIBERACE OF THE LAW' RETURNED THE COMPLIMENT BY DISMISSING WHITLAM ON REMEMBRANCE DAY 1975 AND LATER DISGRACED HIMSELF BY GETTING FAMOUSLY DRUNK AT THE MELBOURNE CUP IN 1977.

He was as drunk as a lord, too, as he slurred and fumbled his way through the prize-giving. Cup Day was (and still is) the national blow-out day, the day of 'get rich quick', and Kerr was booed and jeered from the saddling paddock. But he was also recognised as one of us – a dreamer and a toper and a bit greedy for something more. It was power that he wanted, within a role that was traditionally symbolic.

With the Dismissal, Kerr had made his grab, and so he'd had his 1980s moment five years before the decade actually rolled around. Widely held in contempt, he served out his term with the air of a defiant outcast – the man who suffered his hangover before the party actually began.

There was an atmosphere building up through the remainder of the seventies of bending the rules, finding loopholes, of making all things possible for all people. The signs and wonders were everywhere. Within three months of the Dismissal the headlines said 'Gold For Everyone!' and Australians learned that they could now own, buy and sell any quantity of gold, following the removal of government restrictions. Before this date all gold, except for certain wrought objects and gold coins, had to be delivered to the Reserve Bank within a

OH HOW COSMOPOLITAN WE HAD BECOME! HERE AT THE DAILY PLANET TWO YOUNG HOSTESSES INSTRUCT A RELUCTANT CUSTOMER IN THE FINER POINTS OF AQUATIC SPORTS. THIS 'ESTABLISHMENT' SITUATED AT HORNE STREET, ELSTERNWICK, WAS MELBOURNE'S FIRST LEGAL BROTHEL. ITS ADDRESS WAS A GREAT SOURCE OF AMUSEMENT TO ITS MOST FAMOUS CLIENT, SIR LES 'YA WITH ME?' PATTERSON.

month of its acquisition. Now it was possible for everyone to be like Scrooge McDuck and take a bath in gold; and men with scrolls of silver chest-hair didn't just drape their wives and mistresses in gold, or wear chunky gold jewellery themselves (which they could do more and more as the seventies matured without being branded queer), but they could keep gold ingots under the bed if they wanted to, or bury it in the backyard, and the tax-man need never know.

In the same year, 1976, the hint about greed was taken by six bandits armed with sub-machine guns, who burst into the Victorian Club in Melbourne while bookmakers were settling bets after the Easter race meetings. The $1.4 million stolen in the raid made it Australia's biggest armed robbery to that time.

The encouragement to 'let it all hang out' was starting to feel official. The old wowserism got in the mood, too, and a handful of unofficial nude beaches were given the official nod. Legislation was passed in New South Wales in 1977 by virtue of which discrimination based on sex, race and marital status was rendered unlawful. It prepared the ground for women to take charge, if they could. The aim was to get rid of bias. Employers could no longer indicate that they were looking specifically for a female, or for a male, in their employment advertisements. Men-only and women-only areas in restaurants and the like were prohibited. Lending institutions could no longer refuse loans to single women, de factos and divorcees, or require that husbands sign as guarantor. No more bias!

Actually, 'bias' was a nice old-fashioned word that would soon be overtaken by a new buzz-word, 'discrimination'.

One of the big buzz-words was buzz-word. We'd never heard of the word 'buzz-word' before, but suddenly buzz-word became a buzz-word.

Another buzz-word was sexual harassment, or harassment. That term derives from Harris, the inventor of tweeds, Harris Tweeds. So if a fellow happened to drop his Harris Tweeds accidentally in front of his secretary she deemed herself to have been 'harassed'. A lot of people got complaints about it but it never happened to me. Not one of my research assistants – horn bags, ceiling inspectors, girls Friday – ever moaned about it. Well, they moaned, but not about that.

It became possible even to buy people in the lead-up to the eighties, when buying everything and everybody would become commonplace. The trend was started by the multimillionaire media heir, Kerry Packer, who before the seventies finished bought one of the great national symbols of individuality and personal achievement – the Australian cricket team. It was a move as cheeky and unlikely as buying into any other sacred national institution (such as Qantas or Arnott's Biscuits, which both had to wait until the nineties to be sold). Mr Packer bowled the first ball in 1977, by signing up 13 members of the Australian squad while they were touring England. And then he signed up England's captain, Tony Greig, just to round it off. Where would it all lead? Even the British (under Margaret Thatcher by then but not completely adjusted to the idea that everything publicly owned had its price) were asking the same question. Who knows, next thing Australian businessmen might arrive in England and buy up whole slabs of the country – like villages and landed estates!

Other toilers in industry knew what they wanted, too – but they didn't always get it.

[The character] Lance Boyle was as delightful to act as he was repulsive to watch. While performing him in 1978 it was amusing to scan the stalls and pick out the pious pinkos gazing up ecstatically at the unsavoury opportunist on stage. Their poor little pinched faces always fell most entertainingly when they realised that the odious operator on the boards was one of their own sacrosanct, self-sacrificing trade union lefties …

Lance (on phone to secretary): 'Point one: my trip! I was on that flight from Sydney to Honkers, in economy for the whole trip, with a lot of screaming Indonesian brats. I got off the flight rooted. Now, you remember them meaningful discussions we had with the minister? The minister himself gave me his firm assurance that I would be upgraded from economy to first class and I was bloody not. You remember when they were in deep shit with that new Commonwealth building in Melbourne? The minister told me that if I squared that job away on the quiet he would do everything he could to make this little trip of mine quote "fruitful" unquote. He reckoned the Department would kick the tin on this trip. The result was 9 hours in economy next to the dunnies watching a Charles Bronson fillum I'd seen before with Maureen and the kids at the local drive-in. And to rub my nose in it, I get a squiz through the curtains at first class and there's Rupert bloody Murdoch and Kerry Packer poncing around with glasses of champagne in their hands.

Now, for that little breach of trust, Leone, I want you to ring Clive Hanley first thing in the morning and get him to pull all the machine-maintenance men off the big new Qantas job in Sydney … What do you mean, they're already off? Well pull them off when they get back on.'

Australian trade unionist Lance Boyle takes a break during a fact-finding mission as general secretary of the A.C.U.N.T. He was accompanied on the trip by two members of the Show Girls Union. The Boyle character first appeared in *Isn't It Pathetic At His Age* (1978). Barry Humphries delighted in the moment when 'pious pinkos' in the audience realised that this remarkably offensive man was 'one of their own sacrosanct, self-sacrificing trade union lefties'.

As the seventies compass swung toward the eighties there were still people who couldn't be bought. They were people who would not have done well in the eager eighties, perhaps. But for two of them there was no chance to find out. They were shot … or otherwise disposed of.

One was the anti-drugs campaigner and furniture-store owner Donald Mackay, of the town of Griffith in New South Wales. He was executed gangland-style early one evening as he left his local hotel after buying a wine cask. The evidence of blood on the ground near his Mini Minor van indicated a shooting, but his body was never found.

Coincidentally, someone else who couldn't be bought had connections to the furniture trade too. Juanita Neilsen was heir to the Mark Foy's department store business. She lived in Sydney's Kings Cross, in

SYDNEY'S VICTORIA STREET WAS NEVER SAVED IN THE WAY PUBLISHER JUANITA NEILSEN (above) ENVISAGED. HER CAMPAIGN AGAINST DEVELOPMENT LED TO HER DISAPPEARANCE AND PRESUMED MURDER IN 1975.

beautiful but dilapidated Victoria Street, and her passion was the preservation of that part of Sydney from the developers' hammer. She ran an anti-corruption newsletter, entitled *Now*, with a call to action that brought a murderous response: get rid of her. She was last seen getting into a car with two men in broad daylight in the centre of the Cross. Her body was never found. One supposition is that she was fed down the garbage disposal unit of a local motel.

The 1970s ended with New South Wales pubs being allowed to open on Sundays, bringing them into line with several other states. This was the last impediment to week-long pleasure-seeking. It set the scene for year-long pleasure-seeking, too, and just to symbolise the moment further a new gambling game, Lotto, was introduced by the lotteries authority. It was to be an appropriate threshold to the 1980s.

the

the

the '80s

PARTY of a LIFETIME

1988: THE BICENTENARY

Join the Celebration!

This was the decade

that rolled over in reaction to the hippy-clad seventies and said goodbye to living on dreams without bread. It was when the headband could be thrown away and the long flowing locks of the 'love is all' male could be replaced by the short-back-and-sides of the go-getter. It was when women discovered power dressing; when the Indian cotton shirt could be crumpled into a rag ball and used for buffing the Mercedes-Benz. It was when the tie and the business suit could be worn again with a certain pride. It was when square became hip.

Australian tailoring came of age in the eighties. Most of the suits seen in Sydney and Melbourne were that smart they looked like JR's cast-offs from 'Dallas'. One of our sartorial innovations was the undulating jacket hem. That is to say, the back of an Australian handcrafted mohair and terylene suit coat was always shorter than the front by up to 6 inches, affording extra ventilation to the posterior. Coloured shirts with white collars and cuffs were also popular with merchant bankers and wine tasters.

But don't run away with the idea that we never wore a dinner suit. The only risk was at Canberra cocktail parties when some dickhead might have mistaken you for the drinks waiter. Getting into penguin gear you had to watch out for the sub-tropical weather, particularly when you were sitting in some prestige Yartz venue listening to Roger Woodward or Dame Joan bawling their skulls off. Up-market music on a hot night could make you sweat like buggery, and you could easily rust up the clips on your bow tie.

It was the 'greed is good' decade – and Australians couldn't get enough of it while it lasted. It was the time when wealth meant rocks on the fingers, granite in the kitchen, shirts by

AUSTRALIAN CULTURAL ATTACHÉ SIR LES PATTERSON (right), RESPLENDENT IN A DINNER SUIT, REJOICES IN THE EXCESSES OF THE EIGHTIES. **Previous pages:** PERTH SOCIALITE ROSE HANCOCK (main photo) DISPLAYED ESSENTIAL EIGHTIES ELEGANCE. THE GRIM REAPER (inset right) WAS A POTENT SAFE-SEX SYMBOL THAT ALSO HAD BROADER IMPLICATIONS IN A DECADE WHEN PEOPLE THOUGHT THEY WOULD NEVER HAVE TO FACE THE CONSEQUENCES OF THEIR ACTIONS. A GARISH POSTER (inset below) PROMOTED THE DECIDEDLY ANGLO 'CELEBRATION OF A NATION' IN 1988.

Membery, appliances by Mièle, Möet by the magnum, and mortgages approved by Mooney's. It was the decade when wealth was created overnight and yet the banks owned everything. Super-salesman reigned supreme – even inside people's heads, selling them on the idea that there was something to be had for nothing. It didn't have to be dug from the ground, worked by the hands, carried on the back or earned by the sweat of the brow. For a time, it seemed that everyone had a *scam*.

Where did the idea come from, that something could be had for nothing? One source was financial deregulation. Government controls were lifted, foreign banks were allowed in, the old-fashioned state banks modernised themselves, and building societies were allowed to trade like proper banks. Staid, conservative bank managers

DAME EDNA AND HER MANAGER BARRY HUMPHRIES CAPTURED DURING A QUIETER MOMENT IN THE PARTY DECADE. DAME EDNA, TECHNICALLY A SQUILLIONAIRESS, COPED WITH HER GRIEF OVER HUSBAND NORM'S DEATH BY SPENDING LAVISHLY DURING THE EIGHTIES. SHE USED MONEY AS A SEDATIVE AND WHEN THAT DIDN'T WORK THERE WAS ALWAYS CHAMPAGNE.

were encouraged to 'get with it' and banks advertised themselves in competition with each other and threw their doors wide open. Interest rates went sky-high – as in banana republics and other foreign settings not commonly associated with Australia. But did we notice? Yes. Did it matter? Possibly not – or not yet, anyway.

Money was there for the taking, like a bucket of jewels. Yet something nagged. Was it conscience? Nerves? No, it was just fear of having less than the next person. 'He who dies with the most toys wins.'

Where did the idea come from, that taking out an expensive bank loan would solve all the problems involved in paying it back? It started as a whisper, until it could no longer be refused.

Buy a property on credit. Sell whatever movable assets come along with it. Hold the property for a while, then sell it for more than you paid for it, and start again. Do this all over the place. For you it might

Above: THE CLASSIC EIGHTIES SCAM-MERCHANT, CHRISTOPHER SKASE FLED THE COUNTRY OWING MILLIONS OF DOLLARS AFTER HIS TOURISM AND MEDIA EMPIRE COLLAPSED.

be the house or farm next door; for someone else it might be a construction company, an airline, a brewery, a hotel chain, a scruffy block of land in a tropical backwater that can be promoted as exotic. Despite the effect of the new capital gains tax, this will be highly profitable. Just make sure you get a tax deduction on the interest bill. Show that you are 'solid' by the way you live. Live well. But don't be dull. Pay negative tax and stash away any worthwhile profits in ironclad trusts. Be a caring, loving father and see that your children are well provided for. Ditto in respect of your wife, ex-wife and mistresses. To do a proper job of this, use a Swiss banker to create a trail of assets-shifting that cannot be traced, not even by the most vicious bankruptcy investigator. And bear in mind that if in the end you are asked to pay the ultimate price, and go behind bars, your loved ones will support you, be there for you when you get out, and see that your early dreams come true again … thanks to you.

The buzz-word was *entrepreneur*. It was another word for businessman – but the kind with a disregard for conventional routes to success, a new breed spawned seemingly overnight. If you weren't one, you could become one. In Victoria, clubs for entrepreneurs were established where, for an annual fee, a would-be could hopefully find someone with money to back him.

The big names – those who succeeded, for a while at least – mostly lacked formal education and were defiantly proud of it. These were the corporate cowboys. A few, such as George Herscu, chief executive of the Hooker Corporation, came to the 'greed is good' scene already fully cashed up from earlier careers. They brought their millions with them because they were not content to live quietly and comfortably – they wanted more. Others, such as Alan Bond, of America's Cup fame, originally arrived on the scene with little more than their native cunning and determination. The entrepreneurs applauded stamina and the wisdom of the street. Ethics took a back seat because, as one of them asked, 'Were we going to be good guys, or were we going to be successful?' The thing was to barge through.

The word 'entrepreneur' later acquired such a bad odour that financial journalists stopped using it.

It is not famous names but somewhat faded names that recall these years of froth and bubble. Most of us stood around in stunned wonder as self-selected notables – whether entrepreneurs or otherwise – lived out our fantasies for us. Bond, Edelsten, Capper, Connell, Goward, Hancock, Hawke, Herscu, Hogan, Renouf, Skase – and quite a few others. Where are they now? Some are in Hollywood. Some are in gaol. One is a diplomat emeritus. Some are still jousting with the law from far distant locations, such as Spain. Some are on late-night television, recycling their opinions. Some have cashed in their chips and lie six feet under.

One of the notables, a man few had heard of previously, bought a football team. He bought a pink helicopter too. His name was Geoffrey Edelsten, a doctor who had made money by overturning the genial, low-key image of the general practitioner and establishing a chain of 24-hour clinics. They were the medical equivalent of service stations or Seven Eleven convenience stores, enticing the halt and the lame through doors resembling

Above: ONLY IN THE EIGHTIES AND ONLY IN SYDNEY ... TO THE HORROR OF THE MELBOURNE FOOTBALL ESTABLISHMENT, WHO HAD LENT THE GAME TO NEW SOUTH WALES, THE SYDNEY SWANS INTRODUCED AMERICAN-STYLE CHEERLEADERS, THE SWANETTES, WHO WOULD GO INTO A RAPTUROUS AND RAUNCHY ROUTINE EVERY TIME ITS PIN-UP BOY, PLAYER WARWICK CAPPER, KICKED A GOAL OR REDUCED HIS SHORTS SIZE.

those of Gold Coast casinos. As 1980s enterprises went, the Edelsten clinics were at the honest end of the business curve, or so it seemed. But they needed promotion and Edelsten, having married a fun-loving young wife, Leanne, built a palace for her on several acres of outer-suburban land, and then set about not just buying a Melbourne football team but establishing it in Sydney, where Victorian football was traditionally ignored if not despised. He called his team the Sydney Swans. There was an Ugly Duckling feel to the story, and also an impression that he was doing it for Leanne – or at least indulging 'his and hers' whims.

(At first, attendances at the Swans' home-ground matches were disastrous. But a decade later, long after Geoffrey Edelsten had lost the lot and gone into the entrepreneurs' recovery ward – in his case to gaol for perverting the course of justice – the cultural surgery he performed was deemed successful and the Sydney Swans drew big crowds.)

Footballers were promoted like pop stars by Edelsten's company. At his peak he marketed Warwick Capper, a young leaper with femininely blond hair who invariably wore male hotpants, on the field and off. The hotpants

IF AN ORDINARY BLOKE LIKE BOB HAWKE COULD BECOME PRIME MINISTER THEN AN ORDINARY SIGNWRITER LIKE ALAN BOND COULD BORROW OTHER PEOPLE'S MONEY AND BECOME AN 'ENTREPRENEUR'. HAWKE (LEFT), AT THE LAUNCH OF THE *ENDEAVOUR* PROJECT IN 1987, DISMISSED CRITICISM OF 'BONDY' (RIGHT) AS 'NONSENSE'. BOND WOULD LATER BE DECLARED BANKRUPT AND BE GAOLED FOR CORPORATE CRIMES.

started as Capper's playing gear. Initially he'd worn size-14 footy shorts but nipped them to size 10 to 'hold the Niagaras in'. It was the first time in Australian history that a man's balls were what it took to be briefly famous and passingly fashionable.

Young girls screamed and tried to touch Capper as he toured shopping malls promoting pavlovas. He went to a party at the home of Lady (Mary) Fairfax, where players ran amok and frolicked in the spa. He went on television with the Edelstens as a kind of house pet. We saw him getting dressed in pink, a kind of moving, grooving male centrefold. He was seen in the Edelsten house, training with his long-time girlfriend, Joanne. He was seen playing pool in a white suit and driving a pink Alpha … and then, just as he was on the edge of being forgotten, he got married.

Later an older and wiser Capper recalled the day: 'I got married in '88. I wore a pretty lavish outfit … I saw it in one of the magazines. Joanne said: 'Oh, that'd be great!' So I got one made up in Melbourne. It cost me about $5000 for the outfit, but it was great. It was all skin and leather with big tails. And the tails could come off – after I got married I could still wear it. So instead of John Travolta, it was Warwick Revolting.'

Edna's Eighties

I had a wonderful time in the eighties, but it was an extravagant time. I've always been upfront about my money and I was a squillionairess, technically, according to my Swiss bankers. I was throwing money away with both hands. I suppose, looking back, it was to block my grief over the death of my husband. Norm hadn't been gone very long and I think I used money as a sedative. Spending, spending! Did I spend! I even had a graduate to scatter my scatter cushions. I had a private plane, all that travel, all those clothes, all those holidays, all those staff. I even spent money on my little companion, Madge Alsop (below).

But did it all buy me happiness? The answer, very simply, is yes, yes, yes! 👓

We leapt as high as Warwick Capper in the eighties – and if we dived lower, wasn't it still a 'buzz'?

The ladies' lunch, once held discreetly, perhaps in a city hotel dining room, was now likely to find itself with a national audience. The wives and mistresses of the high-fliers gained celebrity status. 'Red' Bond and 'Pixie' Skase threw the sort of lavish parties at which New York's Ivana Trump would draw the line. The separation between 'old' money and 'new' money blurred. Social columns were filled with the doings of the two 'ladies': Lady (Susan) Renouf, the thrice-married ex-wife of the young parliamentarian Andrew Peacock, of whom it was said that she combined the Australian obsessions of romance and real estate; and Lady Fairfax, of the family that owned, but was about to lose, the venerable *Sydney Morning Herald*. Apart from having football players frolic in her pool, Lady Fairfax also had her own television show.

As the parties raged there were spoilers at work in the corridors of power. In distant Canberra they adjusted the legislative buttons to reflect the social changes going on outside in the real world. It was a full-time job for the nation's many public servants. The Attorney-General's Department was particularly busy drafting legislation. Canberra became the world capital of Repetition Strain Injury (RSI) as old typewriters were thrown out and computer keyboards replaced them. The epicentre of the problem was the Attorney-General's, with the Department of Health running a close second as the whole idea of RSI was researched and investigated. Did it really exist, or was it a way of escaping boring and repetitive work?

GEOFFREY EDELSTEN'S LAVISH MEDICAL CLINICS BOASTED CHANDELIERS AND GRAND PIANOS. THE GOOD DOCTOR (above) MADE SO MUCH MONEY OUT OF MEDIBANK, THE SUPPOSEDLY EGALITARIAN NATIONAL HEALTH SYSTEM, THAT HE BOUGHT THE SYDNEY SWANS FOOTBALL TEAM. ITS STAR FORWARD, WARWICK CAPPER, IS PICTURED (below) WITH WIFE JOANNE ON THEIR WEDDING DAY. THE WHOLE WORLD WAS INVITED TO ANOTHER FAMOUS WEDDING IN THE EIGHTIES WHEN CHARLENE MARRIED SCOTT (right) DURING AN EPISODE OF THE TELEVISION SOAP 'NEIGHBOURS'. TEENAGERS KYLIE MINOGUE AND JASON DONOVAN, WHO PLAYED THE TWO CHARACTERS, WENT ON TO BECOME INTERNATIONAL RECORDING STARS. DAME EDNA HAD BABYSAT THE YOUNG JASON IN MELBOURNE AND PREDICTED HIS SUCCESS FROM A NAPPY READING WHICH REVEALED LOTS OF NUMBER 1'S AND EVEN THE ODD NUMBER 2.

We learnt about a lot of new diseases. One of them was whiplash injury which generally affected Turkish or Greek taxi drivers, enabling them to make great compensation claims. God love them, and the Lord be good to them! The other thing was RSI, which became fairly fashionable. I got RSI at the RSL, funnily enough. But then there was truck driver's bum – a lot of truck drivers had to wear their arses in a sling. And housemaid's knee, penis elbow ... you name it. There was another horrible thing and it was called vibratory white finger. A lot of the blokes working the jackhammers used to get it – you know, clenching their hands, cutting off the blood supply and then going snow white. Amazing.

I once copped that without even using a jackhammer. It happened this way. At one of the nude beaches I created, I happened to be lying in the blazing sun one day in the nuddy with one of my girl Fridays or research assistants, and we were lying pretty close just enjoying ourselves as young people do and I must have fallen asleep because I woke up at the end of the day and I was bright red. Red as a lobster, from head to foot. But funnily enough my finger was completely white.

Dame Edna Puts Scams in the Frame

A big business in the eighties was picture-framing. You could go to the smallest little town and even if there was only one shop it would be a picture framer. Sometimes there wasn't even a store or a police station. Not even a public convenience. But there would always be a picture framer. I wonder who ever got all those pictures framed? People must have been in a constant state of getting things framed. And yet oddly enough, although there were all these framers, I never saw anyone go into a picture framer, or come out of one. I never heard anyone say, 'Oh, Edna, you must come and see our lovely picture frame' or 'We've just had it framed'. Perhaps these people were just whistling in the wind. Perhaps it was a tax loss. It could have been. It could have been a little bit of a scam. That was an eighties word. And there wasn't anyone who wasn't into it. ∞

Australia was not yet like England in having social legislation dismantled. The Labor Party totally dominated Australian politics, and still had plans for bettering the nation through government. Of 22 state and federal elections contested between the years 1981 and 1990 the only win for the (conservative) Liberal Party on the Australian mainland was in New South Wales in 1988. Of course, the shift to Labor, after decades of federal Liberal rule under Menzies (who died in 1978 at the age of 83) and his successors, had been dramatic, but not as radical as some feared and others hoped. In general, Australian politics in the eighties was a battle for the middle ground. As Labor adopted positions more usually associated with the conservatives it became increasingly difficult to define the major political parties in terms of traditional policy positions and philosophies. As a union leader in the sixties and seventies, Bob Hawke had stood his (middle) ground and pushed Labor towards the Left. In 1980 he resigned as ACTU (Australian Council of Trade Unions) leader and was elected to federal parliament. Becoming prime minister in 1983, Hawke remained in the middle and the Liberals shuffled to the Right.

Jack Mundey, instigator of the famous 'green bans' of the seventies, union leader and active environmentalist, felt that the Australian Labor Party in the eighties had sold out. Of Hawke and the party at this time he says: 'We all remember seeing footage of Bob Hawke saying, "My very good friend Alan Bond and my very great friend Kerry Packer" – things you don't expect union leaders to say. Hawke got too close to the corporate sector – and the wrong section of the corporate sector. Keating in many ways continued the same practice. They snuggled in too much with big business, to the detriment of ordinary workers.'

Labor-inspired legislators of the 1970s and 1980s laid the groundwork for an Australia in which women would have more opportunities in the workplace – if they could only manage to stop having fun at lunch. Some had already left the table and pursued a career, postponing or in some cases abandoning altogether the idea of marriage, rejecting the idea of children in favour of a profession, and turning their back on the prospect of family life. Most men offered them platitudes and hollow praise while refusing to change their own ways, and a woman who asserted her ambition was still commonly referred to as a ball-breaker.

Divorce became almost fashionable in the 1980s – which shows what a decadent period it was. There was a lot of high-profile divorces. I suppose the divorce of my daughter Valmai from her husband Mervyn Gittis was pretty big news. As was the divorce of my good friend the Queen's daughter, Anne, from Captain Mark Phillips. The

PRIME MINISTER FOR MOST OF THE DECADE, BOB HAWKE (MIDDLE) AND HIS TREASURER AND SUCCESSOR-IN-WAITING, PAUL KEATING (RIGHT), HAD LITTLE IN COMMON. PICTURED HERE AT OPERA IN THE PARK IN SYDNEY'S DOMAIN, THE SPORTY, BLOKEY, HAIL-FELLOW-WELL-MET HAWKE WAS THERE FOR THE PEOPLE, WHILE THE AESTHETE KEATING WAS THERE FOR THE CULTURE.

Queen and I went through one of the most traumatic experiences a woman can have. Psychologists have said that, for a woman, divorce is a trauma between a hysterectomy and moving house. Or in the Queen's case, moving palace. I feel sorry for Mervyn, who I hadn't much liked, and the children, because they never saw Valmai again. Except occasionally, very occasionally, on 'Crime Stoppers' on TV, holding up a bank … sometimes, sadly, a sperm bank. 👓

In the matter of dealing with broken marital relations the decade opened badly, with the assassination, at point-blank range, of Justice David Opas of the Family Court. He answered a ring on his doorbell and died within minutes, in what was described as an act of revenge on the part of an obviously angry male. Australia was not accustomed to violence from this direction. But the relaxing of divorce rules and the giving of more attention to women's needs to the custody of children led to a further series of attacks. Gelignite became a favoured instrument used in bombings of the homes of Family Court judges, killing the wife of one, damaging the home of another, and devastating the Parramatta (Sydney) premises of the court itself. To the men behind the attacks it seemed that women had taken the power away from them, and they lashed out.

12
INCHES
OF
LES
THE ALBUM

A Live Performance by
Dr. Sir Leslie Colin Patterson, K.B.E.

THE DEMISE OF THE VINYL RECORD BEGAN WITH THE RELEASE OF THE COMPACT-DISC FORMAT IN 1982. SIR LES PATTERSON HELD OUT AGAINST THE ENCROACHMENT OF THE CD WITH HIS 1985 VINYL RELEASE, *12 INCHES OF LES* (left), WHICH INCLUDED HOT TRACKS SUCH AS 'GIVE HER ONE FOR CHRISTMAS' AND 'NEVER TRUST A MAN WHO DOESN'T DRINK'. BARRY HUMPHRIES HIMSELF LET IT ALL HANG OUT AS *CLEO* MAGAZINE'S NOVEMBER 1982 CENTREFOLD (below), IN WHICH HE WAS PHOTOGRAPHED IN EXTRAVAGANT EIGHTIES REPOSE. BARRY RECALLS AT FIRST REJECTING THE INVITATION TO POSE NUDE, BUT THEN BEING PERSUADED BY THE LARGE AMOUNT OF MONEY ON OFFER.

Traditionally, the way out for a much-abused woman, finding little sympathy in the law, had been to kill the bastard and do time. Now, through the courts, women were fighting back.

Australia was a long way from Britain but Margaret Thatcher was seen as a paragon in the sphere of women's power-broking. She mangled the Australian television journalist George Negus, who came to their interview complete with affable manner and 'snag' (Sensitive New Age Guy) moustache to tell the Iron Lady that he regularly met people in the street in England who called her pig-headed. She responded by asking Negus with icy detachment: 'Would you name

them? Which people? Where? When? Who?'

Negus bravely faced her, but had no ready answer.

For a new generation of men, snag-dom meant making concessions and compromises that their fathers had never dreamed of. They found themselves changing nappies

Sir Les Brasses Off

Being a conservationist, as befits the Yartz Portfolio, I'm into nostalgia. I reckon it's a pity we couldn't have saved a few of those old Art Deco 'toilet-style' drinking haunts instead of tarting them up with wall-to-wall carpets, chairs and deodorisers in the dunnies, and giving them phoney olden-day names like 'Captain Cook's Hideaway'. Of course, times have changed and those lovely old colonial-style bars, all tiles for easy cleaning, are now about as hard to find as a pork chop in a synagogue. Now everything's called a brasserie, with Abba and the Bee Gees coming in through holes in the ceiling and a slopey sheila with a nose-stud and a herpes carrier with a moustache dishing out pâté and lasagne to the bourbon-and-coke brigade. I reckon if you went into one of those joints and asked for a beer and a T-bone, they'd give you the bum's rush.

But the beauty of Australian tucker is that it's clean. I generally pick a restaurant that's just been raided by the health authorities. That way you'll be pretty sure a meal there won't give you a dose of the threepenny bits.

and spending several hours at a time alone in the company of their small children. Television was full of the news that fathers were not the fumbling fools we once thought them to be. Dads did the washing up and it began to be conceivable that young men, when they moved away from home, would do their own clothes-washing instead of hauling it back each weekend to be washed by Mum. Men shopped, cooked, and attended prenatal classes. Scientists suggested it might even be possible for men to breastfeed babies. These were the new men, the sensitive men who were (in a phrase first used in public in the eighties) 'discovering their feminine side'. Where would it all end? There was a backlash as documentaries showed men bringing society to a standstill by having to leap from the car and supervise children's toilet stops. Perhaps the confusion was well illustrated when the first crisis centre for men was established (in Canberra, of course) in 1986. And to the sniggers and scoffs of feminists, the Men's Movement began.

But where would the men gather for their meetings? Why not over lunch …

What Australians were in those not-so-distant days was also what they ate. Personal identity was not complete without being seen (preferably on TV) lunching in prominent (if short-lived) eateries.

Food became a social cement and the celebrity chef a fixture. There was a last-ditch stand by the Australian Meat and Livestock Board to maintain older values in city brasseries and boutique dining places, and to insist (with the help of the painfully sincere advertising guru John Singleton) that vegetarianism was next to homosexuality and drug-taking, and that meat and beer were what the 'normal person' ate and drank. But it didn't take on – those days were over. We knew better in the eighties. Gluttony took too many attractive forms to be restricted to just one.

The idea of concluding business over lunch was not a new concept in Australian cities. Until the treasurer in the Hawke Government, the youthful and Honourable Paul Keating, introduced unpopular measures to render the traditional business lunch non–tax-deductible, lunch was the business at hand. The idea was to get 'monumentally drunk' for the rest of the afternoon and recover the shreds next morning. With eating places proliferating, business and pleasure could be combined almost anywhere around the country. Churches, warehouses and derelict wharves became trendy restaurants where 'snow peas and quenelles of roulade au coulis' could be washed down with the obligatory bottle of heavily wooded chardonnay.

Salads were not salads without some contribution from a florist. Elle Macpherson, an embryonic fashion icon, was seen on television toying with a lettuce leaf. Was she a thing of the future, or of the past?

Salad days or not, gross was good in the 1980s and there were some things that only serious money could buy. When the entrepreneurs came to marrying off their daughters or showing off their houses, they had lavish dinners. When they served the soup, it was graced with floating gold leaf. If the caterers' bills (running into the millions for single events) were never paid, what did it matter? My gross was better than your gross.

This was the scene at home in Australia. VIPs visiting London, especially Buckingham Palace, encountered a quite different millieu.

Australian business, of course, had long forgotten the cruelties of World War II, and traded wool, wheat, coal and iron ore with Japan by the shipload. Japan returned the favour with cars, consumer goods, tourists ... and finally with food. The 1980s were when Australians swallowed their pride, tensed their stomachs and ate raw fish for the first time. There was deep suspicion of seaweed as a foodstuff, too, but the publicity given to a business operation in Tasmania that harvested Australian varieties to send to Japan made things easier. If it was ours it must be alright.

As well, the guilt that came from greed could be disciplined by small dollops of pleasure – as patrons of the new cuisine were to find.

> **Dame Edna on Froth and Bubble**
>
> Mineral water was another big thing in the eighties. It was a clever man who could tell you that what came out of the tap wasn't good for you. Instead it was supposed to be more wholesome if it came out of a bottle and tasted of old knives and forks. You could get it fizzy or you could get it plain. Personally I think it's very overrated, but the fizzy stuff was the Earl Grey of mineral water.
>
> And that was another thing that happened in the eighties. When you said, 'Could I have a cup of tea, please?', people would say, 'What kind?' Do me a favour! 🕶

Nouvelle cuisine was where they served you little tiny things. Minimalism, really. It was an eighties thing – particularly in food. Some of this nouvelle cuisine could barely be seen on the plate. You paid through the nose for something you could probably inhale through the nose. 🕶

Coming from the outfield, though, was something *big*. It was a dish that made its way on to certain menus. Not that Australians ever ate it themselves. But there was nothing we liked better than to serve to tourists something we despised without knowing anything about. It was 'croc', the flesh of a very large reptile.

Attacks by northern Australian crocodiles were a scary theme throughout the 1980s. The species' numbers had grown rapidly since the introduction of protection in 1971. An American visitor, Ginger Meadows, was taken as she was swimming at Kings Cascades on the Prince Regent River, in the Kimberley region. Elsewhere, a hunter named Rodney Ansell made a lucky escape, and was flown south for talk shows. The most spectacular case involved an environmentalist, Val Plumwood, attacked while canoeing at the start of the rainy season in Kakadu National Park. Pursued on the water, she tried to climb into the branches of an overhanging tree. But the crocodile grabbed her and took her through an underwater

TOURISTS ATTRACTED TO THE OUTBACK BY THE MOVIE *CROCODILE DUNDEE* NEEDED TO BE REMINDED NOT TO SWIM WITH THE CROCODILES. UNFORTUNATELY, NOT EVERYONE HEEDED THE WARNING.

'death roll'. She broke free, but the animal caught her and again forced her beneath the surface. Remarkably, she escaped to the river bank and managaged finally to claw her way to safety. Val Plumwood suffered horrific bite wounds and lacerations and spent much time in hospital. She offended public opinion by calling for the croc's life to be saved, arguing that in trying to eat her it was only doing its duty.

Plumwood escaped celebrity but attracted blame. Finally she was forgotten, not because she seemed to know what she was talking about, or because she openly admitted a rather foolhardy affinity with the natural world, but because she wouldn't play the publicity game to the hilt and feed the 1980s hunger for myth-making. If a story could not be appropriated for fun and profit, then it was no use at all. For the moment, the ferocious crocodile had replaced the cuddly marsupial as our national symbol, and that was that.

Someone who knew all about this was the actor/comedian Paul Hogan, who saw the young adventurer Rodney Ansell on the TV programme 'Parkinson in Australia', and spun a tale from it. Ansell's account of his mauling in tropical wetlands ended up as an integral part of the film *Crocodile Dundee*. Ansell went back to the Northern Territory to muster cattle while Paul Hogan went to live in Hollywood, where the simple story of a man and his croc made Australia 'the flavour of the month' and earned a sequel.

We had come a long way from the fifties and sixties, when Australian reporters waited on the airport tarmac to ask visiting American stars what they thought of Australia before they had even swatted their first fly. Now Australian reporters jetted to the States and asked Americans the same question …

'We're different, aren't we? Don't our actors prove it?'

The answer from Hollywood agents was that they liked Australian actors because they fitted in with the American marketplace – not because they differed! One agent, when queried, couldn't think of any names. Weren't we all called Brian or Bruce?

There was an Australian actor in Hollywood more different than most, however. His name was Neil Bell, and he cornered the market in dog impersonations. He said he would do anything, almost, to get a part in a film. But he missed out on the big one – playing Australia's most wanted dog.

The facts were simple, weren't they?

PAUL HOGAN MIMICKED THE LACONIC AUSSIE IN THE HIT FILM *CROCODILE DUNDEE*. HE GOT THE IDEA FOR THE MOVIE AFTER HEARING STOCKMAN RODNEY ANSELL TELL OF HIS MAULING IN THE OUTBACK BY A CROC. WHILE HOGES WENT TO LIVE IN HOLLYWOOD, ANSELL WENT BACK TO HIS JOB MUSTERING CATTLE.

In August 1980 a tourist camping near Ayers Rock, central Australia, raised an alarm. Mrs Lindy Chamberlain, wife of a Seventh Day Adventist pastor, said she saw a dingo leaving the tent where she had left her baby and the older children. At first she thought it might have bitten the baby and taken something else from the tent. There was blood inside, but no baby. Mrs Chamberlain felt among the bedding on the ground. She ran out screaming, chasing the dog, but it disappeared into the darkness.

Initial police reports supported Mrs Chamberlain's account. But, by its very nature, the incident was shrouded in mystery. 'Whatever happened,' said a police officer on the spot, 'there is no chance the baby could have survived the night in the freezing temperatures after it was taken.'

It was a tragedy, a joke, the birth of an Australian tall story: 'By jingo, a dingo got my baby.' Public opinion ran one way and then another like a chook with its head cut off. The Chamberlains were practitioners of devil worship. The baby's name, Azaria, was peculiar. What sort of people would give a baby such a name? Didn't it mean 'sacrifice in the desert'? On balance, most Australians believed that the dingo didn't do it. Dingo experts said a dingo *could* do it, but what did that prove to anyone?

The inquest of the Alice Springs coroner found that the baby had been taken by a dingo, but that Azaria's body had been disposed of 'by a person or persons unknown'. The coroner totally exonerated the

Chamberlains and stated that the couple had been subjected to 'probably the most malicious gossip ever witnessed in this country.'

If it felt like an end to the matter for the exhausted Chamberlains, they were wrong. A year later the inquest was reopened. Sensational new evidence was brought forward – with expert witnesses – relating to presumed blood found in the Chamberlains' car. Another year passed. In 1982 Lindy Chamberlain, convicted on a charge of murder, was sentenced to life imprisonment with hard labour. Her husband Michael was found guilty of being an accessory after the fact. The plight of the Chamberlains and the guilt or innocence of the dingo made any other dinner-party conversation redundant. A docu-drama was made, using dramatised scenes based on transcripts of court reportage except for one fictionalised grab – a scene in the desert where Lindy tells her husband that she did it.

Three years and four months later the evidence was discredited, and Lindy was released from gaol. Most of those Australians who had contributed to a wave of public guilt-hysteria now believed that not-guilty was the case. Dingo-lovers were filmed patting their pets and saying that they had received letters asking them not to testify. Another year passed, and the Chamberlains were pardoned by the Northern Territory Government.

'I am not interested in a pardon for something I haven't done,' said Lindy. 'Somebody up there must be confusing granting a pardon with quashing a conviction – it's not even remotely the same.'

Somebody else up there must have taken the point. In September 1988, six years after the trial, the Northern Territory Court of Criminal Appeal quashed the couple's convictions.

One famous Australian, displaying a high degree of empathy with Lindy Chamberlain and her suffering, later chose to satarise the confused national mood over the affair.

When Azaria Chamberlain was abducted by a dingo – and I happen to know it was a dingo – I felt such a strong sense of identification because my own daughter, Lois, had been stolen from me. I'd missed the early-morning feed and Lois was taken from me by a rogue koala. They found the footprints on the verandah and in the bush nearby. My daughter has never reappeared – in the same way as Azaria. My theory and that of many zoologists is that she could still be with a caring koala family. I hope so, and I hope one of those koalas is watching this programme and that my daughter comes back to me. She will not be as she was, bless her heart. She'll be older and of course she'll be feral. She will reek, certainly, of eucalyptus leaves, but she'll be my daughter all the same and she'll be very, very welcome.

Of course, since Lois was stolen, I suppose the koalas – I don't know what kind of communication lines there are between koalas and dingoes, but I think the abduction was a copycat case. I think so. However, there is a chance – another option – that my daughter was taken by aliens. And so, you'll have to excuse me, but I have to go and watch the 'X Files', because she might crop up there. 🎭

OPPOSITE: BEFORE *CROCODILE DUNDEE*, THE TRAGIC CASE OF BABY AZARIA CHAMBERLAIN AND THE DINGO HELPED PUT AUSTRALIA'S FAUNA ON THE MAP. THE ENSUING TRIALS AND THE CONVICTION OF HER MOTHER LINDY (PICTURED HERE WITH HUSBAND MICHAEL AND A PHOTOGRAPH OF AZARIA) WERE FAVOURITE TOPICS OF CONVERSATION. IN 1988 LINDY WAS EXONERATED AND MERYL STREEP WENT ON TO PLAY HER IN THE MOVIE *EVIL ANGELS* (RELEASED INTERNATIONALLY AS *A CRY IN THE DARK*).

Sir Les and the Heroic Signwriter

One of the greatest moments in my life was standing there with Bondy watching *Australia II* come around the finishing line and winning that magnificent trophy. There's our Bondy – just a miserable little pommy. A signwriter coming out to Australia, making good, buying the boat, winning the big race. I hugged him. 'You beauty, Bondy,' I said. 'You're a national hero. You're an honorary Australian now, pal. You can do whatever you like. You can screw Australia for everything they've got as far as I'm concerned.' Well, the silly bastard took my advice. Now he's enjoying the vertical suntan – he's in gaol, and what is he now? A pommy bastard again.

While Americans discovered Australia through dingo mythology, *Crocodile Dundee*, and *Mad Max* movies (in which an unknown actor called Mel Gibson wrecked cars in a futuristic outback populated by shaggy motorcycle gangsters), Australians found a long-lost parallel universe of their own.

It was on Australian soil.

Western Australia was, like Australia to the Americans, always too distant to visit. It languished, unknown and undervalued, for decades. Occasionally a prominent easterner would be revealed to have originated in 'the West'. The great wartime prime minister, John Curtin, had come from there. So had a number of prominent novelists, poets and painters. But suddenly the word got out. Something more interesting than art and politics was happening in 'WA' and the rest of the country scented profit. Money was being reinvented. People in Perth, the state capital, were reputed to follow the fortunes of their millionaires as other people followed their football teams. They watched the television news nightly, to see yet another old shack being bulldozed on the banks of the Swan River to make way for houses that were acres in extent. The millionaires all lived in much the same street, all in the same suburb, Peppermint Grove, and they competed with each other to detail their houses in the fullest 1980s style, with gold-plated plumbing, marble halls, uncountable bathrooms, and gardens transformed by instant full-size trees.

In the mad old eighties I loved going abroad: England, France, America, Western Australia. We in Sydney and Melbourne never thought about Perth until the eighties – until suddenly Perth was the place where there were such things as tycoons. They were people we'd never heard of. They had ordinary names. They used to pull down a whole street of suburban houses and they'd call it a super-block for some reason, and they'd build a great big, rather tasteless home there. Of course, most of them, poor loves, ended up in prison getting what they call the vertical suntan.

But in those days their parties were legendary. Whenever they bought a post-impressionist painting they had a party. Whenever they bought a yacht or won a race there'd be a lovely party. The flowers would be flown in from Melbourne, the frocks and the socialites from Sydney. The oysters, the lobsters – it was incredible. It was another world. It was Babylon. It was Hollywood in the thirties. We'd go there, and there'd be the Skases and the Connells and Rose Hancock and her late husband – when he was still alive.

And the Bonds, of course, lording it over everybody – that legendary couple. They had marvellous parties in their mansion and I'd be there in the midst of it all. I was a much sought-after guest. I was on the 'A' list, of course, whereas my bridesmaid was on the 'F' list. It was quite a way down. I said to Alan: 'Oh, can't you nudge her up just a few?

PERTH'S EILEEN 'RED' BOND WITH THE AMERICA'S CUP (above), WON BY HUSBAND ALAN'S *AUSTRALIA II* (left) IN 1983. THEIR YACHTING VICTORY PUT WESTERN AUSTRALIA ON THE MAP – AND HELPED BOND REAP MILLIONS FROM INVESTORS. THE BONDS WERE A 'LEGENDARY COUPLE', ACCORDING TO DAME EDNA, WHO ATTENDED MANY OF THEIR LAVISH PARTIES IN THE EIGHTIES. UNFORTUNATELY FOR BONDY THE PARTY CAME TO AN ABRUPT HALT AND HE ENDED UP GETTING THE 'VERTICAL SUNTAN' IN GAOL.

You know, to the 'C' list for example?' He said: 'Well, why, Edna?' I said: 'She is my bridesmaid, or significant other.'

But that's not true, really, because Madge Alsop could hardly be called a significant other. More like insignificant other, when you come to think of it.

But they were the eighties – they were mad!

The living legend of the West was a roughly spoken, monstrously wealthy old-timer named Lang Hancock. As a young minerals opportunist, Hancock had the ruthlessness needed to grab a mountain of iron ore in the Pilbara region and to do deals that pushed aside other parties who were there before him – including local Aboriginal people and anyone else who got in his way or wouldn't play his game. Hancock badgered parliaments with a development philosophy of the kind that twentieth-century Australian governments had never been able to resist. He drew sky-pictures of railroads, ports, towns and even cities flourishing where

IRON-ORE MAGNATE LANG HANCOCK MET HIS FLAMBOYANT WIFE ROSE (AT LEFT, WITH HER DAUGHTER) IN THE PHILIPPINES WHERE HE HAD GONE IN SEARCH OF A WOMAN TO TEND TO HIS GERIATRIC NEEDS. THE YOUNGER BRIDE COMFORTED THE AGEING MAGNATE UNTIL HE DIED AND THE INEVITABLE BATTLE OVER HIS ESTATE BEGAN.

there were just bare rock, a few shady waterholes, and fierce heat most of the year. It was in the region of Marble Bar, the hottest place in Australia.

Eventually Hancock saw the planned mines and railroads operating day and night, shipping ore from Hamersley Iron's Mt Newman site to Port Hedland, and he had his millions totting up daily. But it wasn't enough for him. He proposed using nuclear bombs to blast new harbours along the coast. He proposed all sorts of unpleasant solutions, too, to the problem of environmentalists, communists, radicals, homosexuals and just plain ordinary folk who bothered his thinking. He was the mining industry's Dr Strangelove, and strangely enough it was love that reduced him to size.

Although not strictly a Lady, Rose Hancock was Perth's own Imelda Marcos figure, and in making her his second wife the iron Lang proved to be putty. Like many other ageing Australian men who were dissatisfied with the feisty, independent-minded women produced by the bra-burning generation, Hancock had gone to the Philippines in search of a docile, domesticated second partner. He returned with a homemaker, but one who matched his tendency to plan things on an immense scale. Nor was she docile. Towards the end of her husband's life, when he was raking in at least $12 million a year in royalties from Hamersley Iron alone, Rose had few problems in helping him spend it. But just before he died there were reports that Hancock had obtained a restraining order against her, and immediately following his death there were rumours that he may have been poisoned or drugged. The funeral was delayed while Gina, Hancock's daughter from his first marriage, wrangled with Rose over who should be in charge of the burial arrangements. In his will Hancock had stipulated that any beneficiary contesting the will would be disentitled to a share. It made both women sizzle.

The Recently Released Daryl Dalkeith

DARYL DALKEITH, PICTURED ABOVE WEARING TRADEMARK MAGNUM SUNGLASSES AND WITH THE UBIQUITOUS MOBILE PHONE AT THE READY, WAS THE ARCHETYPAL EIGHTIES ENTREPRENEURIAL SPIV. HE FIRST APPEARED IN HUMPHRIES' 1993 SHOW *LOOK AT ME WHEN I'M TALKING TO YOU.*

Allo! Daryl Dalkeith, Dalkeith Holdings. Dazza, I'm generally called. I come from Perth. It must be something about the Indian Ocean, the influence of the mysterious East striking that coast, that we produce a remarkable number of visionaries.

I had a very nice property in Palm Beach that I no longer own – it's now owned by the receivers. But it's the old 'tall poppy' thing for Australia's visionaries. Bondy warned me it would happen. In another age I would have been knighted. Us visionaries were victims of an orchestrated, relentless and unremitting politcal vendetta. We should have complained to Amnesty International. We were all working in the national interest then, only the nation didn't know it.

They've tipped the bucket on us but I've remained very, very loyal to Australia.

I'm back on the road. Never been fitter. That slammer was like a health farm. It's better than Camp Eden.

I was born with this entrepreneurial streak. I've always been a winner and I've had the advantage of having a low profile, of being a silent achiever, and now I'm back in business. Like Paul Keating, I'm interested in the big picture. I'm not a bitter man. I've lost a lot but I'll build my empire again.

My wife Trish came from Sydney. She was a hostess on TAA: another high-flier, and still serves a nice cup of coffee. She's skiing with Ashley and Nicholas. We are separated. 'It's not much fun living with a tall poppy' were her final words to me. ✍

Tania Verstak, Russian migrant and Miss Australia 1961, also married a successful Perth businessman, Peter Young, and settled in the West. She remembers Perth in the eighties as an exciting era. 'We had all the big names and the big parties. And of course, the America's Cup being won by Alan Bond, the whole city came alive with celebrations. He put Fremantle on the map. There were some fantastic parties.'

When it came to high-flying with style, nobody could compete with Alan Bond, the English-born signwriter who had migrated to Australia as a young teenager and had risen to the role of knockabout prime ministerial companion. In 1983, the year that his fellow West Australian, Bob Hawke, became prime minister, Bondy headed the syndicate that successfully raced *Australia II* in the America's Cup. Bondy and Hawkie made it a national event, which the novelist Patrick White described as 'the

AS PRIME MINISTER FOR MOST OF THE EIGHTIES, BOB HAWKE GOVERNED WITH A SHARP TONGUE AND A POPULAR STYLE. 'HAWKIE' WAS A MAN OF THE TIMES: CHEERLEADER FOR THE CORPORATE BUCCANEERS AND A SNAG WHO COULD CRY AT THE DROP OF A HAT AND ADMIT TO HIS MARITAL INFIDELITIES ON NATIONAL TELEVISION.

overheated fizz of artificially inseminated patriotism'. After the victory the famous cup was brought to Perth, but the Americans won it back four years later, and the imprint of excitement was gone from our national psyche as if it had never been stamped there.

Bondy was not content just to enjoy whatever credit could buy, but soared to new heights. While Dr Edelsten toyed with his pink helicopter, Bond soared above Australian cities in an airship. At the peak of his reputation he paid $80 million dollars for Van Gogh's 'Irises', demonstrating unchallengeable love of art. It was world news. Film of the auction showed Bond straining for words to describe the qualities of painting that made *these* flowers just so bloody splendiferous. Then, to confirm a tendency in the intellectual direction, Bond founded his own fully fee-paying tertiary institution, Bond University, on the Gold Coast. Perth's multimillionaires were on the world map. They were backed to the hilt by local politicians, who didn't dare ask themselves if there was actually any money there at all.

It was suggested by the Melbourne *Age* that the Western Australian premier, Brian Burke, affectionately known as Burkie, had put a new spin on the Westminster system by helping to reinvent it as 'WA Inc'. Said the *Age*: 'Parliament became a shelf company run mostly for the convenience of colourful business identities. Burkie took the ideology out of statecraft: it was, he demonstrated, merely commerce under another name. And he arranged the marriage that most of us thought impossible. He coaxed Labor, formerly the angel of the battlers, into bed with the fast money men and a certain amount of rough handling ensued.'

Elsewhere, the bad signs were there from the start for those who cared to look – or smell. So-called 'bottom of the harbour' tax schemes exposed in 1982 showed that respected citizens were involved in tax rorts, selling companies to sham directors and sinking their tax liabilities in the process. Public figures

Right: DAME EDNA IN THE SPECTACULAR GLADIOLI DRESS WHICH WAS A *HAUTE COUTURE* HIGHLIGHT OF THE DECADE. THE MOONEE PONDS MEGASTAR WAS THE ESSENTIAL EIGHTIES WOMAN AND ALMOST A PERSONIFICATION OF THE PERIOD. LIKE LINDY CHAMBERLAIN SHE HAD LOST A BABY, ALTHOUGH FEW EVER HEARD THE STORY OF HOW LOIS WAS TAKEN BY A FERAL KOALA. EDNA ALSO SUFFERED THROUGH THE DIVORCE OF HER OTHER DAUGHTER, VALMAI, A TRAUMATIC EXPERIENCE FOR ANY MOTHER. HOWEVER, SHE DIDN'T SHARE THE NATION'S RELISH FOR *NOUVELLE CUISINE*. 'YOU PAID THROUGH THE NOSE FOR SOMETHING YOU COULD PROBABLY INHALE THROUGH THE NOSE,' SHE SNIFFED.

had their little schemes, too. The Builders' Labourers Federation, a national union, was deregistered in 1986, a year after its Melbourne-based general secretary, Norm Gallagher, was gaoled for taking bribes from developers.

But Sydney could hold its head high as the place where it all began.

I have to tell you I find Sydney liberating. When I was a housewife/actress in Melbourne I was asked to come up here. My friends and advisers – including Barry Humphries, my early mentor before he started putting his hand in the till – all advised me: no one will get the point of you in Sydney. They said: 'You're far too genteel and far too Melbourne.' Anyway, I came to Sydney and, if anything, I was received better than in Melbourne. Quite frankly, just between you and me, I've always felt a little bit freer in Sydney; my skirts are a little bit shorter, my language is a little freer than it usually gets.

When I came to Sydney I began to throw gladdies in a backhand sort of way at the audience, which I hadn't done in Melbourne. I, who can't throw a tennis ball across a room, can get a glad to the gods!

So my backhand has got better in Sydney – the city of backhanders, of course … where the backhander was invented. 🎭

Other states looked on smugly as Sydney identities paid for their wrongdoing. Even the NSW Chief Stipendiary Magistrate saw the inside of the clink for attempting to pervert the course of justice. Eventually the prisons minister himself, Rex Jackson, was given seven years for conspiracy in matters concerning the prisoner early-release scheme. Later his sentence was increased to 10 years.

Roughness at the bottom demanded a touch of roughness at the top. While the decade began with Malcolm Fraser as prime minister, his hold on power was already shaky, and predictions that he would become another Menzies had proved false. Bob Hawke swept into power in the 1983 federal election with a career and a persona that appealed to the broader social base that Labor had been targeting since Gough Whitlam was party leader.

The prime minister, Bob Hawke, was a man my mother would have described as C-O-M-M-O-N, and my mother wasn't the only person who would so describe the little darling. But I like a sensitive man in politics. I like a man who can cry. Though he later confessed to me (and he was crying even when he confessed to me) that the reason he used to burst into tears so often was that he, and only he, knew how much money Australia owed the World Bank. And he was crying at the thought of the next prime minister going through the books and finding out.

I like a man who cries. I like making men cry. In fact I like making women cry – and children. It's just a gift I've got. It was given to me. It's rather marvellous, actually. 🎭

If Australian men were releasing their emotions and trying out their identity as snags, then they had their perfect role model. The son of a Methodist minister, Bob Hawke was a Rhodes Scholar and a unionist, a crusader against the White Australia Policy and a supporter of multiculturalism, a hero of the underdog and respected by business. He was also a sports fanatic with an appeal to women voters, a leader whose image fused strength with the common touch. He was a dedicated drinker who swore off alcohol during his time in office, and earned the admiration of a nation of boozers for doing so.

WHILE REVEREND FRED NILE LED GOD-FEARING HOMOPHOBES IN PRAYERS FOR RAIN, SYDNEY'S HOMOSEXUAL COMMUNITY TOOK TO THE STREETS FOR THE ANNUAL GAY AND LESBIAN MARDI GRAS PARADE. IN THE 1989 EVENT NILE BECAME A CENTRAL SATIRICAL FIGURE WHEN HIS HEAD WAS CARRIED ON A PLATTER – ACCOMPANIED BY THE SISTERS OF PERPETUAL INDULGENCE.

Well, old Bob Hawke was, and is, a sipper. Good luck to him. The Lord be good to him; God love him. But I said to him and I said it frank: 'If you want my input you'll knock off the grog and go on the wagon.' Well, he has – more or less, on and off. Whereas I don't drink at all. I never drink – unless I'm thirsty. In case thirst should overtake me I always have a nice chilled bottle of chardonnay in the bathroom, sitting in the cistern right behind the throttling pit. I just lift the white porcelain lid and there it is – it's delicious. The other morning I got a bit thirsty, so I lifted the lid, poured a glass and drank it straight down. The wife's set of false teeth happened to be in that glass and I swallowed them whole. Consequently, Lady Patterson can't go to state occasions these days, and I have to be careful if I sit down or I could bite me bum.

Bob Hawke's vulnerabilities, it seemed, were everyone's. He cried while talking about his daughter's drug problems. He cried about the students in Beijing's Tiananmen Square. He cried over his wife's plastic surgery. In one of the decade's most embarrassing television moments, he said that Kissinger's statement on power as an aphrodisiac hadn't worked for him. But he stumbled on, and confessed his marital indiscretions to a confessor – his probing biographer, eventually to be his second wife, the author Blanche D'Alpuget.

Bob Hawke's sentimentalism was matched by a vigorous public style that responded to the dominant rough-house events of the day. As the decade partied on, word leaked out that the new breed of entrepreneur was not necessarily a role model for all Australians. In order to quash this unhappy idea, it was necessary for Hawkie to issue a prime ministerial statement about Bondy: 'There's a lot of sloppy talk going around this

'Marsha and the Pollies Girls' at the Gay Mardi Gras parade. No amount of moral indignation was going to stop these girls from having a good time.

country at the moment that somehow there should be no place in the concerns of a federal Labor government for the Alan Bonds of this world. Now, I want to repudiate that nonsense unequivocally. It would be an entirely perverse concept if we didn't recognise the enormous contribution of Alan Bond and the other great entrepreneurs and risk-takers of our country.'

Winning the America's Cup had been worth it. We all had our memories. Isaac Newton's 1680s aphorism, that for every action there is an equal and opposite reaction, applied just as well in the 1980s. After a while, those who had dashed West for the parties of the century could barely remember where Perth was on the map. The spotlight flicked back to Sydney, where in 1978 the first Gay Mardi Gras had been held. By the mid 1980s the Mardi Gras was a national event, and would eventually be televised live by the national broadcaster, earning it the homophobic soubriquet, the 'Gay-Bee-Cee'.

Thanks to commerce, what used to be a consensual act committed behind closed doors or in darkened doorways was henceforth seen as pivotal to Australia's sophistication as a world nation. Putting it another way, by the mid 1980s it was clear that money could be made from gay spenders. While laws were slow to change – Tasmania would not cease outlawing homosexuality until 1997 – prejudice took a holiday when the dollar sign was waved, and around Mardi Gras time the mass migration of homosexuals from all over the world, but particularly from wealthy America, was a business bonanza too good to miss.

Previously inconceivable alliances came out of the closet and on to the open street, as the language of contempt became words of pride in Mardi Gras banners such as 'Dykes and Poofters for Jesus'.

Other Christians, caring little for money, were incensed at the turning of Sydney's Oxford Street into an advertisement for deviance. They prayed for rain. They prayed for the wrath of God and Just Vengeance. Australia's most relentless homophobe, the Reverend Fred Nile, flaunted his opinions by walking around with placards reading: 'God made Adam and Eve, not Adam and Steve.' The Reverend Nile was a spoiler. The party had only just begun and he wanted it finished.

He joined the AIDS argument. There was no doubt in the minds of Mardi Gras critics that AIDS, a disease unknown before the eighties, was a disease of gays and sprang directly from homosexual behaviour (evidence of heterosexual transmission notwithstanding). Australia's first AIDS-related death occurred in Melbourne in

THE FIRST AIDS-RELATED DEATH OCCURRED IN MELBOURNE IN 1983. AFTER FIVE YEARS OF DEBATE ABOUT THE SO-CALLED 'GAY PLAGUE', THE GOVERNMENT LAUNCHED AN ADVERTISING CAMPAIGN WITH IMAGES LIKE THIS, HIGHLIGHTING THE DANGERS OF UNPROTECTED SEX. SAFE SEX HAD BECOME OFFICIAL GOVERNMENT POLICY.

1983. A year later, with AIDS hysteria spreading, the Federal Government established a national AIDS Task Force to research the issue and educate the public. It proved effective, although in Tasmania and Queensland, each a hotbed of conservative politicians, there was resistance to both information and condoms, and panic mounted about a 'gay plague'.

The move didn't stop the party, however. What the curmudgeonly critics didn't realise was that another kind of social change was coming, in which it sometimes *helped* to be gay. When the young star of 'Neighbours', Jason Donovan, on the eve of releasing a new album, issued a press statement to prove that he was both hetero and retro, his song sank without trace. On the other hand a dab of heterosexuality did no harm to Jason's screen buddy, Kylie Minogue. After deciding that her innocent image was no sort of alternative to Madonna's underwear flaunting, Kylie appeared in her own underwear and soon afterwards was crowned 'Woman of the Decade' by the model Jerry Hall and the television host Clive James.

IN THE EARLY EIGHTIES BILLBOARD-USING GRAFFITISTS AGAINST UNHEALTHY PROMOTIONS (BUGA UP) WAS THE NEMESIS OF CIGARETTE AND ALCOHOL ADVERTISERS. ITS ACTIVITIES REFLECTED, ALBEIT ILLEGALLY, WIDESPREAD COMMUNITY SENTIMENT WHICH EVENTUALLY RESULTED IN THE BANNING OF TOBACCO ADVERTISING.

'In the eighties,' James recalled later, 'Australia was turning into the world's paradise. It already was a paradise, but the world had started to know. They'd seen the shrimps go on the barbie, they'd heard about the food and the wine. They thought Australia was heaven. And they were absolutely right ... The things we thought were missing in the fifties, and the things we became hysterically self-conscious about in the Whitlam era, and after the Whitlam era, had settled down into an existence which was simply unmatched in the western world. And remains so. You're more wealthy and more equal in Australia at less social cost than anywhere else on the planet. This is simply the truth. There are problems, of course, but they're not like the rest of the world.'

A rather less official task force called BUGA UP (Billboard-Using Graffitists Against Unhealthy Promotions) also found success in pricking consciences and altering national attitudes. BUGA UP focused on the national hero Paul Hogan who, thanks to his tobacco-advertising efforts, they said, was about as heroic as a man selling poisoned candy to a child. Hogan was the face promoting Winfield cigarettes whose slogan, 'Anyhow, 'ave a Winfield', was inseparable from Crocodile Dundee's laconic style. Every time his billboard face went up in an Australian city or town it was attacked with spray cans and given the sick, sorrowful features of a terminal smoker. Charged with vandalism, BUGA UP injected a note of morality into the mood of the times – the 'Hoges' billboards themselves, the organisation said, were an act of vandalism. So the law was changed and television commercial breaks became filled with advertisements for matches instead. The slogan for Redheads (Australia's most popular brand) was 'Strike up a friendship'. Now, what was to be lit from that? Obviously a cigarette.

Paul Hogan went on from cigarette advertising to spruiking for Foster's lager. It was a big winner while it lasted. Whereas Russia exported Communism, the United States exported Capitalism, Australia exported Fosterism throughout the world. As a national icon it was somehow appropriate. We were no longer content to export our national mythologies of kangaroos, bushmen and bronzed Aussies. We were promoting a product far closer to the nation's soul: booze.

Then, when Paul Hogan's image needed a rest from booze, he proceeded to sell Australia as a tourist destination. For this he was named Australian of the Year.

Money wasn't the only preoccupation of the 1980s. There was also sex. If the years were, hopefully, the last decade in which people were convinced they couldn't live without smoking, they were also the time when many feared they would be asked to live without sex. The sixties and seventies had allegedly cleared the air on the matter, but for the randy male the eighties were a minefield of sexual taboos – his dominance in the field was passing – and yet for the hopeful female they were a desert empty of worthwhile opportunities. One of the most popular television shows of the period, 'Perfect Match', saw young people, who invariably liked windsurfing and raging, partnered with those of like mind. Sent away for weekends together, couples returned with their specifications for the perfect partner still intact. Mostly the result was a slightly miserable mutual disdain. Meanwhile, the predatory employer, the typing-pool prowler, learned – in a somewhat puzzled and picked-upon fashion – that his personal pleasure in the grope wasn't what it was all about.

As the hangover followed the party, and indigestion followed the business lunch, the financial orgy of the eighties was bound to have its own nasty end.

The tycoons of the day did not go down without screaming and kicking. They saw themselves shift from being public role models and Masters of the Universe – heroes of the gossip columns – to being much-derided butts of the finance pages, and *Wasters* of the Universe. The huge stock-exchange crash on 20 October 1987 has been credited with doing away with many fortunes, but the process took a little more time than that, and some of the bigger fish managed to twist and turn until the decade was finally over and so were they.

Spokesman for the new mood was the federal treasurer, Paul Keating, a man of vision, feeling, and many contradictions. Keating had served in the Whitlam Government while in his twenties, and was still in his thirties when Labor came into power again, under Hawke, in 1983. He was a working-class boy with a taste for antiques. He was a socialist who believed in a deregulated economy. He was an aesthete and also a streetfighter who introduced terms like 'scumbag' and 'slime-bucket' into parliamentary language. But in 1986, the year of Halley's comet, Keating saw bad omens coming out of the endless party mood. A recession was on the way, he said, if it hadn't arrived already. Harsh wage and spending restraints were needed. Gross foreign debt was above $100 million, amounting to 34 per cent of gross national product. He remarked: 'This is going to be a long haul out for Australia.'

Paul Keating was a real killjoy. We called him the Undertaker. Kybosh Keating was another name, because he put the kybosh on all the fun we were having in the golden days of Gough. Those beautiful long expense-account lunches at the taxpayer's expense. Those trips up to Surfers Paradise – fact-finding missions with hornbag secretaries and a bevy of raunchy little ceiling inspectors at our bidding. All over – finished. But in the good old days I put my secretary down under expenses. She came under office furniture – and so did I.

Entrepreneurs who were keeping afloat by stripping their corporations of assets were putting on a brave face. But they couldn't escape that sinking feeling. Alan Bond put on the bravest face of all. He acknowledged massive losses but put his faith in faith, and said: 'We're looking at a good year. We will surprise the critics.' (One of the critics was the ABC's investigative TV programme 'Four Corners', whose reporters gave an example of Bond's accounts: a property in Rome selling for a $74 million profit to a company in Canberra with assets of $2.)

GAUDY, JINGOISTIC AND HUGELY SUCCESSFUL, KEN DONE'S ART BECAME THE AUSTRALIANA OF THE EIGHTIES. JAPANESE TOURISTS COULDN'T GET ENOUGH OF HIS CUTE MARSUPIALS AND PASTEL PRINTS. WHILE THE KNOCKERS SUGGESTED HIS ART WAS 'OVER-DONE', IT WAS CERTAINLY IN TUNE WITH THE TIMES.

Critics were a favourite complaint of the tycoons. If it weren't for their critics, they would still be rich! One scourge was Ross Gittins of the *Sydney Morning Herald*, who observed the entrepreneurs going down: 'Now, it seems, there's no greater swearword than entrepreneur. Today, an entrepreneur is a good-time Charlie who built a paper empire which is about to collapse – if it hasn't already. At the rate we are going, it will not be long before it is defamatory to call a businessman an entrepreneur. Unless, of course, you wait till he has fallen over, when the quality of his entrepreneurial talent is plain for all to see. You don't need to be an entrepreneur to realise what they didn't: that this happy game of pass-the-parcel could not go on forever.'

Amanda Muggleton as Chrissie (left), Jane Clifton as Margo (centre) and Val Lehman as Bea (right) in the campy television soap 'Prisoner'. Set in the fictional Wentworth Women's Prison, the long-running series achieved a cult-status following in Britain, where it was retitled 'Cell Block 13'.

The tycoons' losses made a dismal rollcall, with damage totalling around $16.5 billion. Alan Bond's estimated losses were fully a third of this, at $5.3 billion. Even so, Bondy was estimated to have salvaged between $30 million and $70 million through asset-shifting. While *he* would later go to prison, his family would nevertheless do well. Gaol finally came when Bond was sentenced for inducing a fellow businessman to help rescue the troubled Rothwells Bank without telling him that Bond Corporation would get a $16 million fee for the transaction. Still later, Bond would serve another, much longer term, this time for dishonesty in the buying of Van Gogh's 'Irises'. Bond's opinions about art might have been rather ordinary – not unusual enough to suffer for in the time-honoured artistic tradition – but as a bull-artist, Bond suffered for his art.

THE BICENTENNIAL CELEBRATIONS OF 1988 MARKED 200 YEARS OF WHITE SETTLEMENT IN AUSTRALIA AND INCLUDED A RE-ENACTMENT OF THE ARRIVAL OF THE FIRST FLEET IN SYDNEY HARBOUR.

When the whole country was in debt to the tune of hundreds of billions with no recovery in sight, what did a caring socialist government do? It handed out $200 million and threw a party.

The Bicentennial celebrations of 1988 commemorated the white settlement of Australia – the arrival of the First Fleet, under Captain Arthur Phillip, on 26 January 1788. On that day convicts and gaolers spilled on to dry land at Farm Cove, a couple of hundred metres from where the Sydney Opera House now stands. There they engaged in an orgy of booze, licentiousness and harsh recriminations. Memory of the event leaves most Australians with mixed feelings, to say the least. Where, on that day, were any of the qualities (except for a love of drink and a lust for women and real estate) that marked Australians as genial fair-minded people?

The day had always been rather low down on the scale of Australian national days – certainly nothing as significant as Anzac Day, commemorating defeat at Gallipoli in 1915, and solemnised as a day of remembrance for losses in two world wars. Nor did it offer anything like the excitement of the Melbourne Cup, a truly joyous national event. Australia Day had always been a bit dull, a day for civic costume dramas at the hottest time of year, attended by a few worthy notables, and for the rest of the population an excuse for a day off work and a trip to the beach before schools returned from their summer holidays a few days later. At best it made people feel passingly glad they were Aussies. They all loved their country in their own way, but had a mistrust of high-minded official expressions of it. At worst the celebration of Australia Day made many Australians feel left out – a feeling that was magnified almost to crisis level when time for the Bicentennial came round. Celebration of a Nation became Emanation of Confusion.

For several years the office of the Australian Bicentennial Authority had struggled to put a unified face on its celebration plans. To make sure of including all Australians it asked for submissions of celebratory ideas – books, plays, films, pageants, cultural centres, road projects, bridges, T-shirts, marathons, remembrances – and ended juggling innumerable contradictory agendas. Australians discovered that, despite unspoken assumptions, there appeared to be no clear national identity that could be expressed by the Bicentennial Authority, and attempts to fabricate one by academics, cultural advisers and bureaucrats only made matters worse. It was an uneasy unity that showed up – perhaps uneasier than anyone guessed, or would fully understand until the next decade, when the deep race divisions in Australian society would come closer to the surface and not be so buried in platitudes.

Les Patterson on the Heterocentennial

SIR LES PATTERSON PICTURED ON BONDI BEACH (WITH RESEARCH ASSISTANTS/GIRLS FRIDAY) DURING A GOVERNMENT-BACKED BRAINSTORMING SESSION ON THE BICENTENNIAL CELEBRATIONS.

I remember one day going into Bob Hawke's office, and it's as vivid now as it was then. I walked into his office, in regard to the Bicentennial celebrations, and I said, 'Bob, don't go any further,' I said, 'this word Bicentennial, it's got bad connotations.' He said, 'What do you mean, Les?' I said, 'Bi – just think about it.' He said, 'I don't quite get it.' I said, 'Listen, you'll get the wrong types flocking to Australia. You'll be getting the mattress munchers, the pillow biters, the Vegemite drillers – they'll all be flocking to Australia.' I said, 'We've got enough of them as it is. Can't you just call it the Heterocentennial?' He said, 'Now you're telling me? We've had the T-shirts printed, the oven mitts, the mugs. It's all rolling.' I said, 'All right, forget it, Bob.'

Then I said, 'Hang on, I've got another idea. You should get condoms printed.' He said, 'How do you mean?' I said, 'It could all be done tastefully. You should get condoms issued on the occasion, saying: "Three cheers for the Australian Heterocentennial celebrations and may they last forever and everyone have a very good time".'

He said, 'Aw, c'mon, Les. You'll never get all those words up the side of a frenchie.'

I said, 'You speak for yourself!'

The stark truth was that Australia was founded on an invasion of someone else's territory, and the survivors of that displacement were very much still around – vocal, angry, and not in any mood to play white man's games on Sydney Harbour. They made the point that should have been made from the start – that the Bicentennial was all about the past, and so couldn't avoid shooting itself in the foot.

When the day came, it seemed that almost every minority group in Australia considered itself excluded from the Authority's agenda. Aborigines were invited to take part, but most rejected proffered funding as 'blood money'. The most memorable Bicentennial event was unofficial, and happened in England, when the Aboriginal actor and activist, Burnum Burnum, went to the White Cliffs of Dover and claimed Britain on behalf of the Aboriginal people. He promised, however, not to launch an invasion of Britain, poison British waterholes, lace flour with strychnine, pickle skulls for public display, sterilise young women or separate children from their families.

Back home, while 2 million people jammed Sydney Harbour foreshores to view a waterscape jammed with small boats and the tall ships sailing in, Aborigines camped at Lady Macquarie's Chair, overlooking

Sir Les Patterson on Moomba

We've got this festival of Moomba which has been celebrated in Melbourne for generations. Moomba is an Aboriginal word meaning 'let's get together and have fun'. The Aborigines gave us this word because they have no further use for it.

Above: AT THE ANNUAL MOOMBA FESTIVAL AN ELEPHANT PUMPED FULL OF GAS TAKES PRIDE OF PLACE IN THE STREET PARADE. THERE COULD BE NO BETTER METAPHOR FOR THE EIGHTIES EXPERIENCE.

Farm Cove, and with their supporters held a counter-demonstration of 20 000 marching into nearby Hyde Park to commemorate colonisation.

Out on the harbour it was a great day, though. It was almost possible to walk from Sydney to Manly on an unbroken field of boat-decks without spilling a drop of champers. It was a fun day, but it made only a shallow impression on the national psyche. It was, wrote the former judge and politician Jim McClelland, like a long, drawn-out Peter Stuyvesant commercial and also a great day for the kiddies – a day in keeping, it might be said, with the impact of the 1980s overall. Clive James, commenting on the Bicentennial celebrations, felt that it all got too big since there was nobody in charge of keeping it small. 'And how can anyone celebrate for 365 days, except the town drunk.'

A party, a hangover, but what did it leave us in our hands?

ABORIGINAL PROTESTERS FLY THEIR FLAG AT MRS MACQUARIE'S CHAIR ON SYDNEY HARBOUR DURING THE BICENTENNIAL CELEBRATIONS. TO THEM, THE CELEBRATIONS COMMEMORATED AN INVASION WHICH SAW THEM DRIVEN FROM THEIR LANDS, MURDERED AND SUBJUGATED. TO MARK THE BICENTENARY, ABORIGINAL ACTIVIST BURNUM BURNUM CLAIMED BRITAIN ON BEHALF OF HIS PEOPLE.

Migrant Australians of non-British background saw the Bicentennial as an 'Anglo' event. Women saw it as a chance to show off boys' toys – massed fly-pasts, military tattoos, tall ships' regattas. Real men thought there were too many soft and fuzzy activities dragged in – quilting parties, poetry readings, gala concerts. Those who lived beyond the New South Wales perimeter, in the five other states and the Northern Territory, felt that Farm Cove was not *their* place. Many of them noted that the states had all been separate colonies of Britain until Federation, and accordingly believed that 1901, the year of establishment of the national parliament, was the year that should be celebrated. They felt that Western Australia, South Australia, Victoria and the rest had little more cause to be in on the show than, say, New Zealand. Even laconic Australian national icon Paul Hogan said: 'We're going to get so sick of the Bicentenary it will be like the America's Cup and we'll be glad we lost it. We'll be thinking of giving this land back to the Abos.'

Added to all this, the very forces that might have been most content with the idea – the mainstream mercantile figures of industry, mining and commerce – attacked the plans because they believed the celebrations were focusing too much on diversity and too little on what unified all Australians. And yet they were hard put to say what that unity was, or what symbolised it, except for a vague nagging feeling, most consistently expressed by the politician John Howard, a future prime minister, that Australia would only get it right when the whole country fitted into some sort of perceived WASP mould. There was a feeling that we

should turn the clock back to 1950, when we could all agree to stand for the national anthem, and accept that whatever the government decided for us was best.

Clive James turns the viewing glass the other way and analyses the eighties from a fifties perspective. 'In the eighties not only had all the things we'd dreamed of in the fifties come true, but things we weren't capable of dreaming in the fifties had come true. Nobody ever knew that life could be that civilised, that sweet. That you could eat so well, drink so well, see the plays, the operas, make the movies. It was all beyond what anyone had ever envisaged – and to our lasting benefit, and the envy of the world.'

It would be nice to end this account of the 1980s on such an upbeat note. But 1989, the first full year of white Australia's third century, decided to dampen the high spirits of celebrating citizens, and perhaps to punish them for the excesses of the decade.

Justice Muirhead, sitting as a Royal Commission, opened to public awareness the grievous history of Aboriginal deaths in custody – in police cells and in prisons. Thirteen people fell to their deaths after a high-altitude collision between hot-air balloons near Alice Springs, in the Northern Territory. Hundreds of airline pilots lost their jobs (many of them for good) when a prolonged pay dispute collapsed around them. Twenty-four people were killed and more than 50 injured in a series of horrific bus accidents on New South Wales's infamous Pacific Highway. And to top it all off, in the closing days of the decade Australia's strongest-ever earthquake devastated the centre of Newcastle, long one of the country's leading steel-making towns.

Thus sobered, Australians felt their way into the 1990s. It would be a different decade altogether, quieter, facing troubling indications of social and economic health, adjusting to the idea of 'engagement with Asia', and all with the great overhanging cliff of the new millennium not far ahead. Yet there would be progress too, and maturity … of a sort.

We've copped a lot of stick lately for political corruption. But isn't this progress? Australia's in the big league now. We've got organised crime, racial prejudice, cable TV, AIDS, disabled toilets, and under-age drug abuse, second to none. A touch of political corruption here and there is just another harmless symptom of our national maturity …

Opposite: The eighties were a decade when Australians seemed to lose sight of their roots. Here Barry Humphries is captured by photograher Lewis Morley during a pilgrimage to the home suburb of Edna Everage. Like a Buddhist travelling to Bodhinath or a Hindu to Varanasi, he was seeking the source of it all. At the Moonee Ponds railway station Barry made off with this souvenir of a place that is a sort of Australian Shangri-la.

selected works of Barry Humphries

theatre shows

Call Me Madman!, with Melbourne Dada Group, Union Theatre, Melbourne, 1952

Return Fare, Union Theatre, Melbourne, 1955

Mr and Mrs, Phillip Street Theatre, Sydney, 1956

Around the Loop, Phillip Street Theatre, Sydney, 1956–57

Waiting for Godot, with Peter O'Shaughnessy, Arrow Theatre, Melbourne, 1957, Independent Theatre, Sydney, 1958

The Bunyip and the Satellite, with Peter O'Shaughnessy, National Theatre, Melbourne, 1957 and Independent Theatre, Sydney, 1958

Rock 'n Reel Revue, with Peter O'Shaughnessy, New Theatre, Melbourne, 1958

The Demon Barber, Lyric, Hammersmith, London, 1959

Oliver!, New Theatre, London, 1960, Imperial Theater, New York, 1963, Piccadilly Theatre, London, 1967 and London Palladium, 1997

A Nice Night's Entertainment, Australian tour, 1962

The Bed-Sitting Room, The Duke of York's Theatre, London, 1963

Barry Humphries, The Establishment Club, London, 1963

Merry Rooster's Panto, Wyndham's Theatre, London, 1963

A Kayf Up West, Theatre Royal, Stratford East, 1964

Maggie May, Adelphi Theatre, London, 1964

Excuse I, Australian tour, 1965

Treasure Island, Mermaid Theatre, London, 1967

Just a Show, Australian tour, 1958 and Fortune Theatre, London, 1969

A Load of Olde Stuffe, Australian tour, 1971

At Least You Can Say You've Seen It, Australian tour, 1974

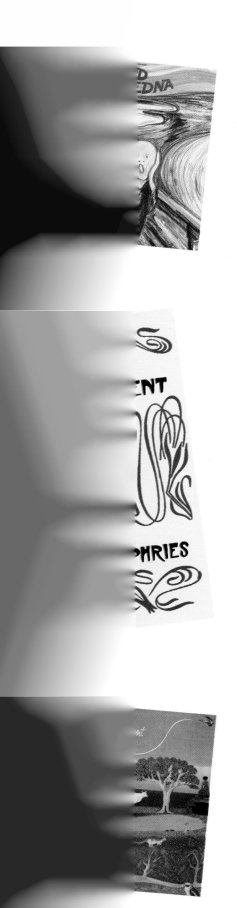

Housewife-Superstar!, Apollo and Globe Theatres, London, 1976 and
　　Theater Four, New York, 1977

Isn't It Pathetic At His Age, Australian tour, 1978

A Night With Dame Edna, Piccadilly Theatre, London, 1978–79

An Evening's Intercourse with Barry Humphries, Regent Theatre, Sydney,
　　Her Majesty's Theatre, Melbourne, 1981 and Theatre Royal, Drury Lane,
　　London, 1982

Last Night of the Poms, with Carl Davis, Albert Hall, London, 1981;
　　then as *Song of Australia*, Regent Theatre, Sydney and Melbourne
　　Concert Hall, 1983

Tears Before Bedtime, Australian tour, 1983; then as *Back With a Vengeance*,
　　Strand Theatre and Theatre Royal, London, 1987–88

The Life and Death of Sandy Stone, Australian tour, 1990

Look At Me When I'm Talking To You, London, 1993
　　and Australian tour, 1993–94

Dame Edna uber Deutschland, German tour, 1996

Dame Edna – The Spectacle, Theatre Royal, London, 1998

Dame Edna's The Royal Tour, Theater On The Square, San Francisco, 1998

Remember You're Out!, Australian Tour, 1999

books

Bizarre, Elek Books, London, 1965

The Barry Humphries Book of Innocent Austral Verse, Sun Books,
　　Melbourne, 1968

The Wonderful World of Barry McKenzie, with Nicholas Garland,
　　Private Eye/André Deutsch, London, 1969

Bazza Pulls It Off, with Nicholas Garland, Sun Books, Melbourne, 1972

The Adventures of Barry McKenzie, with Bruce Beresford, Sun Books,
　　Melbourne, 1973

Bazza Holds His Own, with Nicholas Garland, Sun Books, Melbourne, 1974

Dame Edna's Coffee Table Book, Harrap, London, 1976

Bazza Comes Into His Own, with Nicholas Garland, Sun Books,
　　Melbourne, 1978

Les Patterson's Australia, Sun Books, Melbourne, 1979

Barry Humphries' Treasury of Australian Kitsch, Macmillan, Melbourne, 1980

A Nice Night's Entertainment, Currency Press, Sydney, 1981;
　　Granada, London, 1981

Dame Edna's Bedside Companion, Weidenfeld & Nicolson, London, 1982

The Humour of Barry Humphries, selections by John Allen,
　　Currency Press, 1984

The Traveller's Tool, Sir Les Patterson, Macmillan,
    Melbourne, 1985
The Complete Barry McKenzie, with Nicholas Garland,
    Methuen, London, 1988; Allen & Unwin, Sydney, 1988
Shades of Sandy Stone, The Tragara Press, Edinburgh, 1989
My Gorgeous Life, Dame Edna Everage, Macmillan,
    Melbourne, 1989
The Life and Death of Sandy Stone, edited by Collin O'Brien,
    Macmillan, Melbourne, 1990
Neglected Poems and Other Creatures, Angus & Robertson, 1991
More Please, Viking, 1992
Women In The Background, Reed, 1995

recordings

Wild Life in Suburbia, 1958
Wild Life in Suburbia, volume two, 1959
Sandy Agonistes, 1960
A Nice Night's Entertainment, 1960
Chunder Down Under, 1965
Barry Humphries, 1970
Barry Humphries' Savoury Dip, 1971
The Barry Humphries Record of Innocent Austral Verse, 1971
A Track Winding Back, 1972
Barry Humphries at Carnegie Hall, 1972
Housewife-Superstar!, 1976
The Sound of Edna, 1978
12 Inches of Les, 1985
More Please, 1992
My Gorgeous Life, 1995
Women In The Background, 1995

television shows

'Wild Life and Christmas Belles', Melbourne, 1958
'Trip-Tease and High C's', Melbourne, 1959
'Comfort Station', Melbourne, 1966
'The Barry Humphries Scandals', London, 1970
'The Barry Humphries Show', London, 1976
'A Summer Sideshow', London, 1977
'An Audience with Dame Edna', London, 1980
'Another Audience with Dame Edna', London, 1984

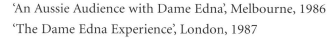

'An Aussie Audience with Dame Edna', Melbourne, 1986

'The Dame Edna Experience', London, 1987

'Dame Edna's Christmas Experience', London, 1987

'One More Audience with Dame Edna', London, 1988

'The Dame Edna Satellite Experience', London, 1989

'A Night On Mount Edna', London, 1989

'Dame Edna's Hollywood', Los Angeles, 1991–92

'Dame Edna's Neighbourhood Watch', London, 1992

'Dame Edna's Work Experience', London, 1996

'Sir Les and the Great Chinese Takeaway', Hong Kong, 1997

films

Bedazzled, 1967

The Adventures of Barry McKenzie, 1972

Barry McKenzie Holds His Own, 1974

The Great McCarthy, 1974

The Getting of Wisdom, 1977

Dr Fischer of Geneva, 1984

Les Patterson Saves the World, 1987

Immortal Beloved, 1994

The Leading Man, 1996

Spice World – The Movie, 1997

art exhibitions

The First Pan-Australasian Dada Exhibition,
   Melbourne, 1951

The Second Pan-Australasian Dada Exhibition,
   Melbourne, 1953

Barry Humphries, Victorian Artists Society Gallery,
   Melbourne, 1958

Ten Little Australians, Myer Mural Hall, Melbourne, 1958

Barry Humphries Retrospective, Bonython Galleries,
   Sydney, 1968

A Brief Glimpse: Barry Humphries the Painter,
   Golden Crust Gallery, Melbourne, 1989

Barry Humphries Dada Artist, National Gallery of
   Australia, 1993

further reading

general

Australia Through Time (Mynah, 1995)

Manning Clark, *A History of Australia* (Melbourne University Press, 1981)

Peter Coleman, *The Real Barry Humphries* (Robson Books, 1990)

Ann Curthoys, A.W. Martin & Tim Rowse (editors) *Australians From 1939* (Fairfax, Syme & Weldon Associates, 1987)

John Lahr, *Dame Edna Everage and the Rise of Western Civilisation: Backstage with Barry Humphries* (Bloomsbury, 1991)

Peter Luck, *This Fabulous Century* (Lansdowne Press, 1980)

the fifties

Peter Beilby, *Australian TV* (Thomas Nelson/Cinema Papers, 1981)

Brian Carroll, *The Menzies Years* (Cassell Australia, 1977)

Jacqueline Kent, *Out of the Bakelite Box* (Angus & Robertson, 1983)

Stella Lees & June Senyard, *The 1950s* (Hyland House, 1987)

Bob Rogers, *Rock 'n Roll* (Cassell Australia, 1975)

Helen Townsend, *Baby Boomers* (Simon & Schuster, 1988)

Richard White, *Inventing Australia* (George Allen & Unwin, 1981)

The Australian Dream: Design of the Fifties (Powerhouse Museum, 1993)

the sixties

Robin Boyd, *The Australian Ugliness* (Cheshire, 1960)

Brian Carroll, *The Menzies Years* (Cassell Australia, 1977)

James Cockington, *Mondo Weirdo* (Mandarin, 1992)

Robin Gerster and Jan Bassett, *Seizures of Youth* (Hyland House, 1991)

Donald Horne, *The Lucky Country Revisited* (J.M. Dent, 1987)

Greg Langley, *A Decade of Dissent* (Allen & Unwin, 1992)

Craig McGregor, *People, Politics and Pop* (Ure Smith, 1968)

Craig McGregor, *Profile of Australia* (Hodder & Stoughton, 1966)

Richard Neville, *Hippie Hippie Shake* (William Heinemann Australia, 1995)

Bob Rogers, *Rock 'n Roll* (Cassell Australia, 1975)

Richard White, *Inventing Australia* (George Allen & Unwin, 1981)

the seventies

James Cockington, *Mondo Bizarro* (Mandarin, 1994)

Frank Crowley, *Tough Times* (William Heinemann Australia, 1986)

Germaine Greer, *The Female Eunuch* (Paladin, 1970)

Greg Langley, *Decade of Dissent* (Allen & Unwin, 1992)

Richard Neville, *Hippie Hippie Shake* (William Heinemann Australia, 1995)

Peter Wilmoth, *Glad All Over: The Countdown Years 1974–1987* (McPhee Gribble, 1993)

the eighties

Paul Barry, *The Rise and Fall of Alan Bond* (Bantam Books, 1991)

Paul Kelly, *The End of Certainty* (Allen & Unwin, 1994)

Peter Wilmoth, *Glad All Over: The Countdown Years 1974–1987* (McPhee Gribble, 1993)

acknowledgments

television

Producer
John McLean

Director
David Mitchell

Writers
Barry Humphries
David Mitchell

Editor
John Pleffer

Associate Producer
Geraldine McKenna

Line Producer
Jo-anne McGowan

Script Consultants
Ian Davidson
Michael Cordell

Legal & Copyright Advisers
Simpsons Solicitors

Produced with assistance from:
The Australian Film Commission
NSW Film & Television Office
HarperCollins*Publishers*
PolyGram Filmed Entertainment
Sony Music Entertainment

A John McLean production
in association with the
Australian Broadcasting Corporation
© Copyright MCMXCVIII Flashbacks Pty Ltd

publishing

Project Director
John McLean

Publisher
Angelo Loukakis

Project Editor
Susan Gray

Editor
Devon Mills

Art Director
Russell Jeffery

Designer
Melanie Feddersen

Project Coordinator
Geraldine McKenna

Picture Research
Wendy Canning,
Geraldine McKenna

Captions
Peter Lalor, Roger McDonald,
John McLean

picture credits

95 David Liddle
96 *The Herald and Weekly Times*
97 News Limited
98 Mitchell Library
99 Orlando Wyndham
101 The Fairfax Photo Library
102 *(left)* Lewis Morley
102 *(right)* Speedo Australia/Powerhouse Museum, Sydney
102/103 *(spread)* ACP Library
103 *(top right)* Reginald Davis
104 News Limited
105 The Fairfax Photo Library
106 Mitchell Library
107 Bruno Benini/Powerhouse Museum, Sydney
108 Pat Purcell/UNSW Archives
109 The Fairfax Photo Library
110 Coo-ee Picture Library
111 The Fairfax Photo Library
112 The Fairfax Photo Library
113 Coo-ee Picture Library
114 Coo-ee Picture Library
115 The Fairfax Photo Library
117 Barry Crocker
118 Rennie Ellis
120 Mitchell Library
121 Rennie Ellis
123 The Fairfax Photo Library
124 Coo-ee Picture Library
125 Lewis Morley
127 From *Hippie Hippie Shake* by Richard Neville (Bloomsbury UK/Random House Australia, 1995)
128 Barry Humphries and Nicholas Garland
129 From *Hippie Hippie Shake* by Richard Neville (Bloomsbury UK/Random House Australia, 1995)
130 The Fairfax Photo Library
131 Miss World Organisation
132 Coo-ee Picture Library
133 The Fairfax Photo Library
134 The Fairfax Photo Library
136 Lewis Morley
137 Cash Harmon Television
138 The Fairfax Photo Library
140 David Liddle
141 Picnic Productions/NFSA
142 The Fairfax Photo Library
143 John McLean
144 Rennie Ellis
146 Performing Arts Museum, Victorian Arts Centre
147 The Fairfax Photo Library
148 *(top)* Lewis Morley
148/149 *(spread)* Neil Holbrook/ACP Library
149 *(bottom)* Australian Bicentennial Authority/Mitchell Library
149 *(top)* Commonwealth Department of Health & Aged Care
150 Barry Humphries
151 News Limited
152 Australian Picture Library/*BRW*

153 Australian Picture Library/J. Carnemolla
154 News Limited
155 Barry Humphries & Lewis Morley (Madge)
156 *(top)* ACP Library
156 *(bottom)* Baker Smith All Sports Management
157 Grundy Television
159 The Fairfax Photo Library
160 *(top)* Barry Humphries
160/161 ACP Library
164 Australian Picture Library/J. Carnemolla
165 Australian Picture Library/UPP
166 The Fairfax Photo Library
169 *(left)* ACP Library
169 *(right)* ACP Library
170 ACP Library
171 Barry Humphries
172 Australian Picture Library/J. Carnemolla
173 John Timbers
175 The Fairfax Photo Library
176 Elio Loccisano
177 Commonwealth Department of Health & Aged Care
178 Lewis Morley
180 ACP Library
181 Grundy Television
182 Coo-ee Picture Library
183 News Limited
184 Australian Picture Library/G. Lewis
185 Australian Picture Library/O. Strewe
186 Lewis Morley
188–191 Courtesy Nicholas Pounder Bookseller

Front cover images appear in the book and are acknowledged accordingly.
Back cover: *The Age*
Spine: Sellheim Estate/Josef Lebovic Gallery

Disclaimer
Every effort has been made to trace and acknowledge the original source of copyright material contained in this book. Where the attempt has been unsuccessful, Flashbacks Pty Ltd would be pleased to hear from copyright holders to rectify any omissions.

barry humphries

Barry Humphries was born in Melbourne in 1934. While a student he began writing and performing in university revues, joining what would later become the Melbourne Theatre Company. Here, in 1956, he created his best-known character, Edna Everage, later adding Sandy Stone, Barry McKenzie and Les Patterson to an impressive list of stage and screen personalities.

Barry gained particular notoriety and international acclaim when he first brought Edna Everage to the British stage for 'Just A Show' in 1969. Other theatrical hits followed, including: 'Housewife-Superstar!', 'A Night With Dame Edna'; 'An Evening's Intercourse', two seasons of 'Back With A Vengeance', and 1998's 'Dame Edna – The Spectacle'. Success crossed over to television; his numerous series and specials ranging from 'The Naked Bunyip' for Channel 7 Melbourne and 'The Barry Humphries Scandals' for the BBC, to 'The Dame Edna Experience' LWT chat show and 'Dame Edna's Hollywood' for the NBC network.

In addition to his numerous recordings, Barry is the author of 18 books, including an autobiography, *More Please*, Dame Edna's autobiography *My Gorgeous Life* and, most recently, *Women in the Background*. He was awarded the Order of Australia in 1982 and was recently voted one of Australia's 'Living Treasures'.

roger mcdonald

Roger McDonald was born in rural New South Wales in 1941. A wide-ranging author, his writing has been awarded Australia's most prestigious literary prizes, including the National Book Award and the Age Book of the Year. *Mr Darwin's Shooter*, his sixth novel, is the fifteenth book in a career that encompasses poetry, fiction, travel writing, essays and screenplays. Two of his books have been hailed as contemporary classics: *1915*, set in World War I, and *Shearer's Motel*, an account of working as a shearer's cook in outback Australia. Both have been filmed for television.

For most of his adult life Roger has lived in Braidwood in southern New South Wales, where he has at different times raised sheep, planted trees, and been both a keen participant and observer of the extremes of the Australian experience. He now divides his time between Sydney and the bush.

david mitchell

David Mitchell was born in Melbourne in 1948. He is the co-writer and director of the critically acclaimed four-part television series, 'Barry Humphries' Flashbacks', which accompanies this book. After writing for two classics of Australian television, 'The Mavis Bramston Show' and 'Number 96', he has become one of the country's most experienced and successful television writers and producers.

David was program consultant on both series of 'The Dame Edna Experience' and on 'The Dame Edna Christmas Experience', and still regularly collaborates with Barry Humphries. He has also worked extensively with Clive James, serving as program consultant on several of James' shows, including 'The Late Clive James', and developing the format for 'Saturday Night Clive'.

Other career high points include the three-hour special '35 Years of Television' in 1991, 1994's 'The Beatles in Australia: 30th Anniversary Special' and, for the last three years, Australia's most popular television series, the Nine Network's 'This Is Your Life'. He is also the author of the recently published book, *This Is Your Life: True Stories of Great Australians*.